Praise for

multipliers

"*Multipliers* is a great manifesto for today's leaders. The author provides a hands-on guide showing leaders how to make their total organization smarter by tapping the brainpower of everyone at all levels. A very timely and insightful book."

—Noel Tichy, coauthor of *Judgment* with Warren Bennis, and Professor of Management and Organizations at the University of Michigan

"We've all known Multipliers—people who bring the best, not the worst, out of everyone around them. They're a company's greatest resource. If you want to learn how to become a Multiplier or transform others into genuine Multipliers, read on. If you want to enhance your own career and strengthen your company, read on."

—Kerry Patterson, bestselling author, *Crucial Conversations*

"A fascinating book that shows how mindsets shape the way people lead. This book will forever change the way we think about leadership."

—Carol Dweck, Lewis and Virginia Eaton Professor of Psychology, Department of Psychology, Stanford University, and author of *Mindset*

"Liz Wiseman's insights are helpful, practical, and relevant. Any leader who needs to get more done with the same (or fewer) resources will find this book a gift and a valuable resource."

—Dave Ulrich, professor, the Ross School of Business, the University of Michigan

"This book will speak to every CEO and CFO. Multipliers get so much from their people that they effectively double their workforce for free."

—Jeff Henley, chairman of the board, Oracle Corporation

"*Multipliers* is a compelling read. A must-have manual for any in a leadership position or aspiring to become a leader. It's obvious Liz Wiseman did the homework, and those of us who read *Multipliers* are all the better for it."

—Byron Pitts, *ABC Nightline*

"This engaging and subversive book asks a vital question: 'How can we grow and harness human talent to address the great issues of our day?' *Multipliers* makes us rethink many of our old assumptions."

—Gareth Jones, visiting professor, IE Madrid, and coauthor,
Why Should Anyone Be Led by You?

"This book touches upon such a fundamental truth about leadership—one that has been waiting to be named, explored, and finally addressed. Liz Wiseman has created a language that will be with us for a very long time, impacting millions."

—Verne Harnish, founder, Entrepreneurs' Organization (EO),
and author of *Scaling Up (Rockefeller Habits 2.0)*

"*Multipliers* is brilliant and extraordinarily timely! It belongs on the bookshelf of every leader—and every leadership scholar."

—Roderick M. Kramer, William R. Kimball Professor
of Organizational Behavior, Stanford University School of Business

multipliers

REVISED AND UPDATED

multipliers

REVISED AND UPDATED

How the Best Leaders
Make Everyone Smarter

Liz Wiseman

HARPER
BUSINESS

An Imprint of HarperCollins*Publishers*

HarperCollins books may be purchased for educational, business, or sales promotional use. For information, please email the Special Markets Department at SPsales@harpercollins.com.

ORIGINALLY PUBLISHED IN 2010 BY HARPER BUSINESS, AN IMPRINT OF HARPERCOLLINS PUBLISHERS.

Revised and Updated Edition published 2017.

Designed by Joy O'Meara

Library of Congress Cataloging-in-Publication Data has been applied for.

ISBN 978-0-06-266307-8

18 19 20 21   DIX/LSC   10 9 8 7 6 5 4

To my children,
Megan, Amanda, Christian, and Joshua,
who have taught me to lead and shown me
why being a Multiplier matters.

Contents

Foreword

by Stephen R. Covey

I had the opportunity to work with a Multiplier when I was in my early twenties. It profoundly shaped the rest of my life. I had decided to take a break in my education to provide extended volunteer service. The invitation came to go to England. Just four and a half months after my arrival, the president of the organization came to me and said, "I have a new assignment for you. I want you to travel around the country and train local leaders." I was shocked. Who was I to train leaders in their fifties and sixties? Some of these individuals had been leading twice as long as I had been alive. Sensing my doubt, he simply looked me in the eye and said, "I have great confidence in you. You can do this. I will give you the materials to help you prepare to teach these leaders." It is hard to overstate the impact this leader had on me. By the time I returned home, I had begun to detect the work I wanted to devote my life to.

His particular ability—to get more out of people than they knew they had to give—fascinated me. I have reflected on this many times, wondering, *What did he do to get so much from me?* The answer to this question is contained in these pages.

Liz Wiseman has written a book that explores this idea more deeply than anything I have read elsewhere on this subject. And her timing couldn't be better.

New Demands, Insufficient Resources

At a time when many organizations do not have the luxury of adding or transferring resources to tackle major challenges, they must find the capabilities within their current ranks. The ability to extract and multiply the intelligence that already exists in the organization is red-hot relevant. Across industries and organizations of all kinds, leaders now find themselves in what David Allen has summarized as "new demands, insufficient resources."

For some forty years I have worked with organizations that were grappling with "new demands, insufficient resources." I have become convinced that the biggest leadership challenge of our times is not insufficient resources per se, but rather our inability to access the most valuable resources at our disposal.

When I ask in my seminars, "How many of you would agree that the vast majority of the workforce possesses far more capability, creativity, talent, initiative, and resourcefulness than their present jobs allow or even require them to use?" the affirmative response is about 99 percent.

Then I ask a second question: "Who here feels the pressure to produce more from less?" Again, a sea of hands goes up.

When you put those two questions together, you can see the challenge. As stated in this book, indeed, people are often "overworked and underutilized." Some corporations have made hiring the most intelligent individuals a core strategy on the basis that smarter people can solve problems more quickly than the competition. But that only works if the organizations can access that intelligence. Organizations that figure out how to better access this vastly underutilized resource won't just be more enjoyable places to work; they will outperform their competitors, which, in this global environment, might well make the difference between companies that make it and those that don't. And, as with so many business challenges, leadership is clearly a critical force for leveraging the full capability of the organization.

The New Idea

Multipliers: How the Best Leaders Make Everyone Smarter represents nothing less than the leadership paradigm necessary for accessing the intelligence and potential of people in organizations everywhere. It unearths and explains why some leaders create genius all around them while other leaders drain intelligence and capability from an organization.

Peter Drucker spoke of what is at stake when he wrote:

The most important, and indeed the truly unique, contribution of management in the 20th century was the fifty-fold increase in the productivity of the manual worker in manufacturing.

The most important contribution management needs to make in the 21st century is similarly to increase the productivity of knowledge work and the knowledge worker.

The most valuable assets of the 20th-century company were its production equipment. The most valuable asset of a 21st-century institution, whether business or non-business, will be its knowledge workers and their productivity.[1]

This book explains with great clarity the kinds of leaders who will answer the promise outlined by Drucker and those who will not.

As I read this book, a key insight was that Multipliers are hard-edged managers. There is nothing soft about these leaders. They expect great things from their people and drive them to achieve extraordinary results. Another insight that resonated with me was that people actually get smarter and more capable around Multipliers. That is, people don't just feel smarter; they actually become smarter. They can solve harder problems, adapt more quickly, and take more intelligent action.

People who understand these ideas will be well positioned to make the shift the authors describe from genius (where they may try to be the smartest person in the room) to genius maker (where they use their intelligence to access and multiply the genius in others). The power of such a shift is difficult to overstate. It is a night-and-day difference.

What I Love About This Book

I admire the work and insights in this book for several reasons.

First, the journalistic integrity and sheer tenacity required to analyze over 150 executives across the Americas, Europe, Asia, and Africa, and for giving us a book full of rich and vivid examples gathered from all over the world.

Second, it focuses the discussion on just those few things that really differentiate intelligence Multipliers and intelligence Diminishers. This isn't a general book on leadership, with all good qualities on one side and all bad qualities on the other. It is more precise than that, identifying and illustrating only the five most differentiated disciplines.

Third, its "range of motion." This book names a phenomenon the way Malcolm Gladwell seems to be able to, but also goes down several layers, to provide practical insight into exactly how to lead like a Multiplier.

Fourth, the way it seamlessly combines cutting-edge insights with timeless principles. Many books do one or the other. Few do both. This book will relate to your life today and it will connect to your conscience, too.

An Idea Whose Time Has Come

Multipliers is relevant for the entire world. Corporate executives will immediately see its relevance, but so will leaders in education, hospitals, foundations, nonprofit organizations, entrepreneurial start-ups, healthcare systems, middle-size businesses, and government at the local, state, and national level. I believe this book is relevant to everyone from first-time managers to world leaders.

And it comes to the world at a time when it is greatly needed, a time of "new demands, insufficient resources," when CFOs and HR directors are surprisingly in synch about the need for an approach that better leverages current resources. The principles in this book will always be true, but in this economic climate they will win in the marketplace of ideas. Their relevance will give them life and attention that is deserved. These are ideas that matter *now*, and, as Victor Hugo once said, "There is nothing more powerful than an idea whose time has come."

I have a vision of thousands of leaders discovering they have unintentionally diminished the people around them, and taking steps toward becoming a Multiplier. I have a vision of schools with diminishing cultures being reinvented around Multiplier principles, to the benefit of the whole community. I have a vision of world leaders learning how to better access the intelligence and capability of those they serve, to address some of the world's toughest challenges.

And so I challenge you to recognize the opportunity that is in your hands. Don't just read this book; pay the price to really become a Multiplier. Don't let this become a mere buzzword in your organization. Use the principles to reinvent your organization toward a true Multiplying culture that gets more out of people than they knew they had to give. Choose to be a Multiplier to people around you, as that president was to me in England all those years ago. I have great confidence in the good that can come from such an approach to leadership in your team and in your entire organization. Just imagine what would happen to our world if every leader on the planet took one step from Diminisher to Multiplier.

It can be done.

Preface

This book began with a simple observation: *There is more intelligence inside our organizations than we are using.* It led to the idea that there was a type of leader, those I came to call Multipliers, who saw, used, and grew the intelligence of others, while other leaders, whom I labeled Diminishers, shut down the smarts of those around them.

When the book was released in 2010, this idea struck a chord with managers around the world, perhaps because it came on the heels of a global recession, at a time when a tectonic shift was occurring in management and the ground was moving under all our feet. What was once predictable and manageable had become volatile, uncertain, complex, and ambiguous. With the explosion of information, for example, doubling every nine months in science and technology,[1] there is simply too much for any one person to know. Consequently, the role of leader has shifted, too—moving away from a model where the manager knows, directs, and tells and toward one where the leader sees, provokes, asks, and unleashes the capabilities of others.

Ideas that were once considered subversive are the new normal. Diminisher bosses still exist, but, like old BlackBerry phones, it is only a matter of time before they become obsolete and people upgrade to newer models. As companies do the math, they realize that they simply can't afford leaders who waste talent, suppress vital innovation, and slow business growth. After all, why would a company pick results-driven leaders who diminish people when they could have leaders who both deliver results and grow people around them? Increasingly, we are seeing diminishing leaders being asked to adapt . . . or leave.

Consider the fate of Jorgen, a general manager for a large, multinational pharmaceutical company.[2] Jorgen was a classic Diminisher who ran a country operation like a dictator and made life miserable for his direct reports. For years his behavior was tolerated because he delivered results, but then the company underwent a significant restructuring to better respond to changes in the marketplace. Instead of a single person calling the shots from the top, they organized around dynamic teams that could span organizational boundaries. Jorgen, accustomed to being the boss, struggled to adapt to this nonautocratic approach. Several months later, Jorgen was called to the corporate office in Europe and told that his style of leadership wasn't working. Jorgen responded with a compelling presentation that detailed his unit's performance. The executive team stopped him and said, "This is purely a style issue. You can no longer be a leader here." Jorgen was removed from his role as general manager and moved into a lower level staff role. His former direct reports celebrated when they heard the news, especially one who was just days away from quitting. But Jorgen wasn't pushed out by staff mutiny; he was a casualty of circumstance. The business environment pushed his company out of the Diminisher camp, and he was left behind. We are seeing more and more senior leaders left stunned in similar scenarios.

While some organizations seek innovation and agility, others are struggling to do more with less. Matthew Haas, deputy superintendent of the Albemarle County public school district in Virginia, said, "We are just running so lean. I can't imagine a world where you could work in silos and not collaborate. You used to be able to isolate yourself, but now efficiency requires collaboration. When you think about what is best for the organization and remove your ego, being a Multiplier is the only way to go."

While the direction may be clear, we clearly aren't there yet. Gallup's State of the Global Workplace study finds that across 142 countries, only 13 percent of people around the world are fully engaged at work.[3] SHRM reports that while 86 percent of Americans were happy with their jobs in 2009, that percentage has been in slow but steady decline ever since.[4]

This lack of engagement isn't just an emotional issue; it implies a waste in the fundamental resource that powers most companies today—intellectual capital. In 2011, after assessing hundreds of executives, we found that managers were utilizing just 66 percent of their people's capability on average. In other words, by our analysis, the managers are paying a dollar for their resources but extracting only 66 cents in capability—a 34 percent waste. When considering only their direct reports, that number increases to 72 percent. As we've tracked this indicator over the last five years, we've seen a slow, steady improvement, rising from 72 percent in 2011 to 76 percent in 2016.[5] And while managers have become better at estimating their diminishing impact on others, most managers are still overestimating their Multiplier characteristics. They believe they are having an enabling, liberating effect on their team, but team members see things differently. We are improving; however, too many organizations are still overmanaged and underled.

In realizing a richer way of working, many critical questions still remain: How fast can we get there? What is the best path to impact? Who can make the shift and who can't? What do we do with those who can't? How do we move and reshape an entire culture? As many authors will confess, the most important insights on a subject tend to come long after the book is written. This new edition incorporates what my colleagues and I have learned as we grappled with these questions and continue to teach and study pioneering companies and their leaders.

Here are the three most essential insights that have shaped this new edition:

1. THE NEED IS UNIVERSAL. In studying leadership, one learns a lot about followership. I've learned that people across cultures, across professions, across industries come to work each day hoping to be well utilized—not by being given more and more work, but through the recognition that they are capable of contributing in significant ways and doing progressively more challenging work. The need for Multiplier leadership spans industries and cultural boundaries; it's not just for innovation centers like Silicon Valley. It is as relevant in industries such as manufacturing, education, and healthcare and in cities like Shanghai, Seoul, and São Paulo. In cultures with high levels of hierarchy, we still find the presence of Multiplier leaders, but we find that the effects of Diminisher leaders are more pronounced—the 2× difference between Multipliers and Diminishers becomes a 3× differential (with the average Diminisher yielding roughly 30 percent of their employees' capability instead of the global average of 48 percent).

And, it's not just for Millennials. Certainly new and younger workers expect, if not demand, to be treated differently than those who came before them. But I'm not convinced Millennials actually need or want anything different than other corporate denizens. Contributors of all ages and stages want their ideas to matter, their voices to be heard, and workplaces where they can grow. Millennials have just been too impatient to wait and too empowered by technology not to speak out. What's good for the Millennials is good for the mainstream.

2. SOMETIMES THE GOOD GUYS ARE THE BAD GUYS. When I began this research, most Diminishers appeared to be tyrannical, narcissistic bullies. But I've come to see that the vast majority of the diminishing happening inside our workplaces is done with the best of intentions, by what I call the Accidental Diminisher—good people trying to be good managers. I've become less interested in knowing who is a Diminisher and much more interested in understanding what provokes the Diminisher tendencies that lurk inside each of us. Chapter 7, "The Accidental Diminisher," is new and offers a glimpse into how our best intentions can go awry and how, with self-awareness and simple workarounds, otherwise good managers can become great leaders. I've added this chapter because our greatest gains in the workplace will not come by reforming hardened Diminishers but by helping Accidental Diminishers become more intentional Multipliers and increasing the number of Multiplier moments in the workplace (perhaps raising their utilization of employee talent from the current average of 76 percent to the target 100 percent).

3. THE BIGGEST BARRIERS ARE CONTEXTUAL AND CULTURAL. To build organizations where intelligence is richly utilized, we need both an offensive and a defensive plan. Most leaders who read the book aspire to lead like Multipliers and find "the better angels of their nature," as Abraham Lincoln once said. However, their efforts are stymied because too much of their mental energy is spent dealing with the devils around them. For others, their diminishing colleagues leave them so enervated that their will to lead excellently is weakened as well. To understand how to counter the effects of shortsighted, absentminded Diminishers, I surveyed hundreds of professionals and interviewed dozens more. I learned that the reductive effect of a Diminisher is not inevitable. While you cannot change another person, you can change your response and smooth the sharp edges of your diminishing boss or colleague. Chapter 8, "Dealing with Diminishers," offers strategies and tactics that help reverse the cycle of diminishing, or at least minimize its effects.

Unlocking individual potential is not just a matter of personal will and individual behavior change; it is a function of entire systems, and reshaping collective will is hard work. To help you navigate the complexities of large-scale change, my team at The Wiseman Group and I have studied organizations that are successfully making this shift. Chapter 9, "Becoming a Multiplier," illuminates the paths that help entire organizations overcome inertia and move from insight to impact.

This new edition also contains some additional resources. There are new Multiplier examples from all around the world and appendix E is a set of experiments to help you develop Multiplier mindsets and practices. Also, the Frequently Asked Questions in appendix B have been expanded and now address the hardest-hitting questions that I've been asked by thousands of readers. These questions include: *What about leading in times of crisis? Does gender play a role? What about the iconic leaders like Steve Jobs with strong diminishing streaks?* . . . and more.

Our world is rapidly changing. To keep up and to create the type of workplaces where people thrive, we need diminishing leaders to be replaced by those who serve as true Multipliers, inspiring collective intelligence and capability on a mass scale. It's immense, both in promise and deed, so let's begin.

—Liz Wiseman
Menlo Park, California, 2017

multipliers

REVISED AND UPDATED

ONE

The Multiplier Effect

It has been said that after meeting with the great British Prime
Minister William Ewart Gladstone, you left feeling he was the
smartest person in the world, but after meeting with his rival
Benjamin Disraeli, you left thinking you were the smartest person.[1]

—BONO

During the summer of 1994, Derek Jones joined the US Navy to escape
his decaying hometown of Detroit, Michigan. Derek, a street-smart,
confident eighteen-year-old, scored high on the navy's aptitude exam
and was slotted to enter its advanced electronics computer program.
Following nine weeks of boot camp in Illinois and eight months of
intense training on missile firing systems, Derek earned advancement
to petty officer third class and was selected for advanced training as
an AEGIS computer network technician. He graduated first in his
class and, in recognition, was able to choose the ship he would serve
on; he picked the navy's newest *Arleigh Burke*–class guided missile
destroyer. Within months, he had established himself among the 210
enlisted men as a superior performer and was recognized by his officers as one of the ship's smartest and hardest-working sailors. On

1

the verge of earning a critical qualification, Derek felt on top of his game—that is, until a new commanding officer (CO), Commander Fredricks, took the helm.[2]

Fredricks was a graduate of the United States Naval Academy, and his assignment as captain of this *Arleigh Burke* destroyer put him in an elite class of officers being groomed for cruiser command. Excepting a major mistake, he was on track to become an admiral. Fredricks had superior knowledge of ships' operations, which he flaunted to his sailors. He managed even the most minute details of the ship's operations, every situation, and every sailor.

In preparation for the ship's first missile exercise under Fredericks's command, Derek's team was to ensure that the ship's weapons systems were 100 percent available. A few days before the exercise, Derek and his peers realized that the ship was missing a critical part, so the sailors secured it through an informal network, then repaired the system and returned it to full operation. Several days later, Fredricks learned of the episode from the CO of a sister ship, who mentioned in passing that his sailors provided the part. Instead of being pleased that the young sailors showed initiative and resourcefulness, Commander Fredricks, evidently embarrassed that his ship required assistance, was livid. Derek instantly became a target of Fredricks's wrath and elevated scrutiny.

During a typical missile exercise, the CO and the ship's tactical action officer (TAO) survey the battle area, find the enemy, determine a firing solution, aim, shoot, and hit the target—all in rapid succession and while being engaged by the enemy. Hundreds of things happen at once that must be processed, prioritized, and decided then acted upon. Success requires intense concentration and keen mental aptitude. These operations can be particularly intimidating because the commanding officer may be standing inches from the AEGIS operator, watching every decision and taking constant notes.

Derek and his team now performed these operations under the wary eye of Fredricks, who publicly mocked their efforts when they failed to immediately determine firing solutions for assigned targets. In the end, Derek didn't just perform poorly in one training evolution, he failed nearly every scenario. He had been stellar in the classroom and during team training, but as Fredricks loomed over his shoulder, managed every detail, and found every mistake, the tension mounted. Derek couldn't think properly and struggled to perform. As the scrutiny continued, Derek and his team became less and less capable. Within weeks, Derek and his chief petty officers were convinced they couldn't operate the ship's combat systems without the CO's intervention. The failure was so clear that Fredricks revoked Derek's qualification to operate the AEGIS console. After that, Derek's performance on the ship fell into a tailspin.

This downturn was interrupted only three months later, when the ship received a new CO. Commander Abbot was also a Naval Academy graduate and was as confident in his sailors as he was in his own abilities.[3] Abbot had worked previously for a high-ranking defense official who assigned him projects stretching him to the limits of his ability. Having been briefed of Derek's troubles with the previous CO, Abbot quickly sought Derek out and informed him that they would be taking the ship to sea for another missile exercise before an extended deployment, saying, "Jones, you are my man in this exercise. Make sure we're ready to ace this test. I'm counting on you, and so are your shipmates." For a week, Derek's team flawlessly exercised the AEGIS systems in every scenario. As they prepared, the new CO provided a watchful eye and was calm and inquisitive. Derek no longer felt like he was being tested but rather, that he was learning and working with the CO on a challenge.

On the day of the exercise, the new CO standing behind him, Derek operated the AEGIS console and provided the correct solutions time after time without error, achieving the highest score any ship had seen in over a year. Commander Abbot announced on the ship's speaker system, "Petty Officer Jones and crew won the battle for us today."

Derek continued to advance on the ship. He was made petty officer second class in record time and became the ship's Sailor of the Quarter, a high honor. Abbot placed Derek in the top 5 percent of the crew and nominated him for the STA-21, or Seaman to Admiral program, where he would earn his college degree and a commission as a naval officer. Upon completing officer training, Derek was promoted each time his record was reviewed. In less than nine years, he was selected to become an executive officer, training and cultivating other officers. Today, he serves in the US Navy as a lieutenant commander, and is destined for success as a commanding officer.

Derek's navy experience illustrates that a change in command can often cause a change in capability. He was stupefied with fear under one leader, but smart and capable under another. What did Fredricks say and do that so diminished Derek's intelligence and capability? And what did Abbot do that restored and expanded Derek's ability to reason and navigate complexity?

Some leaders make us better and smarter. They bring out our intelligence. This book is about these leaders, who access and revitalize the intelligence in the people around them. I call them Multipliers. This book will show you why they create genius around them and make everyone smarter and more capable.

Questioning Genius

There are bird watchers and there are whale watchers. I'm a genius watcher. I am fascinated by the intelligence of others. I notice it, study it, and have learned to identify a variety of types of intelligence. Oracle Corporation, the software giant worth $174 billion, was a great place for genius watching. In the seventeen years I worked in senior management at Oracle, I was fortunate to work alongside many intelligent executives, all systematically recruited from the best companies and the elite universities as top performers. Because I worked as the vice president responsible for the company's global talent development strategy and ran the corporate university, I worked closely with these executives and had a front-row seat to study their leadership. From this vantage point, I began to observe how they used their intelligence in very different ways, and I became intrigued by the effect they had on the people in their organizations.

The Problem with Genius

Some leaders seemed to drain intelligence and capability out of the people around them. Their focus on their own intelligence and their resolve to be the smartest person in the room had a diminishing effect on everyone else. For them to look smart, other people had to end up looking dumb. We've all worked with these black holes. They create a vortex that sucks energy out of everyone and everything around them. When they walk into a room, the shared IQ drops and the length of the meeting doubles. In countless settings, these leaders were idea killers and energy destroyers. Other people's ideas suffocated and died in their presence and the flow of intelligence came to an abrupt halt around them. Around these leaders, intelligence flowed only one way: from them to others.

Other leaders used their intelligence as a tool rather than a weapon. They applied their intelligence to amplify the smarts and capability of people around them. People got smarter and better in their presence. Ideas grew, challenges were surmounted, hard problems were solved. When these leaders walked into a room, lightbulbs started switching on over people's heads. Ideas flew so fast that you had to replay the meeting in slow motion just to see what was going on. Meetings with them were idea mash-up sessions. These leaders seemed to make everyone around them better and more capable. These leaders weren't just intelligent themselves—they were intelligence Multipliers.

Perhaps these leaders understood that the person sitting at the apex of the intelligence hierarchy is the genius maker, not the genius.

Post-Oracle Therapy

The idea for this book emerged from my post-Oracle therapy. Leaving Oracle was like stepping off a high-speed bullet train and suddenly finding everything moving in slow motion. This sudden calm created space for me to ponder about the lingering question: How do some leaders create intelligence around them, while others diminish it?

As I began teaching and coaching executives, I saw the same dynamic playing out in other companies. Some leaders seemed to boost the collective IQ while others sucked the mental life out of their employees. I found myself working with highly intelligent executives who were struggling with their own tendency to either overtly or subtly shut down the people around them. I also worked with many senior leaders struggling to make better use of their resources. Most of these leaders had developed their leadership skills during times of growth. However, in a more austere business climate, they found themselves unable to solve problems by simply throwing more resources at them. They needed to find ways to boost the productivity of the people they already had.

I recall one particularly pivotal conversation with a client named Dennis Moore, a senior executive with a genius-level IQ. As we discussed how leaders can have an infectious effect on the intelligence in their organization and spark viral intelligence, he responded, "These leaders are like amplifiers. They are intelligence amplifiers."

Yes, certain leaders amplify intelligence. These leaders, whom we have come to call Multipliers, create collective, viral intelligence in organizations. Other leaders act as Diminishers and deplete the organization of crucial intelligence and capability. But what is it that Multipliers do? And what do Multipliers do differently than Diminishers?

Scouring business school journals and the Internet looking for answers to these questions, as well as for resources for clients, yielded only frustration. This void set the course for my research into this phenomenon. I was determined to find answers for leaders wanting to multiply the intelligence of their organizations.

The Research

The first major discovery was finding my research partner, Greg McKeown, who was studying at Stanford University's Graduate School of Business. Greg has a curious and tenacious mind and a passion for leadership that gave him my same measure of determination to find the answers. We began our formal research by defining the question that would consume us for the next two years: What are the vital few differences between intelligence Diminishers and intelligence Multipliers, and what impact do they have on organizations? Waking up for 730 days with the same question was like the movie *Groundhog Day*, in which Bill Murray wakes each day to the same time and song on his alarm clock, destined to repeat the events of the previous day. In the singular and prolonged pursuit of this question, we developed a deep understanding of the Multiplier effect.

We began our research by selecting a set of companies and industries in which individual and organizational intelligence provide a competitive advantage. Because these organizations rise or fall based on the strength of their intellectual assets, we assumed the Multiplier effect would be pronounced. We interviewed senior professionals inside these organizations, asking them to identify two leaders, one who fit the description of a Multiplier and one a Diminisher. We studied more than 150 of the resulting leaders through interviews and a quantitative assessment of their leadership practices. For many leaders, we then followed an intensive 360-degree interview process with both former and current members of their management teams.

As our research expanded, we studied additional leaders from other companies and industries, looking for common elements that spanned the business and nonprofit sectors as well as geographies. Our research journey took us across four continents and introduced us to an incredibly rich and diverse set of leaders. We came to know some of these leaders quite well, studying them and their organizations in depth.

Two of the leaders we studied provided a sharp contrast between these two leadership styles. They both worked for the same company and in the same role. One had the Midas touch of a Multiplier and the other had the chilling effect of a Diminisher.

A Tale of Two Managers

Vikram[4] worked as an engineering manager under two different division managers at Intel. Each leader could be considered a genius. Both had a profound impact on Vikram. The first leader was George Schneer, a division manager for one of Intel's businesses.

Manager No. 1: The Genius Maker

George had a reputation for running successful businesses at Intel. Every business he ran was profitable and grew under his leadership. But what most distinguished George was the impact he had on the people around him.

Vikram said, "I was a rock star around George. He *made* me. Because of him I transitioned from an individual contributor to big-time manager. Around him, I felt like a smart SOB—everyone felt like that. He got 100 percent from me—it was exhilarating." George's team echoed the same sentiments: "We are not sure exactly what George did, but we knew we were smart and we were winning. Being on this team was the highlight of our careers."

George grew people's intelligence by engaging it. He wasn't the center of attention and didn't worry about how smart he looked. What George worried about was extracting the smarts and maximum effort from each member of his team. In a typical meeting, he spoke only about 10 percent of the time, mostly just to "crisp up" the problem statement. He would then back away and give his team space to figure out an answer. Often the ideas his team would generate were worth millions. George's team drove the business to achieve outstanding revenue growth and to deliver the profit bridge that allowed Intel to enter the microprocessor business.

Manager No. 2: The Genius

Several years later, Vikram moved out of George's group and went to work for a second division manager, who had been the architect of one of the early microprocessors. This second manager was a brilliant scientist who had now been promoted into management to run the plant that produced the chips. He was highly intelligent by every measure and left his mark on everyone and everything around him.

The problem was that this leader did all the thinking. Vikram said, "He was very, very smart. But people had a way of shutting down around him. He just killed our ideas. In a typical team meeting, he did about 30 percent of the talking and left little space for others. He gave a lot of feedback—most of it was about how bad our ideas were."

This manager made all the decisions himself or with a single confidant. He would then announce those decisions to the organization. Vikram said, "You always knew he would have an answer for everything. He had really strong opinions and put his energy into selling his ideas to others and convincing them to execute on the details. No one else's opinion mattered."

This manager hired intelligent people, but they soon realized that they didn't have permission to think for themselves. Eventually, they would quit or threaten to quit. Ultimately Intel hired a second-in-command to work alongside this manager to counter the intelligence drain on the organization. But even then, Vikram said, "My job was more like cranking than creating. He really only got from me about 50 percent of what I had to offer. And I would *never* work for him again!"

Diminisher or Multiplier?

The second leader was so absorbed in his own intelligence that he stifled others and diluted the organization's crucial intelligence and capability. George brought out the intelligence in others and created collective, viral intelligence in his organization. One leader was a genius. The other was a genius maker.

It isn't how much you know that matters. What matters is how much access you have to what other people know. It isn't just how intelligent your team members are; it is how much of that intelligence you can draw out and put to use.

We've all experienced these two types of leaders. What type of leader are you right now? Are you a genius, or are you a genius maker?

The Multiplier Effect

Multipliers are genius makers. What we mean by that is that they make everyone around them smarter and more capable. Multipliers invoke each person's unique intelligence and create an atmosphere of genius—innovation, productive effort, and collective intelligence.

In studying Multipliers and Diminishers, we learned that at the most fundamental level, they get dramatically different results from their people, they hold a different logic and set of assumptions about people's intelligence, and they do a small number of things very differently. Let's first examine the impact of the Multiplier effect. Why do people get smarter and more capable around Multipliers? And how do they get twice as much from their resources as do the Diminishers?

Multipliers get more from their people because they are leaders who look beyond their own genius and focus their energy on extracting and extending the genius of others. And they don't get just a little more back; they get vastly more.

2× Multiplier Effect

The impact of a Multiplier can be seen in two ways: first, from the point of view of the people they work with, and second, from the point of view of the organizations they shape and create. Let's begin by examining how Multipliers influence the people who work around them.

Extracting Intelligence

Multipliers extract all of the capability from people. In our interviews, people told us that Multipliers got *a lot* more out of them than Diminishers. We asked each person to identify the percentage of their capability that a Diminisher received from them. The numbers typically ranged between 20 and 50 percent. When we asked them to identify the percentage of their capability that the Multiplier extracted, the numbers typically fell between 70 and 100 percent.[5] When we compared the two sets of data, we were amazed to find that Multipliers got 1.97 times more. That represents an almost twofold increase—a 2×️ effect. After concluding our formal research, we continued to pose this question in workshops and with management teams, asking people to reflect on their past Multiplier and Diminisher bosses. Across industries and in the public, private, and nonprofit sectors, we continued to find that Multipliers get at least two times more from people.

What could you accomplish if you could get twice as much from your people?

The reason for the difference is that when people work with Multipliers, they hold nothing back. They offer the very best of their thinking, creativity, and ideas. They give more than their jobs require and volunteer their discretionary effort, energy, and resourcefulness. They actively search for more valuable ways to contribute. They hold themselves to the highest standards. They give 100 percent of their abilities to the work—and then some.

Extending Intelligence

Not only do Multipliers extract capability and intelligence from people, they do it in a way that extends and grows that intelligence. In interviews, people often said Multipliers accessed *more* than 100 percent of their capability. Initially, I pushed back when they would say, "Oh, they got 120 percent from me," pointing out that getting more than 100 percent is mathematically impossible. But we continued to hear people claim Multipliers got more than 100 percent from them, and we began to ask: Why would people insist that intelligence Multipliers got more out of them than they actually had?

Our research confirmed that Multipliers not only access people's current capability, they stretch it. They get more from people than they knew they had to give. People reported actually getting smarter around Multipliers.

The implication of our research is that intelligence itself can grow. This is an insight that is corroborated by other recent research into the extensible nature of intelligence. Consider a few recent studies:

> ► Carol Dweck of Stanford University has conducted
> groundbreaking research showing that children given a
> series of progressively harder puzzles and praised for their
> *intelligence* stagnate for fear of reaching the limit of their
> intelligence. Children given the same series of puzzles but
> then praised for their *hard work* actually increased their
> ability to reason and to solve problems. When these chil-
> dren were recognized for their efforts to think, they cre-
> ated a belief, and then a reality, that intelligence grows.[6]
> ► Eric Turkheimer of the University of Virginia has found
> that bad environments suppress children's IQs. When
> poor children were adopted into upper-middle-class
> households, their IQs rose 12 to 18 points.[7]
> ► Richard Nisbett of the University of Michigan has
> reviewed studies that show: 1) students' IQ levels drop
> over summer vacation, and 2) IQ levels across society have
> steadily increased over time. The average IQ of people in
> 1917 would amount to a mere 73 on today's IQ test.[8]

After reading these studies, I recalculated the data from our research interviews at face value, using the literal percentage of capability that people claimed Multipliers received from them. When factoring this excess capability (the amount beyond 100 percent) into our calculations, we found that Multipliers actually get 2.1 times more than Diminishers. What if you got not only 2× more from your team—everything they had to give—*but also* a 5 to 10 percent growth bonus because they were getting smarter and more capable while working for you?

This 2× effect is a result of the deep leverage Multipliers get from their resources. When you extrapolate the 2× Multiplier effect to the organization, you begin to see the strategic relevance. Simply said, resource leverage creates competitive advantage.

Resource Leverage

Let's take the example of Tim Cook, currently CEO of Apple Inc. When Tim was COO and opened a budget review in one sales division, he reminded the management team that the strategic imperative was revenue growth. Everyone expected this, but they were astounded when he asked for the growth *without* providing additional headcount. The sales executive at the meeting said he thought the revenue target was attainable but only *with* more headcount. He suggested they follow a proven linear model of incremental headcount growth, insisting that everyone knows that more revenue means you need more headcount. The two executives continued the conversation for months, never fully able to bridge their logic. The sales executive was speaking the language of addition (that is, higher growth by adding more resources). Tim was speaking the language of multiplication (that is, higher growth by better utilizing the resources that already exist).

The Logic of Addition

This is the dominant logic that has existed in corporate planning: that resources will be added when new requests are made. Senior executives ask for more output and the next layer of operational leaders request more headcount. The negotiations go back and forth until everyone settles on a scenario such as: 20 percent more output with 5 percent more resources. Neither the senior executive nor the operational leaders are satisfied.

Operational leaders entrenched in the logic of resource allocation and addition argue:

1. Our people are overworked.
2. Our best people are the most maxed out.
3. Therefore, accomplishing a bigger task requires the addition of more resources.

This is the logic of addition. It seems persuasive but, importantly, it ignores the opportunity to more deeply leverage existing resources. The logic of addition creates a scenario in which people become both overworked *and* underutilized. To argue for allocation without giving attention to resource leverage is an expensive corporate norm.

Business school professors and strategy gurus Gary Hamel and C. K. Prahalad have written, "The resource allocation task of top management has received too much attention when compared to the task of resource leverage. . . . If top management devotes more effort to assessing the strategic feasibility of projects in its allocation role than it does to the task of multiplying resource effectiveness, its value-added will be modest indeed."[9]

Picture children at a buffet line. They load up on food, but a lot of it is left on the plate uneaten. The food gets picked at and pushed around, but it is left to go to waste. Like these children, Diminishers are eager to load up on resources, and they might even get the job done, but many people are left unused, their capability wasted. Consider the costs of one high-flying product development executive at a technology firm.

THE HIGH-COST DIMINISHER Jasper Wallis[10] talked a good game. He was smart and could articulate a compelling vision for his products and their transformational benefits for customers. Jasper was also politically savvy and knew how to play politics. The problem was that

Jasper's organization could not execute and realize the promise of his vision because employees were in a perpetual spin cycle, spinning around him.

Jasper was a strategist and an idea man. However, his brain worked faster and produced more ideas than his organization could execute. Every week or so, he would launch a new focus or a new initiative. His director of operations recalled, "He'd tell us on Monday, we needed to catch up with 'competitor X,' and we needed to get it done this week." The organization would scurry, throw a Hail Mary pass, make progress for a few days, but eventually lose traction when they were given a new goal to chase the following week.

This leader was so heavily involved in the details that he became a bottleneck in the organization. He worked extremely hard, but his organization moved slowly. His need to micromanage limited what the rest of the organization could contribute. His need to put his personal stamp on everything wasted resources and meant his division of 1,000 was only operating at about 500 strong.

Jasper's modus operandi was to compete for resources with a larger division in the company that produced similar technology. Jasper's overriding goal was to outsize the other division. He hired people at a breakneck pace and built his own internal infrastructure and staff—all of which was redundant with existing infrastructure in the other division. He even convinced the company to build a dedicated office tower for his division.

Things eventually caught up with Jasper. It became clear that his products were hype and the company was losing market share. When the real return on investment (ROI) calculation was made, he was removed from the company and his division was folded into the other product group. The duplicate infrastructure he built was eventually removed, but only after many millions of dollars had been wasted and opportunities lost in the market.

Diminishers come at a high cost.

The Logic of Multiplication

We have examined the logic of addition and the resource inefficiencies that follow from it. Better leverage and utilization of resources at the organizational level require adopting a new corporate logic, based on multiplication. Instead of achieving linear growth by adding new resources, leaders rooted in the logic of multiplication believe that you can more efficiently extract the capability of your people and watch growth skyrocket by *multiplying* the power of the resources you have.

Here is the logic behind multiplication:

1. Most people in organizations are underutilized.
2. All capability can be leveraged with the right kind of leadership.
3. Therefore, intelligence and capability can be multiplied without requiring a bigger investment.

For example, when Apple Inc. needed to achieve rapid growth with flat resources in one division, they didn't expand their sales force. Instead, they gathered the key players across the various job functions, took a week to study the problem, and collaboratively developed a solution. They changed the sales model to utilize competency centers and better leverage their best salespeople and deep industry experts in the sales cycle. They achieved year-over-year growth in the double digits with virtually flat resources.

Salesforce, a $7 billion software firm that has pioneered software as a service, has been making the shift from the logic of addition to the logic of multiplication. They enjoyed a decade of outstanding growth using the old idea of "throwing resources at a problem." They addressed new customers and new demands by hiring the best technical and business talent available and deploying them on the challenges. However, a strained market environment created a new imperative for the company's leadership: get more productivity from their currently available resources. They could no longer operate on outdated notions of resource utilization. They started developing leaders who could multiply the intelligence and capability of the people around them and increase the brainpower of the organization to meet their growth demands.

Resource leverage is a far richer concept than merely "accomplishing more with less." Multipliers don't get more with less; they get more by using *more*. More of people's intelligence and capability, enthusiasm and trust. As one CEO put it, "Eighty people can either operate with the productivity of fifty or they can operate as though they were five hundred." And because these Multipliers achieve better resource efficiency, they enjoy a strengthened competitive position against companies entrenched in the logic of addition.

We want to strike at the root of the outdated addition logic. Let's turn to the question of how Multipliers access intelligence and get so much from people. The answer is in the mindset and the five disciplines of the Multiplier.

The Mind of the Multiplier

As we studied Diminishers and Multipliers, we consistently found that they hold radically different assumptions about the intelligence of the people they work with. These assumptions appear to explain much of the difference in how Diminishers and Multipliers operate.

THE MIND OF THE DIMINISHER. The Diminisher's view of intelligence is based on elitism and scarcity. Diminishers appear to believe that *really intelligent people are a rare breed* and that they are *of that rare breed*. From this assumption they conclude that they are so special, *other people will never figure things out without them.*

I recall a leader I worked with whom I can only describe as an "intellectual supremacist." This senior executive ran a technology organization employing more than 4,000 highly educated knowledge workers, most of them graduates of top universities from around the world. I joined one of his management meetings, in which twenty members of his senior management team were troubleshooting an important go-to-market problem for one of their products.

As we walked out of the meeting, we were reflecting on the conversation and the decisions made. He stopped, turned to me, and calmly said, "In meetings, I typically only listen to a couple of people. No one else really has anything to offer." I think he saw the alarm on my face because after his words came out, he added the awkward postscript, "Well, of course, you are one of these people." I doubted it. Out of the top twenty managers representing a division of 4,000 people, he believed only a couple had anything to offer. As we walked down the hallway, we passed by rows and rows of cubicles and offices occupied by his staff. Seen through new eyes, this expanse now suddenly looked like a massive brainpower wasteland. I wanted to make a public announcement and tell them all that they could go home since their senior executive didn't think they had much to offer.

In addition to seeing intelligence as a scarce commodity, our research showed that Diminishers regard intelligence as something basic about a person that can't change much; they believe it is static, not able to change over time or circumstance. This attitude is consistent with what Dr. Carol Dweck, noted psychologist and author, calls a "fixed mindset," a belief that one's intelligence and qualities are carved in stone.[11] Diminishers' two-step logic appears to be that *people who don't "get it" now, never will*; therefore, *I'll need to keep doing the thinking for everyone*. In the Diminisher world, there is no vacation for the smart people!

You can probably predict how the executive described above actually operated on a day-to-day basis. You might ask yourself how *you* would operate if, deep down, you held these beliefs. You would probably tell people what to do, make all the important decisions, and jump in and take over when someone appeared to be failing. And in the end, you would almost always be right, because your assumptions would cause you to manage in a way that produced subordination and dependency.

THE MIND OF THE MULTIPLIER. Multipliers hold very different assumptions. If Diminishers see the world of intelligence in black-and-white, Multipliers see it in Technicolor. Multipliers have a rich view of the intelligence of the people around them. They don't see a world where just a few people deserve to do the thinking. In addition, Multipliers see intelligence as continually developing. This observation is consistent with what Dweck calls a "growth mindset," a belief that basic qualities like intelligence and ability can be cultivated through effort.[12] They assume that *people are smart and will figure it out.* To their eyes, their organization is full of talented people who are capable of contributing at much higher levels. They think like one manager we interviewed who takes stock of her team members by asking herself, "In what way is this person smart?" In answering this question, she finds colorful capabilities often hidden just below the surface. Instead of writing people off as not worth her time, she is able to ask, "What could be done to develop and grow these capabilities?" She then finds an assignment that both stretches the individual and furthers the interests of the organization.

Multipliers look at the complex opportunities and challenges swirling around them and think, *There are smart people everywhere who will figure this out and get even smarter in the process.* And they see that their job is to bring the right people together in an environment that liberates everyone's best thinking—and then to get out of their way and let them do it!

How would you operate if you held these assumptions? In the most trying times, you would trust your people; you would extend hard challenges to them and allow them space to fulfill their responsibilities. You would access their intelligence in a way that would actually make them smarter.

The chart below summarizes how these very different sets of assumptions have a powerful effect on the way Diminishers and Multipliers lead others:

How would you:	Diminisher "They will never figure this out without me."	Multiplier "People are smart and will figure this out."
Manage talent?	Use	Develop
Approach mistakes?	Blame	Explore
Set direction?	Tell	Challenge
Make decisions?	Decide	Consult
Get things done?	Control	Support

These core assumptions are essential to unearth and understand because, quite simply, behavior follows assumptions. If someone wants to lead like a Multiplier, he or she can't simply mimic the practices of the Multiplier. An aspiring Multiplier must start by thinking like a Multiplier. In twenty years of watching and coaching executives, I have observed how leaders' assumptions affect their management. When someone begins by examining and potentially upgrading their core assumptions, they will more easily adopt the five disciplines of the Multiplier with authenticity and impact.

The Five Disciplines of the Multiplier

So what are the practices that distinguish the Multiplier? In analyzing data on more than 150 leaders, we found a number of areas in which Multipliers and Diminishers do the same things. Both groups are customer driven. Both show strong business acumen and market insight. Both surround themselves with smart people and consider themselves thought leaders. However, as we searched the data for the active ingredients unique to Multipliers, we found five disciplines in which Multipliers differentiate themselves from Diminishers.

1. ATTRACTING AND OPTIMIZING TALENT. Multipliers are *Talent Magnets*; they attract and deploy talent to its fullest, regardless of who owns the resource, and people flock to work with them because they know they will grow and be successful. In contrast, Diminishers operate as *Empire Builders*, insisting that they must own and control all resources to be more productive. They tend to divide resources into those they own and those they don't, and then allow these artificial separations to hamstring effective use of all resources and restrict growth. People may initially be attracted to work with a Diminisher, but it is often the place where people's careers die.

The Diminisher is an Empire Builder who acquires resources and then wastes them. The Multiplier is a Talent Magnet who utilizes and increases everyone's genius.

2. CREATING INTENSITY THAT REQUIRES BEST THINKING. Multipliers establish a unique and highly motivating work environment where everyone has permission to think and the space to do their best work. Multipliers operate as *Liberators*, which produces a climate that is both comfortable *and* intense. They are able to remove fear and create the safety that invites people to do their best thinking. At the same time, they are creating an intense environment that demands people's best efforts. In contrast, Diminishers operate as *Tyrants*, introducing judgment and a fear of judgment, which have a chilling effect on people's thinking and work. Diminishers try to demand everyone's best thinking, yet they don't get it.

The Diminisher is a Tyrant who creates a stressful environment. The Multiplier is a Liberator who creates a safe environment that fosters bold thinking.

3. EXTENDING CHALLENGES. Multipliers act as *Challengers*, continually challenging themselves and others to push beyond what they know. How do they do this? They seed opportunities, lay down challenges that stretch the organization, and, in doing so, generate belief that it can be done and enthusiasm about the process. In contrast, Diminishers operate as *Know-It-Alls,* personally giving directives to showcase their knowledge. While Diminishers set a direction, Multipliers ensure that a direction gets set.

The Diminisher is a Know-It-All who gives directives. The Multiplier is a Challenger who defines opportunities.

4. DEBATING DECISIONS. Multipliers operate as *Debate Makers,* driving sound decisions through rigorous debate. The decision-making process they foster contains all the information the organization needs to be ready to execute those decisions. Multipliers engage people in debating the issues up front, which leads to decisions that people understand and can execute efficiently. In contrast, Diminishers operate as *Decision Makers* who seem to make decisions efficiently within a small inner circle, but they leave the broader organization in the dark to debate the soundness of the leader's decisions, and with none of the satisfaction of helping to fine-tune and execute them.

Diminishers are Decision Makers who try to sell their decisions to others. Multipliers are Debate Makers who generate real buy-in.

5. INSTILLING OWNERSHIP AND ACCOUNTABILITY. Multipliers deliver and sustain superior results by inculcating high expectations across the organization. They serve as *Investors* who provide the necessary resources for success. In addition, they hold people accountable for their commitments. Over time, Multipliers' high expectations turn into an unrelenting presence, driving people to hold themselves and each other accountable, often to higher standards and without the direct intervention of the Multiplier. In contrast, Diminishers serve as *Micromanagers* who drive results by holding on to ownership, jumping into the details, and directly managing for results.

The Diminisher is a Micromanager who jumps in and out. The Multiplier is an Investor who gives others ownership and full accountability.

The following chart summarizes the five vital disciplines that differentiate Diminishers and Multipliers:

THE FIVE DISCIPLINES OF THE MULTIPLIER

	DIMINISHERS	MULTIPLIERS
SEE	**THE ASSUMPTION** "People won't figure it out without me"	**THE ASSUMPTION** "People are smart and will figure it out"
DO	**THE DISCIPLINES** **1. The Empire Builder** Hoards resources and underutilizes talent **2. The Tyrant** Creates a tense environment that suppresses people's thinking and capability **3. The Know-It-All** Gives directives that showcase how much they know **4. The Decision Maker** Makes centralized, abrupt decisions that confuse the organization **5. The Micromanager** Drives results through their personal involvement	**THE DISCIPLINES** **1. The Talent Magnet** Attracts talented people and uses them at their highest point of contribution **2. The Liberator** Creates an intense enviornment that requires people's best thinking and work **3. The Challenger** Defines an opportunity that causes people to stretch **4. The Debate Maker** Drives sound decisions through rigorous debate **5. The Investor** Gives other people ownership for results and invests in their success
GET	**THE RESULT** $<50\%$	**THE RESULT** $2\times$

Surprising Findings

As we studied Multipliers across the world, we found a remarkable amount of consistency and several patterns that confirmed our early observations. Here are four surprising and intriguing findings that we want to share.

They Have a Hard Edge

One of the most critical insights from our study of Multipliers is how hard-edged these managers are. They expect great things from their people and drive them to achieve extraordinary results. They are beyond results-driven; they are tough and exacting. Indeed, Multipliers make people feel smart and capable, but they don't do it by being "feel-good" managers. They look into people and find capability, and they want to access all of it and utilize people to their fullest. They see a lot, so they expect a lot.

During our research interviews, people oozed appreciation for the Multipliers they had worked with, but the gratitude was rooted in the deep satisfaction found in working with them, not in the pleasantries of a relationship. One person described working with Deb Lange, a senior vice president of taxation at a large firm: "Working with her was like an intense workout. It was exhausting but totally exhilarating." Another said of his manager: "He got things from me I didn't know I had to give. I would do almost anything to not disappoint him." An executive who reported to Derek Williams, executive vice president of Oracle's Asia Pacific region, put it this way: "When you left his office you felt so much taller."

The Multiplier approach to management isn't just an enlightened view of leadership. It is an approach that delivers higher performance because it gets vastly more out of people and returns to them a richly satisfying experience. As one early reader of this book noted, these leaders aren't about "cupcakes and kisses."

They Don't Play Small

People often assume that Multiplier leaders have to step to the side in order to shine a spotlight on others, or that they play small so that others can play big. However, I found that these leaders not only utilize all of the intelligence and talent of the people around them, they use all of their own as well. One of my favorite Multiplier leaders is Magic Johnson. Even back in high school, when he was just Earvin Johnson Jr., he was a phenomenally talented basketball player. His high school coach told him, "Earvin, every time you get the ball, I want you to take the shot." And so he did—and he scored a lot of points as they won every game. They would score 54 points, and Earvin would have made 52 of them. The coach loved it, and the players loved it, because what boy doesn't want to be on an undefeated team? But then after one particular game, as the players were leaving the gym and heading out to their cars, Earvin noticed the faces of the parents who had come to watch their sons play basketball but instead ended up watching this superstar. He said, "I made a decision at this very young age that I would use my God-given talent to help everyone on the team be a better player."[13] And this decision eventually earned him the nickname Magic—for his ability to raise the level of excellence of every team he ever played on and of every person on those teams. It's not that these Multipliers shrink so that others can be big. It's that they play in a way that invites others to play big, too.

They Have a Great Sense of Humor

On a whim, we added "Great Sense of Humor" to our leadership survey. Our suspicion proved right. Not only is this trait prominent among Multipliers, it is one of the traits that is most negatively correlated with the mindset held by Diminishers. Multipliers aren't necessarily comedians, but they don't take themselves or situations too seriously. Perhaps because they don't need to defend their own intelligence, Multipliers can laugh at themselves and see comedy in error and in life's foibles, and their sense of humor has a liberating effect on others. Multiple workplace studies conclude that humor strengthens relationships, reduces stress, and increases empathy. Those who work in a fun environment have greater productivity, interpersonal effectiveness, and call in sick less often.[14] Leaders who operate with a sense of humor create an environment where people can contribute at their fullest.

Think of George Clooney when you think of the humor of the Multiplier—it's a self-deprecating wit and an ability to put others at ease, allowing people to be themselves. As one journalist wrote of Clooney, "After fifteen minutes, he made me feel comfortable in my own house."[15] A Clooney costar said, "He has a way of daring you . . . which can be irresistible." Multipliers use humor to create comfort and to spark the natural energy and intelligence of others.

The Accidental Diminisher

Perhaps one of our biggest surprises was realizing how few Diminishers understood the restrictive impact they were having on others. Most of them had grown up praised for their personal intelligence and had moved up the management ranks on account of personal—and often intellectual—merit. When they became "the boss," they assumed it was their job to be the smartest and to manage a set of "subordinates." Others had once had the mind and even the heart of the Multiplier, but they had been working among Diminishers for so long that they inherited many of their practices and absorbed their worldview. As one executive put it, "When I read your findings, I realized that I have been living in Diminisher land so long that I have gone native." Many people have worked for Diminishers and, although they may have escaped unscathed, they carry some of the residual effects in their own leadership. The good news for the Accidental Diminisher is that there is a viable path to becoming a Multiplier. Chapter 7, "The Accidental Diminisher," is for well-meaning, decent managers who are underutilizing their people, despite having the very best intentions.

The Promise of This Book

As we studied Multipliers and Diminishers, we heard case after case of smart individuals being underutilized by their leaders. We heard their frustration as they told us how little some leaders got from them, despite how hard they were working and how they tried to give more. We learned that it is indeed possible to be both overworked and underutilized. Latent talent exists everywhere. Organizations are replete with underchallenged resources.

Multipliers are out there, and they know how to find this dormant intelligence, challenge it, and put it to use at its fullest. Great Multipliers exist in business, in education, in nonprofits, and in government. Consider just a few whom you will learn more about later.

1. K. R. Sridhar, successful green-tech entrepreneur and CEO, who recruits A+ talent, then gives them an environment with a lot of pressure but very little stress, and allows them to experiment and take risks until the right technology and solutions emerge.

2. Alyssa Gallagher, an assistant superintendent who led a charge to revolutionize learning across her school district by giving ownership to the teachers and letting them be the revolutionaries.

3. Lutz Ziob, general manager of Microsoft Learning, whose team says of him, "He creates an environment where good things happen. He recruits great people, allows them to make mistakes, and ferociously debates the important

decisions. He demands our best, but then shares the success with the whole team."

4. Sue Siegel, former biotech president turned venture capitalist, whose business partner described "a Sue effect. Everything around her gets better and companies grow under her guidance. I often wonder what people are like when they aren't around Sue."

5. Larry Gelwix, head coach of Highland Rugby, whose high school varsity team's record is 392 wins and just nine losses in thirty-four years. He attributes this extraordinary record to a deliberate leadership philosophy that engages the intelligence of his players on and off the field.

Leaders like these provide an aspiration point for those who would be Multipliers.

The promise is simple: You can be a Multiplier. You can create genius around you and receive a higher contribution from your people. You can choose to think like a Multiplier and operate like one. This book will show you how. And it will show you why it matters.

This is a book for every manager trying to navigate the resource strain of tough economic times. It is a message for leaders who must accomplish more by getting more out of their people. As companies shed excess resources, the need for leaders who can multiply the intelligence and capability around them is more vital than ever. This book is also for the raging Multiplier who seeks to better understand what he or she does naturally, as well as for the aspiring Multiplier who wishes to get the full capability and intelligence from his or her people. And it is most certainly for the Diminishers, so they can better understand the negative effects of leadership centered on their own intelligence. It is for every manager seeking the promise of the Multiplier: to increase intelligence everywhere and with everyone.

As you read, you will find a few central messages:

1. Diminishers underutilize people and leave capability on the table.
2. Multipliers increase intelligence in people and in organizations. People actually get smarter and more capable around them.
3. Multipliers leverage their resources. Corporations can get 2× more from their resources by turning their most intelligent resources into intelligence Multipliers.

Before turning our attention to the practices of the Multiplier, let's clarify what this book is not. It is not a prescription for a nice-guy, feel-good model of leadership. Rather, this book discusses a hard-edged approach to management that allows people to contribute more of their abilities. And although there will be much discussion of Multipliers and Diminishers, this book isn't about what they achieve themselves. It is about the impact that these leaders have on others. It is about the impact and the promise of the Multiplier. And lastly, the ideas offered here are not intended to be terms for labeling your diminishing boss and your colleagues. Rather, I offer a framework for helping you to develop the practices of a Multiplier.

This book has been designed as an end-to-end learning experience, offering an opportunity to both understand and implement the Multiplier ideas. This introduction has provided a first glance into the Multiplier effect and an overview of what Multipliers do. Succeeding chapters will clarify the differences between Multipliers and Diminishers and will present the five disciplines of the Multiplier and how you can minimize your Accidental Diminisher tendencies. You'll also gain a set of strategies for dealing with the inevitable Diminishers around you. You will read stories of real Multipliers and Diminishers, but be aware that we've changed the Diminishers' names and the names of their companies, for rather obvious reasons. The book concludes with a road map for becoming a Multiplier leader and for building a Multiplier culture across an entire enterprise.

My Challenge to You

Although the Multiplier/Diminisher framework might appear binary, I wish to emphasize that there is a continuum between Multipliers and Diminishers, with just a small number of people at either polar extreme. Our research showed that most of us fall along this spectrum and have the ability to move toward the side of the Multiplier. With the right intent, the Multiplier approach to leadership can be developed. The good news is that 1) Multipliers are out there, 2) we have studied them to uncover their secrets, and 3) you can learn to become one. And not only can you become a Multiplier yourself, you can find and create other Multipliers. That will make you a Multiplier of Multipliers.

In this spirit, I challenge you to read this book on several levels. At the most fundamental level, it might illuminate what you undoubtedly have experienced—that some leaders create genius, while others destroy it. Or you might go beyond this and reflect on the quintessential Multipliers and Diminishers who have been part of your career and life experience. But perhaps the best way to approach the book is to look beyond the idea that you or your colleagues are Multipliers, and instead spot yourself at times in the guise of Diminisher. The greatest power of these ideas might be in realizing that you have the mind of a Multiplier but have been living in a Diminisher world and have lost your way. Perhaps you are an Accidental Diminisher.

As I have journeyed into the world of Multipliers and Diminishers, I have often seen glimpses of myself—either in the present or from years past—and have found ways to better exemplify the Multiplier in my own work teaching and coaching leaders around the world. I've come to see that most of us have a Diminisher side, or at least a few vulnerabilities, mostly born of the best intentions. I certainly do. While we may not entirely rid ourselves of our diminishing tendencies, we can certainly work to string together as many Multiplier moments as possible.

Multipliers is a guide to those of you who wish to follow the path of the Multiplier and, like British Prime Minister Benjamin Disraeli, leave those you meet thinking they, rather than you, are the smartest person in the world. It is a book for executives who want to seed their organization with more Multipliers and watch everyone and everything get better.

Let me now introduce you to the fascinating and diverse set of leaders we call the Multipliers. They come from all walks of life— from corporate boardrooms and our schools' classrooms, from the executive suite to the fields of Africa. And the leaders we've selected represent diverse ideologies. I encourage you to learn from everyone, even those whose political views you do not share. None of these leaders is perfect, but as we look into some of their finest Multiplier moments, we can discover new possibilities. I hope you will find their stories, their practices, and their impact as inspiring as we did when we entered their worlds.

Chapter One Summary

Multipliers Versus Diminishers

MULTIPLIERS: These leaders are genius makers who bring out the intelligence in others. They build collective, viral intelligence in organizations.

DIMINISHERS: These leaders are absorbed in their own intelligence, stifle others, and deplete the organization of crucial intelligence and capability.

The Five Disciplines of the Multipliers

1. *The Talent Magnet:* Attracts and optimizes talent
2. *The Liberator:* Requires people's best thinking
3. *The Challenger:* Extends challenges
4. *The Debate Maker:* Debates decisions
5. *The Investor:* Instills accountability

The Accidental Diminisher

While true Diminishers are easier to spot, much of the diminishing that transpires in the workplace is a result of well-intended leaders whose honest attempts to lead or be helpful shut down ideas and cause others to hold back.

The Results

By extracting people's full capability, Multipliers get twice the capability from people as do Diminishers.

TWO

The Talent Magnet

I not only use all the brains that I have,
but all that I can borrow.

WOODROW WILSON

When you walk up to the porch of her house in Menlo Park, Cali-fornia, you can sense that Meg Whitman, CEO of eBay, has spent time on the East Coast. With its saltbox shape and white wood, the house looks like it should be in New England. Perhaps it reminds Meg of her time in Cambridge, Massachusetts, while at business school.

It was September 2007, early in the race for the 2008 presidential nomination. There were many interesting candidates vying for the ticket for both parties. That day was a chance for us locals to get a peek at one of the candidates, and for me, it was a chance to extend our research and gain insight into two interesting leaders.

As the guests gathered on her backyard lawn, Meg Whitman took the microphone and began to introduce Mitt Romney as a candidate for president of the United States. Her introduction was simple.

I was a young consultant at Bain & Company and had the good fortune to work for Mitt Romney early in my career. After we were hired, all the new consultants scrambled to get on Mitt's project teams. Why? The word spread that he was the best boss to work for because he knew how to lead a team and he grew his people. Everyone grew around Mitt.

You can imagine Meg, a newly minted Harvard MBA, ready to make her mark on the business world. Like many MBAs, she chose to begin her career at Bain & Company, an elite business consulting firm. She knew landing in the right place inside would determine how quickly she'd learn and advance her career and her value in the marketplace. She heard from one of the more senior consultants, "If you're smart, you'll find a spot on Mitt Romney's team." She didn't quite know why Mitt was such a great boss, but, being savvy, she maneuvered her way onto his team. She learned why when she started working with him.

On Mitt's team, people were engaged. He took the time to get to know each person and to understand the capabilities they brought to the team. This went well beyond reviewing their résumés. Mitt would determine what people were naturally good at and find a way to use those talents with the client engagement. In assigning people to roles, Mitt asked questions like "What is the next challenge for you? What would be a stretch assignment?" It wasn't unusual for someone on Mitt's team to be loaned to another group if their skills could help rescue a troubled project. In one-on-one meetings, Mitt not only asked about the status of project deliverables, he asked about the blockers. A favorite question was "What is getting in the way of your being successful?"

Meanwhile, many of Meg's colleagues didn't get the same guidance and found themselves working for company leaders who appeared more concerned with advancing their own careers than growing the people on their team. Team meetings typically consisted of long briefings from project leaders, followed by the usual project updates from each of the consultants, who reported on progress in their functional area. People stuck to their roles on the team. When one person was struggling, he or she usually just suffered in silence and pulled a few all-nighters rather than solicit help from colleagues. The job got done, but individual efforts were not acknowledged. The only visible recognition came in the form of kudos for the project leader and an increase in the size of his or her organization. As for the destiny of the project members, they were almost certainly guaranteed a role on the next project that closely resembled what they had done on the last project.

In any organization, there are Talent Magnets, people who attract the best talent, utilize it to its fullest, and ready it for the next stage. These are leaders who have a reputation not only for delivering results but for creating a place where young, talented people can grow. They are accelerators to other people's careers.

Mitt Romney operated as a Talent Magnet. He accelerated the career of Meg Whitman, who went on to be CEO of eBay and lead an eighty-eight times increase in revenue. And Mitt has been a magnet and an accelerator in the careers of hundreds of people with similar stories, not only Meg.

Perhaps you are a Talent Magnet. Would your people describe you as someone who recognizes talented people, draws them in, and utilizes them at their fullest? Would they say they have grown more around you than with any other manager they have worked for? Or would they describe you as someone who pulled them into your organization not as a talent to be developed, but more as a resource to be deployed, and then left to languish? Would they perhaps say that they were heavily recruited but not given a meaningful role—just a visible role—and were serving as a showpiece or hood ornament in your organization?

Some leaders are like magnets that draw in talent and develop it to its fullest. Other leaders acquire resources to build their empire. This chapter explores the differences between these two approaches to the management of talent and the impact that both types of leaders have on the people around them.

The Empire Builder Versus the Talent Magnet

Multipliers operate as Talent Magnets to attract talented people and then use them to their fullest capacity, that is, working at their highest point of contribution. Multipliers have access to the best talent, not because they are necessarily great recruiters but because people flock to work for them. As Meg Whitman found Mitt Romney, people seek out a Talent Magnet, knowing that their capabilities will be appreciated and also that their value will appreciate in the marketplace.

In contrast, Diminishers operate as Empire Builders who hoard resources and underutilize talent. They bring in top talent and make big promises, but then they underutilize their people and disenchant them. Why? Because they are often amassing the resources for self-promotion and their own gain. Empire builders accumulate rather than multiply; they collect people like knickknacks in a curio cabinet—on display for everyone to see, but not well utilized.

Each of these approaches produces a self-perpetuating cycle. The Talent Magnet spawns a virtuous cycle of attraction and the Empire Builder spawns a vicious cycle of decline.

A Cycle of Attraction

In 1914, when venerated British explorer Ernest Shackleton decided to embark on an expedition to traverse Antarctica, he placed a recruitment advertisement in *The Times* (London), which read:

*Men wanted: For hazardous journey. Small wages, bitter cold,
long months of complete darkness, constant danger, safe return
doubtful. Honour and recognition in case of success.*

Surprisingly, hundreds of men applied. Shackleton, with the wisdom of an experienced captain, staffed his crew with men of a certain orientation—men who were attracted to adventure and recognition but were also realistically prepared for the hardship they would face. No doubt Shackleton's ability to attract the right team was one key factor in the survival of every member of the expedition.

The cycle of attraction begins with a leader possessing the confidence and magnetism to surround him- or herself with top talent, or "*A* players"—sheer raw talent and the right mix of intelligence needed for the challenge. Under the leadership of the Talent Magnet, the genius of these players gets discovered and utilized to the fullest. Having been stretched, these players become smarter and more capable. *A* players become *A*+ players who are positioned in the spotlight and get kudos and recognition for their work. They attract attention and their value increases in the talent marketplace, internally or externally. *A*+ players get offered even bigger opportunities, and they seize them with the full support of the Talent Magnet.

And then the cycle kicks into hyperdrive. As this pattern of utilization, growth, and opportunity continues to occur, others in the organization and outside notice, and the leader and the organization get a reputation as a "place to grow." This reputation spreads and more *A* players flock to work in the Talent Magnet's organization, so there is a steady flow of talent in the door, replacing talent growing outward.

This cycle of attraction, outlined below, is exactly what happened to Mitt Romney at Bain & Company and why Meg Whitman knew to join his organization.

THE CYCLE OF ATTRACTION

Attract other
A players

Get fully
utilized
and grow

I.
A Players

IV.
Reputation for
"Place to grow"

II.
A+ Players

Offered
opportunities

Get
recognized

III.
Increased
Market Value

Talent Magnets create a powerful force that attracts talent and then accelerates the growth of intelligence and capability in others, as well as themselves. These leaders operate like an electromagnetic force that, through interactions between atoms, propels matter in the universe.

A Cycle of Decline

For many years, I had the pleasure of working closely with Brian Beckham,[1] a brilliant and affable Canadian. Brian had a reputation for being smart, optimistic, and collaborative, and could solve just about any complex problem that got tossed his way. This reputation earned him a key role as the vice president of operations in a rapidly growing division. The problem was that the division was run by an uncontrolled Diminisher and determined Empire Builder.

Brian went to work solving the complex problems of the emerging division but soon found that the senior vice president running the division didn't really want the underlying issues addressed. The SVP wanted only to grow an empire! And he wanted growth at any cost. Brian's role quickly degenerated into window dressing, where he and his team were only tweaking issues on the surface, just enough so the executive committee would continue to fund additional headcount into the organization.

For many months, while Brian continued to pursue his work at full throttle, deep problems were festering at the core of the division. With continued indifference from his manager, Brian became numb and started to settle into mediocrity. He lost good players on his team. When other leaders in the company saw the depth of the problems in the division, Brian's Midas-touch reputation was tarnished. After several years of hanging in there, hoping for things to improve, he found himself stuck in a dying organization, watching his opportunities fade.

Soon Brian became one of the walking dead who roam the halls of so many organizations. On the outside, these zombies go through the motions, but on the inside they have given up. This is called "quit and stay." It was painful to watch this happen to Brian, whom I knew to be an absolute superstar. No doubt you have seen this happen to colleagues in other organizations or have even been there yourself. Is it possible that it is happening inside your own organization?

Empire Builders create a vicious cycle of decline. Talent recruited into their organization soon becomes disengaged and goes stale. The cycle of decline begins much like the cycle of attraction (which is why it is easy to be deceived by Diminishers). Empire Builders seek to surround themselves with *A* players. But, unlike Talent Magnets, they accumulate talent to appear smarter and more powerful. The leader glosses over the real genius of the people while placing them into boxes on the org chart. The *A* players have limited impact and start to look more like *A*– or *B*+. They fail to get noticed for their work, and they lose intellectual confidence. They begin to recede into the shadow of the Empire Builder. Their value in the job market drops and opportunities begin to evaporate. So they stay and wait, hoping things will turn around. This cycle of degeneration impacts not only one person; it infects an entire organization. The organization becomes an elephant graveyard earning a reputation as "the place people go to die." As one technology superstar said of his empty vice president job, "I'm definitely past my sell-by date here." The resignation in his voice made it clear: if he were milk, he'd be curdled.

Empire Builders, having earned their reputation as career killers, continually struggle to get truly top talent into their organizations. Perhaps this is why they labor hard to hoard the resources that they have. Empire Builders may initially be able to attract top talent, but their focus on building themselves and their organizations underutilizes the true talent that they have in their organization and renders it stagnant and inert.

They generate a cycle of decline that spirals downward as illustrated on the following page.

Empire Builders hoard resources and underutilize talent. Talent Magnets attract talented people and use them at their highest point of contribution. Let's explore the world of the Talent Magnet, these Multipliers who create a cycle of attraction and grow intelligence around them.

THE CYCLE OF DECLINE

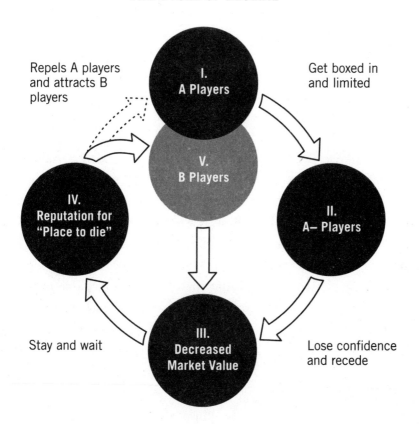

Repels A players
and attracts B
players

Get boxed in
and limited

I.
A Players

V.
B Players

IV.
Reputation for
"Place to die"

II.
A– Players

III.
Decreased
Market Value

Stay and wait

Lose confidence
and recede

The Talent Magnet

The Talent Magnet creates a cycle of attraction that accelerates performance and grows genius. But does this only work for top talent
and for the A players in the market? Or can a true Talent Magnet find
and grow genius everywhere and with everyone?

Hexal AG, a maker of generic drugs, is located in a small village
close to Munich, Germany. Hexal was founded in 1986 by Thomas
and Andreas Strüengmann, twin brothers and self-made entrepreneurs. Andreas, a doctor, is the medical authority, and Thomas is the

international marketing genius behind Hexal. These brothers teamed their expertise to build a successful generic drug company, growing primarily from the local talent pool in the village. What makes the company unique is that its approach to talent is anything but generic, and it is an approach that gets extraordinary results from very ordinary people.

It starts with how these leaders hire people into their company. They explained, "When we consider each person, we ask one or two questions. If they don't fit, we simply don't continue the conversation. If the person is individualistic, we know that he or she won't fit in our culture. When we find someone who will fit with our company, then we spend a lot of time with this person to make sure we understand their capability and what they would bring to our organization." The Strüengmann brothers knew how to spot and attract the right talent.

Once people joined Hexal, they discovered another one of the Strüengmanns' unconventional practices. Hexal doesn't have jobs per se, and they don't have an org chart. This isn't like some elite organizations that choose not to publish their org chart for fear that some other company will snatch up their talent. Hexal didn't have an org chart because the Strüengmanns didn't believe in them. Jobs were loosely created around people's interests and unique capabilities. They called their approach the "ameba model." Here's how it works.

Ursula's responsibility was to assist the customer services manager. In her role, she saw a large number of repetitive requests for the same action and was continually updating people on the status of these requests. She had an idea to use the Internet to create a workflow tracking system. She wrote up a little proposal and sent the idea around to her colleagues in an email asking, "What do you think about it?" Some people replied on email and others stopped by her desk to discuss it in person, but everyone agreed that it was a good idea and wanted to see it happen. She gathered the people she needed, secured some budget, and got the system built through this makeshift team. The team then presented the system to the Strüengmann brothers, who applauded their efforts and Ursula's leadership and initiative. These twin brothers simply believed that if an idea got support from a lot of people, it was a good idea. At Hexal, you could work wherever there was energy.

Through encouraging their employees to use this heat-seeking approach, they were able to utilize people at their highest point of contribution. They didn't box people into jobs and limit their contribution. They let people work where they had ideas and energy and where they could best contribute. They let talent flow, like an ameba, to the right opportunities.

There are clearly multiple reasons for their success, but it is interesting to note that the Strüengmann brothers sold Hexal (along with holdings in another company) to Novartis in 2005 for $7.6 billion; at age fifty-five, they were each worth $3.8 billion. As they led Hexal, the Strüengmann brothers got extraordinary results from very ordinary people. Why? Because these twin Talent Magnets knew how to unleash people's genius into their organization.

How does a Talent Magnet find and unleash genius? In the four practices of the Talent Magnet, we find some of the answers.

The Four Practices of the Talent Magnet

Among the Multipliers we studied in our research, we found four active practices that together catalyze and sustain this cycle of attraction. These Talent Magnets: 1) look for talent everywhere; 2) find people's native genius; 3) utilize people at their fullest; and 4) remove the blockers. Let's look at each to understand exactly what a Talent Magnet does to create genius in others.

1. Look for Talent Everywhere

Talent Magnets are always looking for new talent, and they look far beyond their own backyard. Multipliers cast a wide net and find talent in many settings and diverse forms, knowing that intelligence has many facets.

Appreciate All Types of Genius

In 1904, a test of intelligence that later evolved into the IQ test was developed by French researcher Alfred Binet as a tool for assessing the learning progress of French schoolchildren. His assumption was that lower intelligence signaled, not an inability to learn, but a need for more and different teaching.[2] This tool quickly became ubiquitous as a unilateral determinant of intellectual horsepower. Much work has been done over the last two decades by cognitive psychologists around the world, offering additional methods for identifying and developing intelligence. Whether it is Harvard professor Howard Gardner's theory of multiple intelligences, Daniel Goleman's work on emotional intelligence, or Stanford professor Carol Dweck's work on the effect of mindsets on capability, the message is clear: IQ is a practical but limited measure of the true intelligence of our species. We are simply smarter in more ways than can be measured through an IQ test.

A Talent Magnet knows that genius comes in many forms. Some minds excel at quantitative analysis or verbal reasoning—capabilities measured through IQ, SAT, and other tests of traditional cognitive intelligence. Other minds offer creative genius, innovating through fresh thinking and bold ideas. Some minds are critical, spotting every problem or landmine lurking within a plan; the genius of some others is to find a way to tunnel around these landmines. For example, a successful CEO turned venture capitalist in Tokyo has a rule he applies when listening to a start-up company's management team pitch seeking funding: if all three are engineers, he doesn't entertain the business plan. He looks for diversity, knowing it takes a mix of types of intelligence to start any business, even a technical one.

Bill Campbell, the former CEO of Intuit who passed away in 2016, was one such leader who appreciated the diversity of talent requisite to build a successful company. This economics major and football coach at Columbia University was renowned for his ability to lead and guide Silicon Valley's elite technologists. Bill reflected, "Their minds can do something that mine can't. They have a genius that I don't." He communicated this respect for the intelligence of others through his actions. He readily admitted that he didn't think like they did and that he appreciated what they brought to the table. He listened intently to the ideas and advice of those who offered this perspective he didn't have. And he asked people to teach him what he didn't know. This rich appreciation for the genius of others is how this former football coach became a personal adviser to CEOs at Apple, Google, and many more.

Ignore Boundaries

In their quest to assemble the finest talent, Talent Magnets are blind to organizational boundaries. They see multiple forms of intelligence everywhere. Talent Magnets live in a world without walls and without hierarchical or lateral restrictions. Instead, they see talent networks.

You can often spot Talent Magnets inside organizations because they are the ones who ignore org charts. Such charts are handy for finding out who works for whom and who's in charge if something goes wrong, but these issues are of relative unimportance when you are searching for genius. As far as Talent Magnets are concerned, org charts are irrelevant. Why? Because *everyone* works for them—or at least every person whose genius they can uncover. The mind of the Multiplier works like this: *If I can find someone's genius, I can put them to work.*

The idea is simple. Multipliers understand that people love to contribute their genius. If they put in the effort to figure out someone's genius, they have opened a pathway for that person to contribute. They can utilize them. Multipliers aren't deterred if someone doesn't officially report to them on an org chart. These leaders see an unlimited talent pool that they can draw from. Everyone works for a Multiplier.

For this reason, Multipliers leading cross-functional projects and intercompany ventures may be in key staff roles, or they may be at the top of the org chart. The common denominator is that they look beyond boundaries for talent. A CEO of a high-tech company in Beijing was on the constant prowl for the best talent from universities and the competition. At the end of the working day, he would sit outside a competitor's office in his Uber-registered car and wait to pick up employees. Once in the car together, he would strike up a conversation with them, deliberately hunting for genius. While lurking outside a competitor's office into the dark hours of the night might be extreme, it's a great example of the way Talent Magnets look for talent everywhere and then study that talent to uncover and unlock the real genius that lies within.

2. Find People's Native Genius

As the head of a global function inside a multinational corporation, I spent a lot of time in cross-functional meetings and on task forces. It was almost inevitable that at some point in these meetings, when things would become murky, someone would hand me the whiteboard pen, point to the front of the room, and say, "Liz, lead us through this." I'd readily jump in and do my thing, and at some point hand back the pen. After a while, I started to wonder why I almost never got to be a regular meeting attendee and sit in the back of the room and check email. I thought, *Why do I always get asked to lead these difficult meetings? Why am I always getting put in charge when it isn't even my job?*

After seeing this pattern repeated over many years at work and in other group settings, I realized that I wasn't being asked to be in charge per se—it was a very particular type of "in charge." I would find myself in charge when a group needed more of a facilitative leader and less of a boss. I vividly remember one of my colleagues trying to explain to me why I was always being asked to lead these types of meetings. Ben explained, "It is because you can so easily frame the issue, synthesize what people are saying, and lay out a course of action." What? I stared at him blankly, trying to decipher what he was saying. It sounded like he was telling me that I was good at breathing. It didn't strike me as a particularly big deal or something someone might find difficult. It *was* as easy as breathing, at least for me. What my colleagues were teaching me was that I have a native ability— something that I do both easily and freely.

Look for What Is Native

Talent Magnets know how to uncover and access the native genius of others. By "native genius" I mean something even more specific than a strength or a skill that might be highly rated on a 360-degree leadership assessment. A native genius or talent is something that people do, not only exceptionally well, but absolutely naturally. They do it easily (without extra effort) and freely (without condition).

What people do easily, they do without conscious effort. They do it better than anything else they do, but they don't need to apply extraordinary effort to the task. They get results that are head-and-shoulders above others, but they do it without breaking a sweat.

What people do freely, they do without condition. They don't need to be paid or rewarded to do it and often don't need to be asked. It is something that gives them inherent satisfaction, and they offer their capability voluntarily, even ardently. It is effortless, and they stand ready and willing to contribute, whether it is a formal job requirement or not.

Finding someone's native genius is a key that unlocks discretionary effort. It propels people to go beyond what is required and to offer their full intelligence. Finding people's genius begins by carefully observing them in action, looking for spikes of authentic enthusiasm and a natural flow of energy. As you watch someone in action, ask these questions:

➤ What do they do better than anything else they do?

➤ What do they do better than the people around them?

➤ What do they do without effort?

➤ What do they do without being asked?

➤ What do they do readily without being paid?

Label It

Native genius can be so instinctive for people that they may not even understand their own capability. Perhaps you've heard the phrase "fish discover water last." But if people aren't aware of their genius, they are not in a position to deliberately utilize it. By telling people what you see, you can raise their awareness and confidence, allowing them to provide their capability more fully.

Players for Larry Gelwix, the now retired head coach of the almost unbeatable Highland High School rugby team, often report that he got more out of them than other coaches. Before working with Larry, John saw himself as a good athlete but not a great one. But Larry pointed out something that changed his view of himself. John recalled, "Larry commented publicly about my speed." John was surprised when the coach started talking in front of the other guys about how fast he was. He continued, "I thought I had good speed, but not great speed. But because Larry singled it out, it inspired me to develop a distinct self-concept: *I was fast.* And every time I found myself in a situation where speed was required, I remembered this, and I pushed myself beyond my limits." John not only became fast, he became really fast.

By labeling his genius for him, Larry unlocked this ability for John. Like John, people's first reaction to hearing someone describe a genius of theirs can often be bemusement. You know you've hit a genius nerve when they say, "Really? Can't everyone do this?" or "But this is no big deal!" Finding people's native genius and then labeling it is a direct approach to drawing more intelligence from them.

3. Utilize People at Their Fullest

Once a Talent Magnet has uncovered the native genius of others, he or she looks for opportunities that demand that capability. Some of these are obvious; others require a fresh look at the business or the organization. Once they've engaged the person's true genius, they shine a spotlight on them so other people can see their genius in action.

Connect People with Opportunities

Courtney Cadwell was a seventh-grade math teacher in her first year of teaching at Egan Junior High School in the Los Altos School District. She had a deep and true love of math and science, as well as a penchant for innovation and a drive to experiment with new ideas. What would a typical administrator do with Courtney? Make sure she was happy? Move her to a higher grade level or give her the honors classes? Such actions would surely signal her value to the school and energize her as a teacher.

Courtney's appetite for classroom experimentation and innovation caught the attention of her principal, who had been asked to recommend a teacher to pilot a blended learning solution that would integrate the Khan Academy. You see, the district had established a bold vision to revolutionize learning for all students, and Assistant Superintendent Alyssa Gallagher was assembling a pilot team.

These four teachers, each passionate about rethinking math instruction, jumped in. As they developed new approaches to deeply integrate technology and online learning into their curriculum, they encountered many obstacles and some messy gray areas. Courtney stepped in, asking questions, exploring options, and helping others make sense of the complexity. Alyssa noticed how these messy areas seem to bring out Courtney's natural leadership. But why? Alyssa watched her closely, noting that Courtney had a genius for navigating complexity. Somehow, the grayer the issues, the better Courtney was.

After completing a wildly successful pilot, Alyssa wrangled the funding to take the new blended learning instructional strategies to the next level and spread these practices across all upper-grade math classes involving over fifty teachers. She tapped Courtney to be the district math coach, spending half of her time in her own classroom and the other half guiding the other teachers' ability to implement technology in their classrooms. When these teachers encountered obstacles, Courtney helped them navigate as well. When a teacher couldn't see how to do it without a computer for each student, Courtney asked what could be done with just five computers. Soon they found a way to rotate students. With Courtney's coaching, teachers turned their questions into next steps until the new blended learning strategies were evident in classrooms across the entire district.

By year three, the passion to innovate had become infectious across the school. The parent community took notice and eagerly supplied additional funding for three full-time coaching roles that included a technology integration coach, an innovative strategies coach, and a STEM (science, technology, engineering, math) coach. With Courtney serving as the full-time STEM coach, she was now able to influence all teachers in rethinking instructional practices not only in math but also in science. There was so much interest in the innovation this team was driving, Alyssa organized open-house events for other school leaders to come and learn how they could create blended learning environments and revolutionize learning for their students. And when they came, they had Courtney there helping them navigate the gray areas.

When leaders connect people's natural passions and native genius to big opportunities, those people are used at their highest point of contribution. For Alyssa, this wasn't a lucky discovery; it was a deliberate management approach. She studied Courtney, as well as each of the other team members, noticing what each of them did naturally and freely. She then put them to work at their fullest, tackling the district's aspiration to revolutionize learning for all students.

Are there people on your team who could lead a revolution if they were unleashed on the right opportunity? Are there people on your team who aren't being used at their highest?

Shine a Spotlight

Each summer in the Sierra Mountains of California, roughly seventy-five teenage girls eagerly gather for an annual girls' camp— a week of fun, adventure, and camaraderie that often serves as a watershed event in their young lives. The camp is run entirely on the volunteer efforts of sixty leaders. For the last six years, Marguerite Hancock has served (also as a volunteer) as the camp director at the helm of this incredible group of youth and leaders.

Marguerite is the executive director at the Computer History Museum and was previously a Stanford University research director. She is smart, accomplished, and extraordinarily capable, a strong leader with strong ideas of her own. One of her assistant directors said, "Marguerite is so capable, she could do virtually any aspect of girls' camp herself." But what is interesting about Marguerite isn't that she could—it is that she *doesn't*. Instead, she leads like a Multiplier, calling forth brilliance and dedication among the other fifty-nine leaders who make this camp a reality.

Marguerite begins by building a "dream team" carefully recruited for each person's individual genius. One of the assistant directors told us, "Marguerite studies people. She watches them until she figures out what they are great at. She chose her assistant directors not only for their strengths but because we each had strengths in areas where she was weak." She then finds a place where each person's genius will shine. For some, it is working with the girls one-on-one; for another, it is managing the sports program; for another it is leading the nightly campfire. But each role is carefully cast to draw upon the unique talents of every person on the team.

Marguerite then makes it clear to each person why she has been selected for that role. She not only notices their talent; she labels it for them. One camp leader said, "She tells me the talent she sees in me and why it matters. She tells me why girls' camp will be better because of me and my work." But Marguerite doesn't stop there. She lets everyone else know, too. It is typical for her to introduce someone to the group by saying, "This is Jennifer. She's a creative genius, and we are so fortunate to have her leading our art program."

With her talented cast assembled, Marguerite then goes to the back of the room, takes control of the spotlight, and begins shining it on others. She is effusive with praise, but it is never empty. Her praise of others' work is specific, and it is public. The other leaders at camp can see the direct link between their work and the success of the camp. A camp leader said, "She not only tells you that you are doing a great job, but she tells you why it matters to these girls. I know my work is appreciated."

Marguerite finds other people's genius and then shines a spotlight on it for everyone to see their talent in action. What is the result? A character-building, life-changing experience for seventy-five young women, and also a deeply rewarding, growing experience for the fifty-nine leaders who serve alongside Marguerite.

4. Remove the Blockers

Talent Magnets are attracters and growers of talent and intelligence, and leaders who serve as Multipliers provide both the space and the resources to yield this growth. But Talent Magnets go beyond just giving people resources. They remove impediments, which quite often means removing people who are blocking and impeding the growth of others. In almost every organization there are people who overrun others, consuming the resources needed to fuel the growth of people around them. Like weeds in a garden bed, they choke the development of the intelligence around them.

Get Rid of Prima Donnas

Bloom Energy, located in the heart of Silicon Valley, had developed a fuel cell system that produces clean, reliable, and affordable energy. As venture capital firm Kleiner Perkins Caufield & Byers's first green-tech venture, Bloom Energy has become a leader in their industry. Leading Bloom Energy is K. R. Sridhar, renowned aerospace and environmental scientist and an energy thought leader.

When Sridhar started Bloom Energy, he began with what he calls "gene pool engineering." K. R. explains, "*A* players attract other *A* players. Their smarts and passion make other smart, passionate people want to work here. So your first fifty employees are the most important, and hardest." When Bloom Energy needed to hire their first fifty employees, there was no established green-tech industry at the time. So K. R. broke down each technology they would require to build their energy generators and identified the leading company in this technology. He then researched and found the person inside each company that the company would least want to lose. He reached out to these people, explained the bold challenge Bloom Energy was undertaking, and recruited them to join the company. In this way he engineered a "gene pool" of elite technical talent who were the best in their respective fields. He established one rule: No prima donnas— leave your ego at the door and work as a team. He now had the talent he needed, and the work of building a team that would deliver an integrated energy technology began.

Within this elite team, one technologist was particularly indispensable. Stefan, an outstanding scientist, was the world expert in the technology that was the lynchpin in their solution. As the team worked, it became clear that Stefan couldn't collaborate and had become entrenched in his position about the technical direction the company should pursue. Tensions mounted in the team because the company had just committed to an important beta release in eighteen months. K. R. pulled Stefan into his office and explained the situation, but Stefan wouldn't back down. Knowing how essential he was to the technical viability of the venture, he made it clear to K. R.: it was either him or the team. K. R. explained the options, but Stefan's ego wouldn't allow him to let go of the issue.

K. R. contemplated the issue and the risks involved. Within the hour, he had made his decision. He chose the team. He walked Stefan to the door, then walked over to the rest of the team and explained his actions. "I have put us at significant risk, but I know we have it in us to overcome this. I trust that we will get through this, but there will be significant delays," he explained. Initially the group was silent, stunned that K. R. was willing to let go of their top technologist. One team member broke the silence and said, "There will be no delays. We will do things we have never done before to get this done." With renewed energy, the team worked weekends and extraordinary hours. They brought in consultants with the critical expertise they lacked. They kept up the pace for eighteen months while people grew to fill in the gap that was created by Stefan's departure. They delivered the product successfully, missing their original deadline by only two days!

This incident became the foundation for how the company would operate: the best talent in the industry, but not a single prima donna. K. R. Sridhar accelerated the development of the intellectual assets of this company by getting rid of the prima donna who was impeding the intelligence of the whole organization. Today, Bloom Energy is thriving and is often cited as the reason Kleiner Perkins continues to expand their green-tech portfolio.

Individual genius can be deceptive. At first look, it would appear costly to remove one supersmart player, even if she has a diminishing effect on a team. But one needs only to do the math to see the high cost of destructive genius. Our research consistently confirmed that Diminishers cause people to operate at about 50 percent of their full intelligence and capability. Removing a highly intelligent employee or leader can be difficult, but it can have huge payoffs. On a work team of eleven people, removing a Diminisher can give back the equivalent of five full-time people, with ten people operating at 100 percent. You may lose one mind, but you gain back five. It is a law of numbers.

Leaders most often know who the blockers are. The most common mistake they make is waiting too long to remove them. Is it possible that your smartest people are impeding the smarts of your organization? And is it possible you are waiting too long to remove the blockers? If you want to unleash the talent that is latent in your organization, find the weeds and pull them out. Don't do it quietly. Like K. R. Sridhar, huddle the team immediately, and let them know that you've removed someone because he or she was holding back the team. Give people permission to think fully again.

Get Out of the Way

Sometimes a Talent Magnet removes the prima donna who is blocking the intelligence of others. But sometimes the blocker is the leader him- or herself. The late management guru C. K. Prahalad (who passed away in April 2010) was one of my mentors. He once shared with me an old saying in India: "Nothing grows under a banyan tree." It provides shade and is comfortable, but it allows no sun in for growth. Many leaders are banyan trees; they protect their people, but nothing grows under them.

One corporate VP had a favorite saying, quoted often and written on her door: "Ignore me as needed to get your job done." This simple mantra signaled an important trust in the judgment and capability of others. Her people knew that exercising their judgment and getting the job done rapidly was more important than placating the boss. She told new staff members, "Yes, there will be a few times when I get agitated because I would have done it differently, but I'll get over it. I'd rather you trust your judgment, keep moving, and get the job done."

Talent Magnets remove the barriers that block the growth of intelligence in their people.

The world of the Talent Magnet is dynamic. Talent is drawn in by the strong gravitational pull of the Talent Magnet. It is then fully utilized, stretched, made continually ready for new challenges. Life with an Empire Builder doesn't offer the same thrill ride. It is a world of politics, ownership, and limitations.

The Diminisher's Approach
to Managing Talent

Multipliers operate from a belief that talent exists everywhere and they can use it at its highest if they can simply identify the genius in people. Diminishers think *People need to report to me in order to get them to do anything.* One such senior director said the only thing that was wrong with the underperforming IT division was that it reported to someone else. He saw owning the resources himself as the primary solution. Diminishers are owners of talent, not developers of talent. Because they don't actively develop talent, people in their organizations languish and can actually regress.

Here are the ways Diminishers see the world and operate, and a glimpse at how these behaviors affect people and organizations:

ACQUIRING RESOURCES. Empire Builders focus their energy on acquiring resources and slotting them into organizational structures where they are visible and clearly under the command of the leader. For some leaders, this amassing of talent can become an obsession.

Recall Jasper Wallis, the high-cost Diminisher from the first chapter, who was obsessed with the size of his organization relative to those of his peers on the executive team. After years of building his organization with his right hand while masking with his left hand the underlying problems, Jasper succeeded in building an empire complete with a separate office tower, customer visit center, and training campus just for his division. However, his organization had become gangly after such rapid, unrestrained growth and had acquired new problems in integration and coordination. The hole became deeper and deeper until the division was radically scaled back and folded into another group. Like imperial Rome, the empire eventually over-extended itself and collapsed under its own weight.

PUTTING PEOPLE IN BOXES. Divide and conquer is the modus operandi of Empire Builders. They bring in great talent and carve out a fiefdom for them, but they don't encourage people to step beyond these walls. Rather than give broad scope to their management team, Empire Builders ensure that they, themselves, are the point of integration. You can often spot an Empire Builder because he or she either operates exclusively through one-on-one meetings or runs staff meetings as an official report-out from each fiefdom.

One manager was known for making key decisions one-on-one rather than with his team. This fostered a covert and high-stakes game among his lieutenants. Each of them would vie for the coveted one-on-one meeting time—the last meeting on a Friday afternoon. Why? Because everyone knew that he made his decisions by himself over the weekend and announced them in his staff meeting on Monday. People quickly learned that the person who got his ear last on Friday afternoon would have the most influence. His divide-and-conquer approach not only kept people in narrowly defined roles, it was a dangerous and costly way to make decisions.

LETTING TALENT LANGUISH. One way Empire Builders stifle their talent is by hogging the limelight for themselves. They are often prima donnas, insisting that they get maximum time onstage and that scripts are written to feature them. Whereas Talent Magnets give credit, Empire Builders take credit.

Hogging the limelight is an active way Empire Builders hold others back, but the more insidious problem is actually what they don't do—these managers actively acquire talent, but then are passive about growing it. They are, for the most part, oblivious to the development of others. In fact, in our quantitative research, we found that "developing the talent of the team" was among the lowest three skills of the Diminisher.

They also stifle talent by not clearing away the dead wood. One Diminisher we studied was notorious for draining his organization through his inaction. People said, "He and his management team never made decisions. They didn't make waves, they just kept analyzing." Instead of firing toxic or ineffective leaders, he would slowly disable them. One observer noted, "It was torture to watch one of his staff get cut off. It was like a child pulling off the legs of a spider one by one and then watching it hobble away."

When leaders play the role of the Empire Builder, they bring in great resources, but they underutilize them because they fundamentally undervalue them. They continue to operate in a "one brain, many hands" organizational model that stunts the growth of both intelligence and talent around them. Diminishers build organizations where people go to die. This is why Diminishers are costly to organizations. The assets in their portfolio don't increase in value.

Becoming a Talent Magnet

The promise of a Multiplier is that they get twice the capacity, plus a growth dividend from their people as their genius expands under the leadership of the Multiplier. Let's now look at a few starting points for becoming a Talent Magnet.

How do you create this cycle of growth and acceleration inside your organization? You can kick-start the cycle by learning to be a genius watcher and spotting the native genius of everyone around you. Imagine, if you will, a corporate manager "genius watching," observing each member of her team and noticing what they do naturally and freely. Instead of taking inventory of who has done their job, she asks, "How can I use their natural genius to get our most important jobs done?" Or, consider a new high school principal who, having practiced genius watching on his own team for two weeks, now finds himself spotting genius everywhere. While attending a mandatory school district meeting, he notices Ellen, a curriculum coach from a rival high school, who points out a myriad of pitfalls that the schools might encounter in adopting a new program. Her knack for bringing potential problems to the surface had seemed annoying in previous meetings, but now it appears useful. He wonders who on his team has the "pitfall finder" genius and how he can use it.

If you want to get better at seeing, naming, and using the genius of everyone around you, try the following three experiments—each is a critical skill for the would-be Talent Magnet. Appendix E has full worksheets for conducting many of the Multiplier Experiments referenced throughout the book.

1. **NAME THE GENIUS**—Kick-start this cycle by tapping into someone's native genius and unlocking hidden reserves of discretionary effort. You can start by finding the native genius (that which they do easily and freely) of each individual on your team. Or, you might be selective and focus on an individual you are struggling to work with or trying to understand how to utilize. Perhaps you've been wishing you could remove this person from the team. Instead of asking, "Is this person smart?" try asking, "In what way is this person smart?" You might discover something that breaks the cycle of assumptions. Once you have some practice identifying native genius (in both yourself and others), you can conduct this exercise as an entire management team so that each team member understands the native genius of each person on the team.

2. **SUPERSIZE IT**—Try sizing someone's job the way you shop for shoes for a young child. How does the wise parent decide what size to buy? They start by measuring the child's foot,

and then they buy a pair that's a size too big. And how does the parent respond when their child tries on those shoes, awkwardly parading down the store aisle, complaining that the shoes feel weird and too big and that their feet are flopping around in them? The parent reassures them, "Don't worry, you'll grow into them."

Try supersizing someone's job. Assess their current capabilities and then give them a challenge that is a size too big. Give an individual contributor a leadership role; give a first-line manager more decision-making power. If they seem startled, acknowledge that the role or responsibility might feel awkward at first. Then step back and watch them grow into it.

3. **LET GO OF A SUPERSTAR**—Perhaps the only thing harder than watching an *A+* player leave your team is knowing that you were the one who encouraged them to move on. While most managers try to retain their top players, the best leaders know when it's time to let them go. They recognize when a superstar has outgrown his or her environment. Like parents watching their child head off to college, they are full of mixed feelings, but they are clear that the young person needs a bigger stretch and new test. Is there someone on your team who needs a bigger challenge but won't continue to grow unless you let them go?

Up and to the Right

Sue Siegel, former president of Affymetrix and an extraordinary Multiplier, reflected on her pillar experiences as a leader. She said, "My best moments were when team members would call me after accomplishing some tough goal or overcoming a huge hurdle. They were usually tired, but they were brimming with enthusiasm, having grown through the challenge. These moments were exhilarating for them and me." The people who worked for Sue indeed describe the time as a highlight of their career.

Talent Magnets encourage people to grow and leave. They write letters of recommendation and they help people find their next stage to perform on. And when people leave their group, they celebrate their departures and shout their success to everyone. You see, these celebrations become their best recruiting tool.

Jack and Suzy Welch wrote, "The best thing about being a preferred employer is that it gets you good people, and this launches a virtuous cycle. The best team attracts the best team, and winning often leads to more winning. That's a ride that you and your employees will never want to get off."[4] Talent Magnets create a cycle of attraction that is exhilarating for employer and employee alike. Their organizations are coveted places of employment, and people flock to work for them knowing the Talent Magnet will stretch them, grow them, and accelerate their careers. It is a thrill ride with the speed and exhilaration of a roller coaster but one that, like the revenue chart of every CFO's dreams, moves constantly "up and to the right."

Chapter Two Summary

The Empire Builder Versus the Talent Magnet

EMPIRE BUILDERS bring in great talent, but they underutilize it because they hoard resources and use them only for their own gain.

TALENT MAGNETS get access to the best talent because people flock to work for them, knowing they will be fully utilized and developed to be ready for the next stage.

The Four Practices of the Talent Magnet

1. *Look for Talent Everywhere*
   - Appreciate all types of genius
   - Ignore boundaries
2. *Find People's Native Genius*
   - Look for what is native
   - Label it
3. *Utilize People to Their Fullest*
   - Connect people with opportunities
   - Shine a spotlight
4. *Remove the Blockers*
   - Get rid of prima donnas
   - Get out of the way

Becoming a Talent Magnet

1. Name the genius
2. Supersize it
3. Let go of a superstar

Leveraging Resources

	Empire Builders	Talent Magnets
What They Do	Hoard resources and underutilize talent	Attract talent and deploy it at its highest point of contribution
What They Get	A reputation as the person A players should avoid working for ("the place you go to die")	A reputation as the person A players should work for ("the place you go to grow")
	Underutilized people whose capability atrophies	Fully utilized people whose genius continues to expand
	Disillusioned A players who don't reach out to other A players	Inspired A players who attract other A players into the organization
	A stagnation of talent where disillusioned A players quit and stay	A flow of A players attracting other A players as they then move up and out of the organization

Unexpected Findings

1. Both Talent Magnets and Empire Builders attract top talent. What differentiates them is what they do with the talent once it's in the door.
2. Talent Magnets don't run out of talent by moving their people on to bigger, better opportunities, because there is a steady stream of talent wanting to get into their organization.

THREE

The Liberator

The only freedom that is of enduring importance is the freedom of intelligence, that is to say, freedom of observation and of judgment.

JOHN DEWEY

Michael Chang[1] began his career in a small consulting company. As a young manager, he was forceful with his opinions and veered toward brutal honesty. Over time, he saw its damaging effects and reflected, "It certainly doesn't get people to blossom."

Michael began to realize that when you become the leader, the center of gravity is no longer yourself. He had a mentor who taught him that the leader's job is to put other people onstage. As he began to shift his focus to others, he became less controlling and learned to give people space. Where he used to jump in and do it for them, he learned to hold back. He found that not only do other people step up, they often surprise you by producing something better than you would have. As he has grown as a leader, he's learned to be direct without being destructive. He's learned how to create an environment where he could tell the truth and have others grow from it.

Today, this manager is the CEO of a thriving start-up company.

He has developed several practices that give space for others to do their best work. He makes a conscious effort to create a learning environment by recruiting people with a strong learning orientation and by admitting his own mistakes often. This gives others permission to make and recover from their own mistakes. When offering his opinion, he distinguishes "hard opinions" from "soft opinions." Soft opinions signal to his team: *Here are some ideas for you to consider in your own thinking.* Hard opinions are reserved for times when he holds a very strong view.

Here's a leader who began his career headed down the path of a management tyrant but became a Multiplier and Liberator himself. The accomplishment is significant when you consider that the path of least resistance for most smart, driven leaders is to become a Tyrant. Even Michael said, "It's not like it isn't temping to be tyrannical when you can."

Let's face it. Corporate environments and modern organizations are the perfect setup for diminishing leadership and have a certain built-in tyranny. The org charts, the hierarchy, the titles, the approval matrixes skew power toward the top and create incentives for people to shut down and comply. In any hierarchical organization, the playing field is rarely level. The senior leaders stand on the high side of the field and ideas and policies roll easily down to the lower side. Policies—established to create order—often unintentionally keep people from thinking. At best, these policies limit intellectual range of motion as they straitjacket the thinking of the followers. At worst, these systems shut down thinking entirely.

These hierarchical structures make it easy for Tyrants to reign. And in their reign, these managers can easily suppress and constrain the thinking of the people around them.

Consider the fate of Kate, a corporate manager who began her career as an intelligent, driven, and creative collaborator. She was promoted into management and moved quickly from frontline manager to vice president and is now running a large organization. She still sees herself as an open-minded, creative thought leader. But in a recent 360-degree feedback report, she was shocked to find that her people don't seem to agree. As she read the report, she could see that her strong ideas were hampering the creativity and capability of her people. And her drive for results was making it difficult for people to be truthful and take risks. One of the comments read, "It is just easier to hold back and let Kate do the thinking." Kate was stunned.

Every step she had taken up the corporate ladder made it that much easier for her to unintentionally kill other people's ideas. The nature of the hierarchy had skewed power, making every conversation Kate had with a subordinate inherently unequal because the playing field was tilted in her favor. An off-the-cuff remark could be translated as a strong opinion and turned into policy for her division. If she rolled her eyes or sighed sharply after someone's comment, everyone in the room noticed and avoided saying anything they thought would produce the same reaction. She had more power than she had realized. She had become an Accidental Diminisher.

I suspect I saw too many military movies in college, because they all started to look alike. Inevitably there would be a scene where an army private who was privy to some debacle would stand at attention and nervously appeal to the commanding officer, "Permission to speak freely, sir?" I could never understand this strange custom and why someone would need permission to speak freely. After all, I was in college, where thinking and speaking freely were the norm. However, after several years in the workplace, I clearly understood. Formal hierarchies suppress the voices, and often ideas, of those at the bottom.

Multipliers, by contrast, liberate people from the oppressive forces within corporate hierarchy. They free people to think, to speak, and to act with reason. They create an environment where the best ideas surface and where people do their best work. They give people permission to think.

The Tyrant Versus the Liberator

Multipliers create an intense environment in which superior thinking and work can flourish. Tyrants create a tense environment that suppresses people's thinking and capability.

A Tense Leader

Jenna Healy was an SVP of field operations for a large telecommunications company. Even at five feet, three inches, she had a way of towering over the people who worked for her. Jenna was a serious leader and a smart manager with strong experience, but she was an absolute Tyrant.

Her colleagues told us, "She created an environment of hysteria. She created fear all around her and intimidated and bullied people until she got what she wanted. Her primary approach to leadership was 'What more can you do for me?'" When one of her managers said, "She's a bit like the ruthless Miranda Priestly in *The Devil Wears Prada*," I got the picture immediately.

Not only was Jenna a bully, but she struck at random. It was hard to predict what would set her off or who would be the next victim. One person recalled, "You felt like you could be the next guy. I was stressed, on the edge, and at risk around her." Her colleagues joked, "There needs to be a storm warning system for Jenna. People need to know when it is time to duck and cover."

Jenna's quarterly management meeting in Denver was one such time. Jenna had gathered a cross-functional team to review the state of the business in the US market. It was a typical business review with each function, in turn, presenting its "state of the business." After several presentations, Daniel, the manager of the information technology team, began his presentation by showing the managers the data for how their field service staff was utilizing the IT tools that his team had built for them. He then inquired, "In light of these numbers, I wonder if the service teams are taking advantage of the tools that already exist?" Based on Jenna's reaction, you would have thought he had just told her that her team was stupid and lazy. She snapped, "You have no idea what you are talking about," and then berated him in front of the group. The argument got heated and lasted for an uncomfortable ten minutes. When somebody finally signaled that the group was overdue for a break, there was a rapid dash for the door, but Daniel stayed, in an attempt to hold his ground against Jenna. With everyone out in the hall, the argument escalated irrationally and turned to shouting.

While things were heated in the conference room, outside in the hall, there was a distinct chill in the air. Everyone in the hall was quietly cheering Daniel for standing up to the bully, but those who were next up to present were frozen with fear, and you could feel the tension. The fortunate ones who had already given their presentations wished luck to their ill-fated colleagues. These remaining presenters began scrambling to adjust their presentations, taking out anything controversial that might incite the already irascible leader. The presenters watered down their presentations, and they got through the meeting, but nothing much was really said and nothing much was accomplished.

Jenna's organization made modest progress but continually failed to hit its revenue and service quality targets. Eventually, when she went too far and bullied one of their partners, she was exited instantly from the organization. Jenna went to another company as COO. She lasted two weeks before being demoted. Six months later she was asked to leave.

People hold back around leaders like Jenna. Such Tyrants shut down the flow of intelligence and rarely access people's best work. Everywhere they go, they find people doing less than they really can. It is no wonder they resort to intimidation, thinking it will get them what they no doubt want—great thinking and great work. But intimidation and fear rarely produce truly great work.

Let's look at another senior sales and services leader.

An Intense Leader

Robert Enslin is the president of Global Customer Operations for SAP AG, the global software giant. Originally from South Africa, he speaks with a calm confidence. Robert is highly respected with a reputation as a fair, consistent sales leader who grows organizations and delivers results.

Robert operates as a peer to everyone he works with and is accessible to all. One of his managers said of him, "He is very good at disarming you. He is a commoner—one of us. Even if you work three levels below him, he still wants to know what you think." As a result, people are more transparent around him. They don't feel like they have to tell him what he wants to hear. This approachability creates safety for the people around Robert. And that safety is what allows him to run a massive sales organization with no surprises.

Several years ago, Robert was asked to take over the Japanese subsidiary for SAP to address some very specific sales performance issues. When he met with his new leadership team in Japan for the first forecast meeting, he could see the forecasting process was in complete disarray. Instead of playing the authoritarian, judging their failure, and dictating his solution, Robert restrained himself and started a learning process. He helped them realize the limitations of the current process and the advantages of a new approach. He then drew on their knowledge of the Japanese business and asked them, "How can we take this to the next level?" He created space for the team to try new approaches and fix the problem themselves. He stayed with them on the issue for months until they could run a forecast process that delivered solid, predictable results for the business.

Robert was known for his collegial approach and his calm consistency, but this was tested when he took over the North American business in 2008, just as the global economy was melting down. As spending was locking up and large capital purchases were being put on hold, executives everywhere were beginning to panic. You could feel the tension as you walked through the halls of SAP's Newtown

Square office near Philadelphia. There was even more tension, one step past the glass door as you entered the executive conference room.

Inside another conference room, Robert and his new management team were assembled to plan their sales strategy in this new economic environment. Every person on his team knew that Robert had been meeting with the senior executives and was under a lot of pressure. They came to the meeting prepared to feel their share of the pain—after all, this was a sales organization. But Robert was calm and constant, even amid this chaos. His team began to wonder if he hadn't been reading the news or had skipped the executive meetings. He opened the meeting by acknowledging the severity of the economic issues, but suggested they put them aside. He kept the team focused on the issues within their control. He then asked, "What can we do to differentiate ourselves right now?" Safe within their sphere of expertise and control, the group worked to identify the value proposition that would help them position their solutions in the turbulent climate. After the discussion, he asked, "How can we help people consume our products so they get the most economic value?" Again, the group could wrestle this question down and put together a plan.

His team said, "We know he must have been getting pressure from up higher, but he didn't create anxiety for us. He remained calm and just never wigged out. He doesn't create whiplash for his people." Another SAP executive said, "During a crisis, he asks even more questions—the same type of questions that force you to really think through a situation—just more of them. You feel his stealthy hand guiding decisions."

Robert's calmness is not synonymous with softness. He is as intense and focused as any other successful sales executive. The difference is where his focus lies. His fellow executive continued, "He's hard on the issues but easy on people. You believe that he has your back so when you inevitably make a mistake, he'll help you fix it first and not lash out at you. There's an aura that we're in this together, which means the stress is distributed among the larger group so one person doesn't disproportionally feel it." A member of his leadership team said, "With Robert, it isn't about him. He makes it about you and about getting the best work from you."

Robert's steady hand and open environment provide sanity and stability to an organization that could have easily spun into crisis.

Tense Versus Intense

Tyrants create a *tense* environment that is full of stress and anxiety. Liberators like Robert, on the other hand, create an *intense* environment that requires concentration, diligence, and energy. It is an environment where people are encouraged to think for themselves and also where people experience a deep obligation to do their best work.

Diminishers create a stress-filled environment because they don't give people control over their own performance. They operate as Tyrants, overexerting their will on the organization and causing others to shrink, retreat, and hold back. In the presence of a Tyrant, people try not to stand out. Just consider how people operate under the rule of a political dictator. Tyrants get diminished thinking from others because people only offer the safest of ideas and mediocre work.

While a Tyrant creates stress that causes people to hold back, a Liberator creates space for people to step up. While a Tyrant swings between positions that create whiplash in the organization, a Liberator builds stability that generates forward momentum.

The Liberator

The Liberator creates an environment where good things happen. They create the conditions where intelligence is engaged, grown, and transformed into concrete successes. What are the conditions for this cycle of learning and success? They might include:

➤ Ideas are generated with ease.

➤ People learn rapidly and adapt to new environments.

➤ People work collaboratively.

➤ Complex problems get solved.

➤ Difficult tasks get accomplished.

Let's examine three Liberators from very different industries who created these conditions and freed their organizations to think and to perform.

Liberator No. 1: Equity in the Firm

Ernest Bachrach from Argentina is the director and special partner for Advent International, a global private equity firm. With twenty-seven years of experience in international private equity and an MBA from Harvard University, Ernest is clearly an expert. But the source of his genius is the environment he creates to unleash the genius of his organization.

One of his analysts described his approach: "Ernest makes a conscious effort to create an environment. He creates forums for people to voice their ideas. But he holds a very high bar for what you must do before you voice an opinion. You need to have the data. He has a problem with opinions without data."

Ernest builds a learning machine in his organization. When he discovers performance problems, he is quick to give feedback. The feedback is direct and sometimes harsh, but he dispenses the feedback in small enough doses that someone can absorb it, learn from it, and adjust. He teaches his organization that mistakes are a way of life in the investment business. And how does he respond to mistakes? First, he doesn't panic or assign arbitrary blame. One team member said, "He lets us know that when decisions are collective, the mistakes are collective, too. No one person takes the blame." The team then does a postmortem and learns how to avoid the error a second time. It appears that Ernest understands how to create an environment that best leverages the investments he has made in his people.

Liberator No. 2: Close Encounters

Everyone knows Steven Spielberg as an award-winning film director, and it's likely that your list of top ten movies includes one of his films. But why are his movies so successful, grossing an average of $156 million per film? Some would posit that it is his creative genius and his ability to tell a story. Others would point to his work ethic. But the true "active ingredient" may be his ability to elicit more from his crew than other directors do. People who have worked on Spielberg's films say, "You do your best work around him."

One way he elicits the best thinking from people is that he knows what people are actually capable of producing. Though he knows everyone's job intimately, he doesn't do it for them. He tells them that he has hired them because he admires their work. He uses his knowledge of the job and of their personal capabilities to set a standard for demanding their best efforts.

He comes with strong ideas of his own, but he makes it clear that bad ideas are an okay starting point. He says, "All good ideas start as bad ideas. That's why it takes so long." He establishes an open, creative environment, but he still demands extraordinary work from his team. One of his crew members said, "He expects people to be doing their best. And you know it when you aren't giving your best."

And why does Spielberg produce so many successful movies? Because his crew is twice as productive as those of some of the Tyrant directors we studied. Because Spielberg creates an environment where people can do their best work, these artists and staff sign up to work with him again and again. In fact, Spielberg typically manages two projects simultaneously, each in different production stages, because his crew stays with him and rolls directly onto the next project. He gets their best work and 2× the productivity! And they get to create award-winning films along with him.

Liberator No. 3: A Master Teacher

Stop and think about the best teachers you've had. Pause for a moment and identify one or two. What type of learning environment did they create? How much space and freedom of thought did you have? What were the expectations of your performance? In what ways were you stretched and utilized? And how did you actually perform? I asked these questions of a dozen eighth-grade students in Mr. Kelly's class.

Patrick Kelly teaches US history and social studies to eighth-graders at a distinguished California public school. He caught my attention when I learned that every year at middle school graduation ceremony, he not only gets more "shout-outs and thank-yous" from the graduating students than any other teacher, he gets more than all the other teachers combined. He is more talked about, more loathed, more beloved than any other teacher at the school. Why?

I got my first glimpse at the fall parent information night at La Entrada Middle School. It is one of those nights parents with multiple children dread because, with four children, I have to get to seventeen different teachers' classes, many simultaneously, defying laws of physics. My daughter in eighth grade said to me, "Here's my class schedule. Get to as many classes as you can, but be sure to make it to Mr. Kelly's social studies class. And do *not* be late. And do not talk during his presentation. And do not answer your cell phone. And do *not* be late. Mom, did you hear me about not being late?" I entered his classroom both scared and intrigued. After the standard twelve-minute segment with Mr. Kelly, I left enchanted with eighth-grade social studies, ready to quit my job and go back to middle school to learn US history.

How does he affect students and parents alike in such powerful ways?

It begins with his classroom environment. He makes it clear that you are there to work hard, to think, and to learn. One student said, "In his class, he doesn't tolerate laziness. You're always working, thinking things over, and seeing your mistakes so you can learn from them." It's a professional and serious environment, which gets lighter and more fun as the students work harder. In this environment, students are encouraged to speak up and voice their opinions. Equal weight is given to asking a good question and to answering one of his.

Mr. Kelly's expectations for the students' learning are both clear and extremely high. One student said, "He believes that with high expectations come high results. He demands our best. He makes it clear that if we put in our hardest effort, we will succeed." Another said, "He doesn't hide anything from us and lets us know what to improve on. He demands that we work to the best of our ability." No more, no less—just to the best of their ability. There is no homework in his class—nothing assigned, nothing arbitrary. Instead, students are encouraged to do "independent study" to help them understand the ideas and perform well on tests. The students, having made the choice themselves, do the independent study with zeal.

Not all students like Mr. Kelly. Some find him too tough, too demanding, and his expectations unfair compared to other teachers'. For students wanting the easy path, his class can be an uncomfortable environment. But most students are engaged by his intelligence and his dedication and thrive under his leadership. They experience his contagious passion and themselves become passionate about civil rights, the US Constitution, and their role in the political process.

Patrick Kelly is a Multiplier who liberates his students to think and learn. He creates an environment where students can speak out but where they are required to think and perform at their finest. It won't surprise you that 98 percent of students in his class score at the "proficient" or "advanced" levels on standardized state tests, up from 82 percent just three years previously.[2]

A Hybrid Climate

The secret behind the environment in Mr. Kelly's classroom (and Ernest Bachrach's firm and Steven Spielberg's movie sets) is in the duality we consistently found that Liberators embraced. They appear to hold two ostensibly opposing positions with equal fervor. They create both comfort *and* pressure in the environment. In the eyes of the Liberator, it is a just exchange: *I give you space; you give me back your best work.*

Liberators also give people space to make mistakes. They create an environment of learning, but they expect people to learn from the mistakes. Another fair trade: *I give you permission to make mistakes; you have an obligation to learn from the mistakes and not repeat them.*

The power of Liberators emanates from this duality. It isn't enough just to free people's thinking. They create an intense environment that requires people's best thinking *and* their best work. They generate pressure, but they don't generate stress.

Liberators operate with this dual operating system much like a hybrid car that switches over seamlessly between the electric and the gasoline engine. At low speeds, a hybrid operates in electric mode. At high speeds, it draws on gasoline to fuel the extra demands on the engine. Such leaders create an open, comfortable environment where people can freely think and contribute, and when more power is needed, they invoke their demanding side which commands only the best performance from others.

How do Liberators create a safe, open environment, and also relentlessly demand the best thinking and work of those around them? How do they get the full brainpower of the organization? Let's turn to the practices of the Liberator for answers.

The Three Practices of the Liberator

Among the Multipliers we studied in our research, we found three common practices. Liberators: 1) create space; 2) demand people's best work; and 3) generate rapid learning cycles. We'll examine each in turn.

1. Create Space

Everyone needs space. We need space to contribute and to work. Liberators don't take it for granted that people have the space they need. They deliberately carve out space for others to be able to make a contribution. Let's look at some examples of how they do this.

Release Others by Restraining Yourself

It is a small victory to create space for others to contribute. It is a huge victory to maintain that space and resist the temptation to jump back in and consume it yourself. This is especially true in formal, hierarchical organizations where people are accustomed to deferring to their leaders.

Ray Lane, former president of Oracle Corporation and a prominent Silicon Valley venture capitalist, is a master at executive restraint. One of his portfolio CEOs remarked, "Ray has learned the importance of restraint in leadership. He knows that less is more, and he never wastes an opinion."

When Ray goes on sales calls to meet with executives at a potential client's, two things are certain: 1) The client will want to hear from Ray and his vast experience; and 2) Ray will be prepared. But, despite these forces pulling him in, he holds back. He offers a few opening pleasantries, but he lets the sales team do the deal. Issues come up in conversation that Ray has a point of view about, but still he waits. The sales team, knowing full well that Ray could probably be doing a better job than they, continue their work nonetheless. When they are done, Ray then comes into the conversation. He still doesn't unleash his ideas and give a monologue. He has listened carefully and knows exactly what he wants to add. He dispenses his views in small but intense doses.

A longtime colleague of Ray remarked, "He'll often be quiet for long stretches of an important meeting. He listens to what others are saying. And when he does speak, everyone listens."

Ray is well-known as a brilliant strategist and is perhaps one of the most articulate communicators in his business. But instead of overplaying himself and his own ideas, he creates room for others and uses his presence where it can have the greatest potency and impact for the team.

Shift the Ratio of Listening to Talking

Liberators are more than just good listeners; they are ferocious listeners. They listen to feed their hunger for knowledge, to learn what other people know and add it to their own reservoir of knowledge. As the late management guru C. K. Prahalad once said to me, "How smart you are is defined by how clearly you can see the intellect of others." They listen intently because they are trying to learn and understand what other people know.

John Brandon, one of Apple Inc.'s top sales executives, runs an organization that brings in tens of billions of dollars in revenue each year across three regions of the world. John is a high-energy sales leader and maintains an aggressive travel and meeting schedule, so getting time on his calendar can be tough. But when his direct reports meet with him one-on-one, they get his whole presence. John listens intently to them and is keenly interested in understanding their reality—what is really happening on the ground, with customers and with deals. He asks probing questions that get to the heart of the matter. One of his direct reports said, "The difference with John is not that he listens; it is that he listens to an extreme." In a typical conversation, he spends 80 percent of the time listening and asking questions. By listening, asking, and probing, John develops an understanding of the realities of the business and an understanding with his team of the opportunities and problems they face. This collective insight into the market has enabled John's organization to experience a phenomenal 375 percent growth over the last five years. John, who can certainly talk a good game himself, knows when it is time to listen.

Liberators don't just listen a lot of the time, they listen most of the time, massively shifting the ratio and creating space for others to share what they know.

Define a Space for Discovery

John Hoke, Nike Inc's chief of global design, gathered his senior leaders for a week off-site to explore new thinking in design and how leaders can multiply the talent inside their organization, which I helped facilitate. He wasn't expecting to hear that his optimism as a leader was a problem, but he quickly realized that his hopeful style of leadership might be causing some angst. His team explained the extraordinary pressure they felt to deliver flawless design, every time. With the Olympics around the corner and a brand promise to sustain, the group insisted that there simply was no room to fail.

With John's encouragement, his team and I decided to define a space for experimentation. We rapidly laid out their various work scenarios into two buckets: in one, failure was okay; in the other, success had to be assured. The group debated each until they agreed on every scenario. Within an hour, they had created a playground— a safe space for their teams to struggle and potentially fail without harming their stakeholders or their business. With the boundaries clearly defined, John's team didn't require optimism from above; hopeful energy radiated from within.

This thinking rippled across Nike's design community and sparked leaders such as Casey Lehner, senior director of global design operations, to introduce the "risk and iterate" performance goal that encouraged each design operations director to identify something they would take a risk with and then iterate solutions throughout the year. Casey said, "To me it's not about failing, it's about prototyping. If someone on my team has an idea they want to pursue, I tell them to go for it—and I'll provide support if they need it. If it doesn't work, we can still learn and evolve from it."

This "risk and iterate" effort legitimized the possibility of failure and created safety for designers to tackle the scary problems. One of her twenty staff members said, "She empowers us to lean into the tension and take risks." Another team member said, "She strikes this amazing balance between giving us the freedom to try things and always having our backs when we need support." In 2012, Casey Lehner's staff secretly nominated her for the Multiplier of the Year award and then cheered and celebrated her as she won.[3]

Level the Playing Field

In any formal organization, the playing field is not exactly level, and certain voices are inherently advantaged. These usually include senior executives, influential thought leaders, critical organizations like product development or sales, and people with deep legacy knowledge. Unless the situation is managed, other voices, that are perhaps closest to the real issues, can be muffled. Liberators know how to amplify these voices to extract maximum intelligence and give advantage to the ideas and voices on the lower end of the playing field.

Mark Dankberg is chairman of the board and CEO of ViaSat Inc., which he cofounded in 1986. Under his leadership, ViaSat has consistently been one of America's fastest-growing technology companies and was named three times in the Inc. 500 list of fastest-growing private companies. Mark presides over a large firm with $1.4 billion in annual revenue and over 4,000 employees, but he ensures the inherent hierarchy doesn't block the best ideas from being heard and rising up.

Mark operates with the assumption that if you hire really good people, you don't need to be limited by org charts. If someone on the engineering side of the business thinks something is wrong in another area, it is expected that they will speak up and make sure the company does the right thing. At ViaSat, a VP or CEO can be challenged by a first-year engineer right out of college. If fact, junior staff are expected to speak up, and when they do, they are heard. Mark reflected, "Wisdom doesn't just come from the top; it comes from all across the organization. But, as a leader, you have to do more than just not discourage it, you need to actively encourage people to speak up. The leader has to ask questions and invite the most junior people to express their ideas."

Keven is ViaSat's general counsel, who began working with Mark when he was a young attorney in an outside law firm. Keven said, "The funny thing is, regardless of my level, Mark has always treated me the same. With Mark, it's about good thinking and providing your well-thought-out point of view. Titles don't bring you more respect; it's about what you're contributing. When I was younger Mark always listened to my ideas." Keven recalls one day when he was new to ViaSat and working on a holiday. He accompanied his boss into Mark's office to share an opinion on a business matter. The debate that ensued went on for three hours. Keven was deeply impressed that the opinion of a junior attorney mattered to this CEO and has remained emboldened by this experience years later.

When ViaSat's Commerical Mobility business was experiencing rapid growth, the company assembled a team comprising both veteran leaders and junior managers to formulate a growth plan. As the team began making decisions about roles, one veteran manager casually said, "I'll talk to James about the role and see what he thinks." The newer manager looked surprised that a senior executive would consult with a junior employee: "Talk to him? Don't we just decide what he's going to do? It's not a democracy." When he heard about this, Mark clarified, "Well, ViaSat kind of is a democracy. We don't just tell people what their jobs are. We give people choice about what they work on, as long as they perform at the level their co-workers expect."

Liberators begin by creating space, but they do more than create space for others to contribute. They also expect extraordinary work in return.

2. Demand People's Best Work

Henry Kissinger, US secretary of state under Richard Nixon, was a demanding diplomat, but he also had some masterful Multiplier moments. According to one story, his chief of staff once handed in a report he had written on an aspect of foreign policy. When Kissinger received the report, he asked simply, "Is this your best work?" The chief thought for a moment and, worried that his boss would think the report was not good enough, responded, "Mr. Kissinger, I think I can do better." So Kissinger gave the report back. Two weeks later the chief turned in the revised report. Kissinger kept it for a week and then sent it back with a note that said, "Are you sure this is your best work?" Realizing that something must have been missing, the chief once again rewrote the report. This time when he handed the report to his boss he said, "Mr. Kissinger, this is my best work." Upon hearing this, Kissinger replied, "Then this time I will read your report."[4] Here are a few ways that Liberators demand the best from those they work with.

Defend the Standard

Larry Gelwix, the head coach of Highland Rugby, stood at the center of a huddle of rugby players at the side of the field for the team's first game debrief of the season. Larry asked one question: "Did you give your *best*?"

One player enthusiastically spoke up, "Well we won, didn't we?" Not unkindly, Larry said, "That's not the question I asked." Another player jumped in. "We just dominated that team. We won 64 to 20. What more could you ask for?" Larry said, "When you came for tryouts, I said I expected your *best*. That means your best thinking out there as well as your best physical effort. Is that what you gave today?"

One player described one game played on the island of Tonga when he could answer yes to Larry's question. He said, "I had a painful shoulder contusion after a devastating tackle on my opponent. I was ready to quit, ready to let my team down. I couldn't lift my arm and the pain was excruciating. I remember I began to chant the *haka* [a traditional Maori war chant] in my head. I remember looking over at the sunset through the palm trees. At that very moment the game seemed to stop, and I had a choice. A voice told me that I needed to keep going and do my best, not only for myself, but for who I am, and most importantly for the team—for my brothers. The voice was the recollection of countless practices and games when Coach Gelwix simply asked, 'Is that your best?' I finished that game with two tries [each the equivalent of a touchdown] becoming the first high school American to score in Tonga."

As a manager you know when someone is below his or her usual performance. What is harder to know is whether people are giving everything they have. Asking whether people are offering their best gives them the opportunity to push themselves beyond previous limits. It is a key reason why people report that Multipliers get more than 100 percent intelligence out of them.

Distinguish Best Work from Outcomes

Requiring people's best work is different from insisting on desired outcomes. Stress is created when people are expected to produce outcomes that are beyond their control. But they feel positive pressure when they are held to their best work.

K. R. Sridhar, CEO of Bloom Energy, innovator of green-power generators globally, and a renowned scientist himself, has mastered this distinction in his company. "If you want your organization to take risks, you have to separate the experiment from the outcome. I have zero tolerance if someone does not run the experiment. But I don't hold them accountable for the outcome of the experiment. I only hold them accountable to execute." This is one of Bloom Energy's secrets for innovating across complex, integrated technologies.

K. R. understands the distinction between pressure and stress. He cites the famous image of William Tell shooting an apple off his son's head: "In this scenario, William Tell feels pressure. His son feels stress." K. R. keeps the pressure on his team to act, but doesn't create stress by holding them accountable for outcomes beyond their control.

3. Generate Rapid Learning Cycles

In studying Multipliers, I have often wondered, *How smart do you have to be to be a Multiplier?* The answer from Bill Campbell, former chairman and CEO of Intuit, was perfect: "You have to be smart enough to learn."

Perhaps most important, Liberators give people permission to make mistakes and the obligation to learn from them.

Admit and Share Mistakes

When Lutz Ziob took over as general manager of the education business at Microsoft in 2003, it was falling short of its goals for revenue and reach. Lutz needed to make progress fast and could have easily created a stressful environment around him. But he also needed the organization to be creative and take risks if they were to catch up in the market. It was a classic management dilemma. If you take the obvious path, the climate will become tense and your people may become risk averse. But if you lessen the pressure by softening the goals, then your organization becomes complacent. Lutz did neither.

Instead he created an environment that was equal parts pressure and learning. Lutz never backed down from the natural pressure for the business to perform, but he made it safe for people to take risks and make mistakes. He did this by how he responded to both his mistakes and the mistakes of others.

Lutz does not hide his own mistakes or divert them to his staff, he confesses them shamelessly. He loves to tell stories, and his favorites are about his mistakes. When he launched an unsuccessful product, he talked about it openly and what he learned from it. One member of his management team said, "He brings an intellectual curiosity for why things didn't work out." By taking his mistakes public, he made it safe for others to take risks and fail.

Insist on Learning from Mistakes

Lutz creates room for other people to make mistakes. When Chris Pirie, the general manager for sales and marketing working for Lutz, was newly promoted to lead sales for Microsoft Learning, he tried a risky promotion. Unfortunately, it didn't work. But instead of rationalizing the mistake, he went to Lutz and admitted the misstep, diagnosed it, and then tried something different. Chris said, "With Lutz, you get to make mistakes. But you are expected to learn fast. With Lutz, it's okay to fail. You just can't make the same mistake twice."

Lutz loves feedback. He isn't just open to it, he insists on it. A direct report of his recalled a time he had to give Lutz some tough love about a critical project Lutz was particularly excited about. As such, he had been dominating the discussion and had taken over. Lutz's direct report scheduled a one-on-one, sat down in Lutz's office, and delivered the feedback: "Lutz, you are sucking the oxygen out of the room. No one else has any room to breathe. You need to back off." How do you think Lutz responded? How would you have responded if one of your people suggested you were a domineering oxygen hog? Lutz's curiosity was triggered, and his response was simple. He asked, "What does it look like? Who did it impact? How do I avoid doing it again?" After taking the time to understand his mistake, he asked his direct report, "Will you tell me if I do this again?" His final comment to his direct report was, "I wish you would have told me sooner." He really meant it.

Lutz achieved the climate he wanted, even amidst a stressful external environment, by generating rapid learning cycles. As Chris Pirie said, "Lutz creates an environment where good things happen." Even in times of immense external pressure, Lutz created a climate that drew out people's best thinking and work and he maintained a creative intensity.

Tyrants and Liberators both expect mistakes. Tyrants stand ready to pounce on the people who make them. Liberators stand ready to learn as much from the mistake as possible. The highest quality of thinking cannot emerge without learning. Learning can't happen without mistakes. Liberators get the best thinking from people by creating a rapid cycle between thinking, learning, and making and recovering from mistakes in order to generate the best ideas and create an agile organization. As K. R. Sridhar explained, "We iterate fast so we can bring cycle time down. The key to this rapid iteration is creating an environment where people can bring up risks and deal with mistakes sooner." A. G. Lafley, former CEO at Procter & Gamble, said, "You want your people to fail early, fast, and cheap—and then learn from it."

Diminishers don't generate these cycles. They might request—if not demand—people's best thinking, but they fail to establish the environment where ideas are easily expressed and developed to full maturity and efficacy.

The Diminisher's Approach to Environment

Diminishers haven't developed this smooth duality of comfort and pressure. Instead, they jerk the organization around as they swing between two modes: 1) militant insistence on their ideas and 2) passive indifference to the ideas and work of others.

Timothy Wilson is an award-winning Hollywood property master. He and his team set the scene and create context for a movie, and he has worked on some of the biggest and most successful films. He's a creative genius, but he comes at a high cost. Why? Because so few people are willing to work with him *twice*.

One of his staff said, "I'd take any job before working with him." Signing up to work with Timothy means working in fear and stress with little enjoyment. Those who do work for him say, "You don't want to come back to work the next day." From the moment Timothy steps onto the set, the mood changes. People brace for his criticism. As Jeremy sees Timothy walk over to one of the props that he had been working on for the last two days, Jeremy wonders which of the usual insults it will be. Or will he perhaps deliver a rare compliment? Timothy inspects the prop, and delivers his signature critique, loudly and to the whole group, "This looks like a prop for a B movie." And then there are the random things that set him off. If the prop cart isn't organized correctly, he goes crazy. One day he got so tense that he argued with the director of photography and threw his walkie-talkie at him. The set went from tense to tenser as people prepared to duck and cover.

Some leaders create an *intense* environment that requires people's best thinking and work. Timothy created a *tense* environment by dominating the space, creating anxiety, and judging others in a way that had a stifling effect on people's thinking and output.

DOMINATE THE SPACE. Tyrants are like a gas that expands and consumes all the available space. They dominate meetings and hog all the airtime. They leave little room for anyone else and often suffocate other people's intelligence in the process. They do this by voicing strong opinions, overexpressing their ideas, and trying to maintain control. Garth Yamamoto, chief marketing officer at a consumer products company, uses up almost every cubic inch of space in the room. He jumps in and interrupts people's presentations, he expresses very strong and extreme opinions, and either spends his time micromanaging or is noticeably absent. People warn newcomers in his division, "The art of being successful around here is figuring out Garth." One member of his group said, "I think I am atrophying here. I'm probably giving him about 50 percent." That person has since left the organization and is thriving in another company.

CREATE ANXIETY. The hallmark of a Tyrant is their temperamental and unpredictable behavior. People don't know what will set them off, but it is almost certain that the mood will change when they are around. Tyrants impose an "anxiety tax" wherever they go, because a percentage of people's mental energy is consumed trying to avoid upsetting the Tyrant. Just think of the wasted productivity on the set with Timothy. Instead of using their full energy making "A movie" props, Timothy's team worries about the next thing that Timothy is going to say or do or, for that matter, throw.

JUDGE OTHERS. Tyrants centralize their power and play judge, jury, and executioner. In sharp contrast to the rapid learning cycles of the Liberator, Tyrants create cycles of criticism, judgment, and retreat. Like the presenters scurrying to adjust their presentations for Jenna Healy (the telecommunications sales leader who resembled Miranda Priestly in *The Devil Wears Prada*), people retreat to a safe position where their ideas won't be criticized or exposed. The Japanese have a saying for this: *Deru kui wa utareru,* which translates as, "The stake that sticks out gets hammered down."

When leaders play the role of the Tyrant, they suppress people's thinking and capability. People restrain themselves and work cautiously, only bringing up safe ideas that the leader is likely to agree with. This is why Diminishers are costly to organizations. Under the influence of a Diminisher, the organization pays full price for a resource but only receives about 50 percent of its value.

Diminishers believe that *pressure increases performance.* They demand people's best thinking, but they don't get it. They haven't created an environment where people feel safe to truly express themselves or their ideas. An unsafe environment yields only the safest ideas. On the other hand, Multipliers know that people are intelligent and will figure it out. Because they engage people's natural intelligence, people offer them back their full brainpower. Because people have a foundation of safety and comfort, they are free to offer their boldest ideas, not just the safe ideas that will keep them out of the wrath of a Tyrant. The environment of learning has enabled them to take risks, and quickly and inexpensively recover from them.

There is an assumption that underlies the practices of a Liberator: *People's best thinking must be given, not taken.* A manager may be able to insist on certain levels of productivity and output, but someone's full effort, including their truly discretionary effort, must be given voluntarily. This changes the leader's role profoundly. Instead of demanding the best work directly, they create an environment where it not only can be offered, but where it is deeply needed. Because the environment naturally requires it, a person freely bestows their best thinking and work.

Becoming a Liberator

Remember that the path of least resistance is often the path of the Diminisher. As Michael said, "It's not like it isn't tempting to be tyrannical when you can." Becoming a Liberator requires long-term commitment. Here are a few starting points.

The Starting Block

1. **PLAY FEWER CHIPS.** If you want to create more room for others to contribute, and especially if you are prone to dominating discussions, you might consider a good game of poker chips.

Matthew is a smart, articulate leader. However, he often found himself frustrated and running out ahead of his organization, struggling to bring a cross-functional team along with him and his ideas. He was also struggling to be heard. He had great ideas, but he was simply talking too much and taking up too much space in team meetings. I was working with him to prepare a critical leadership forum for his division. He was eagerly awaiting the opportunity to share his views about the strategy for advancing the business to the next level. Instead of encouraging him, I gave him a challenge.

I gave him five poker chips, each worth a number of seconds of talk time. One was worth 120 seconds, the next three worth 90 seconds, and one was worth just 30. I suggested he limit his contribution in the meeting to five comments, represented by each of the chips. He could spend them whenever he wished, but he only had five. After the initial shock and bemusement (wondering how he could possibly convey all his ideas in five comments), he accepted the challenge. I watched as he carefully restrained himself, filtering his thoughts for only the most essential and looking for the right moment to insert his ideas. He played his poker chips deftly and achieved two important outcomes: 1) He created abundant space for others. Instead of being Matthew's strategy session, it became a forum for a diverse group to voice ideas and cocreate the strategy. 2) Matthew increased his own credibility and presence as a leader. By exercising some leadership restraint, everyone was heard more, including Matthew as the leader.

Try giving yourself a budget of poker chips for a meeting. Maybe it is five; maybe it is just one or two. Use them wisely, and leave the rest of the space for others to contribute.

2. LABEL YOUR OPINIONS. As you know, formal organizations can create a strong deference to the opinions and thinking of the leader. One executive described his first week as the newly appointed president of a large company. People came at him from all directions to ask him their pent-up questions. He was new and wanted to be helpful, so he would offer a casual opinion. To his amazement, weeks later he found that his opinions had become a set of disjointed policies. As he unraveled the mess, he learned to carefully label the difference between a random musing, an opinion, and a policy decision.

Try the practice used by Michael Chang, in his shift to Liberator. Divide your views into "soft opinions" and "hard opinions":

➤ *Soft opinions:* you have a perspective to offer and ideas for someone else to consider
➤ *Hard opinions:* you have a clear and potentially emphatic point of view

By doing this, you can create space for others to comfortably disagree with your "soft opinions" and establish their own views. Reserve "hard opinions" for when they really matter.

3. TALK UP YOUR MISTAKES. There is no easier way to invite experimentation and learning than to share stories about your own mistakes. Your acknowledgment, as a leader, of your mistakes will give others permission to experience failure and go on to learn and recover with dignity and increased capability.

Great parents do this with their children. They understand that their children are liberated when they know their parents are human and make mistakes just as they do. They especially appreciate knowing that their parents learned from their blunders and recovered. When we help people see a path to recovery, we spawn a learning cycle.

As you share your mistakes, try these two approaches:

1. **GET PERSONAL:** Let people know about mistakes you have made and what you have learned from them. Let them know how you have incorporated this learning into your decisions and current leadership practices. As a manager of a consulting group, you might share with your team the time you led a project that failed and how you dealt with the irate customer. You can focus on what the experience taught you and how it shaped your current approach to project management.

2. **GO PUBLIC:** Instead of talking about mistakes behind closed doors or just one-on-one, bring them out in the open where the person making a mistake can clear the air and

where everyone can learn. Try making it part of your management ritual.

As a corporate manager, I would often take this practice to the extreme. A regular feature in my staff meetings was "screwup of the week." If any member of my management team, including myself, had an embarrassing blunder, this was the time to go public, have a good laugh, and move on. This simple gesture sent a message to the team: Mistakes are an essential part of progress.

4. MAKE SPACE FOR MISTAKES. Define the space for experimentation in your team's work by clarifying the area where it's okay to fail versus when failure isn't an option. This delineation acts like a ship's waterline (as described by management author Jim Collins): above the "waterline," people can experiment and take risks and still recover; however, mistakes below the waterline are like cannonballs that may cause catastrophic failure and "sink the ship." Creating a clear "waterline" for your team will give them confidence to experiment and take bolder action but will signal to them to be extra diligent where the stakes are high. This distinction will also signal to you when you can stand back and when you need to jump in and rescue.

Each of the steps outlined above is a simple starting point. But these practices, if done consistently over time, can allow a leader to become a powerful force for liberating the intelligence from within an organization.

Free to Think

When people operate under stress, they shut down. With enough stress, they eventually rebel, often overthrowing their despotic leaders. To build organizations where people can think and do their best work, we need to do more than rid our organizations of Tyrants and oppressive dictators. We need leaders who serve as Liberators, giving people space to think and learn while applying enough pressure to demand their best work.

Multipliers liberate people from the intimidation of hierarchical organizations and the domination of tyrannical leaders. Multipliers don't tell people what to think; they tell them what to think about. They define a challenge that invites each person's best thinking and generates collective will. They create an environment where every brain is utilized and every voice is heard. Instead of rebellion, they create a movement.

Chapter Three Summary

The Tyrant Versus the Liberator

TYRANTS create a tense environment that suppresses people's thinking and capability. As a result, people hold back, bring up safe ideas that the leader agrees with, and work cautiously.

LIBERATORS create an intense environment that requires people's best thinking and work. As a result, people offer their best and boldest thinking and give their best effort.

The Three Practices of the Liberator

1. *Create Space*
   - Release others by restraining yourself
   - Shift the ratio of listening to talking
   - Define a space for discovery
   - Level the playing field
2. *Demand Best Work*
   - Defend the standard
   - Distinguish best work from outcomes
3. *Generate Rapid Learning Cycles*
   - Admit and share mistakes
   - Insist on learning from mistakes

Becoming a Liberator

1. Play fewer chips
2. Label your opinions
3. Talk up your mistakes
4. Make space for mistakes

Leveraging Resources

	Tyrants	**Liberators**
What They Do	Create a tense environment that suppresses people's thinking and capability	Create an intense environment that requires people's best thinking and work
What They Get	People who hold back but appear to be engaged on the surface	People who offer their best thinking and really engage their full brainpower
	Safe ideas the leader already agrees with	The best and boldest ideas
	People who work cautiously, avoid taking risks, and find excuses for any mistakes they make	People who give their full effort and will go out on a limb and learn quickly from any mistakes

Unexpected Findings

1. The path of least resistance is often the path of tyranny. Because many organizations are skewed, a leader can be above average in an organization and still operate as a Tyrant.

2. Liberators maintain a duality of giving people permission to think while also creating an obligation for them to do their best work.

3. Multipliers are intense. Leaders who can discern and create the difference between a *tense* and an *intense* climate can access significantly more brainpower from their organizations.

FOUR

The Challenger

The number one difference between a Nobel Prize winner and others is not IQ or work ethic, but that they ask bigger questions.

PETER DRUCKER

Matt McCauley took the reins of Gymboree, a $790 million children's retailer headquartered in San Francisco, at the age of thirty-three, after coming through the ranks of planning and inventory management. This made Matt not only the youngest CEO to head Gymboree in its thirty-year history but also the youngest CEO of a company in Wall Street's Russell 2000 index.

McCauley used his youth to keep him open to the ideas of others. "I love to riff and bounce ideas off of people. Regardless of what their function is, [Gymboree employees] are all talented, bright people," says McCauley. Matt had been a pole vaulter in college. He set one bar at seventeen feet, six inches, which is what he knew he could clear, and always kept a second bar set at twenty feet—the world record at the time—to remind himself of what was possible. Matt took this same approach at work.

RAISING THE BAR. When Matt took over as president, he had the benefit of a recently rejuvenated product line as well as the challenge of some sloppy business operations. He saw an opportunity not only to grow sales but also to vastly increase net income, which at the time stood at $0.69 per share. Using his deep knowledge of operations and inventory optimization, he estimated the upside opportunity, then went to the board and told them he believed the company could achieve $1.00 per share. The board members laughed, but Matt remained convinced of the possibility.

As Matt met with his management team, he explained his rationale for the growth opportunity in both sales and earnings per share. He took them through the calculations for sales and expense optimizations that he had been studying for the last five years and asked if they could indeed be achieved. He then threw out "Mission Impossible"—a net income of $1.00. He asked each member of his management team this question: "What would be your Mission Impossible?" As the management team caught the enthusiasm of this high-bar approach, they began to ask the entire organization to do the same. Soon every person inside this 9,500-person organization had a Mission Impossible goal—a crazy aspiration. It appeared that being asked to identify their personal Mission Impossible ignited the charge to make it possible.

CLEARING THE BAR. A year later Matt announced to the board, to Wall Street, and to every employee in Gymboree that they had achieved not just the "Mission Impossible" goal of $1.00 but had reached $1.19 per share, a 72 percent improvement over the previous fiscal year.

Fueled by this accomplishment, what did Matt do next? He set the bar higher and suggested to the board that they could achieve $2.00 per share. This time the board thought it was outrageous. But he turned to his organization for support, sharing his Mission Impossible task and once again asking every person to create their personal

Mission Impossible needed to achieve $2.00 per share. In fiscal year 2007, they delivered $2.15 per share, an 80 percent improvement.

Again Matt went to the board to suggest $3.00 per share. One year later he announced $2.67 per share, and two years later, in 2008, an incredible $3.21 per share. That is a more than 50 percent increase in earnings per share year over year and an almost fivefold increase in four years.

MISSION IMPOSSIBLE. This young Challenger CEO used his deep knowledge of the business to see both an opportunity and a path for achieving unheard-of levels of business performance. He articulated this opportunity and laid down the challenge for the organization. He then asked each person to join him in attempting the impossible and to analyze how they might achieve it. By setting the bar high, he gave people permission to rethink the business. By asking them to create their personal Mission Impossible, he allowed them to embrace and step into the challenge themselves. And by acknowledging the impossible nature of the mission, he gave people permission to try without fear of failure.

Matt got more out of people than they knew they had to give—not because he convinced them that a goal was possible, but because he invited them to explore the impossible, that uncertain, uncomfortable place that makes us stretch both our imagination and our capabilities.

Consider another executive's approach to setting direction.

The Expert

Richard Palmer founded SMT Systems in the mid-1990s in the United Kingdom to build systems and tools for business process reengineering. Started as Richard's brainchild, the company's intellectual foundation was built from his expertise as a business process analyst and in expert systems. The process reengineering work appealed to Richard's sense of methodology and superior strategy, both developed through years of playing chess as a youth.

Not only was Richard one of England's youngest chess champions (holding a Master rating), but it was common knowledge throughout the company and typically the first thing people mentioned about Richard. Chess champion and Oxford University graduate. He was clearly a genius and the chief genius in the company. He doesn't just share his ideas; he sells them, relentlessly and forcefully. While he thinks he's inspiring others, it is more like he's wearing them down and flogging people into submission. While he gave the title of CEO to someone else, everyone knew that Richard, who remained the chairman of the board, was still the one who called the shots on budget, pricing, products, compensation, and company strategy.

AN ARMY OF PAWNS. The energy changes in a room when Richard enters. It is as if the headmaster has entered the school assembly. People begin to shrink. People react the way they might when the calculus teacher gives a surprise oral quiz, getting smaller—hoping he or she won't call on them and find them lacking. Despite the fact that everyone fears the attention will turn to them, the attention often just stays with Richard, who works to make sure he is seen as the expert and smartest person in the room.

In one executive management meeting, Richard put the company general counsel in the hot seat with a pop quiz about a technical distinction on a very specific legal code regarding corporate governance. Richard had become concerned that his general counsel didn't fully understand the nuances of this particular code that had to be reported to the city, so he began launching questions. One by one, the general counsel answered them until the questions became more precise and delved into nuances and obscure scenarios. The general counsel looked puzzled but answered the questions to the best of his knowledge. This didn't satisfy Richard, who left work in time to stop by a WHSmith bookshop just before it closed. He didn't buy just any governance book, he bought the 600-page manual on the most recently announced corporate governance codes. And he didn't just look up the answer to the question he'd asked, he stayed up through the night reading the entire book. The following day, he called a meeting of the executive team. The topic for this emergency management meeting was, of course, this particular code. Richard professed his newfound knowledge and quite publicly let everyone know everything the general counsel got wrong.

BAD BISHOP. Richard is a master of the Gotcha: he only asks questions that he knows the answer to. He asks questions to test other people's knowledge and to make sure other people understand his point of view. One of his vice presidents said, "I can't think of a single time that he has asked a question when he didn't know the answer."

He is also a master of the Stall, which he uses when he doesn't have the answer himself. He is known for asking frivolous questions during teleconferences to stall the conversation while he googles the answers to get ahead in the conversation. One such stall was during a meeting with an account team that was planning their sales proposal for a deal with British Telecom. The sales team was reviewing the proposed contract. Richard, who appeared not yet to know exactly how the contract should be worded, jumped in with, "How many of you have read British Telecom's field operations manual?" The document was five hundred pages long and not your typical reading for a sales representative. Wondering if this was a trick question, the team tentatively confessed that they hadn't read it. Richard replied with, "How can you even understand this contract and sell to a BT if you haven't read the field operations manual?" The sales process came to a complete standstill while the entire account team, along with Richard, the founder and chairman of the board, read the manual. One team member said, "He wasn't the kind of leader who would say, 'I have an idea. Why don't we look in the manual to better understand the business and the terms of the contract?' Instead, he made us look ridiculous for not doing it."

FOOL'S MATE. It is no surprise when really smart, talented people don't stay long in this organization. Some are asked to leave when the founder finds out they aren't as smart as he'd like. Others "quit and stay," giving up on the idea of making a meaningful contribution. The sharpest people leave because they see the wasted time and talent and know the organization can't grow beyond its founder. Although the company has been able to grow sales under Richard's leadership, most believe that the organization is inherently limited. They remark, "We'll never become a serious company."

One of these two executives operated as a Challenger. The other operated as a Know-It-All. This chapter is about the difference.

The Know-It-All Versus the Challenger

The approach of these two executives captures the essential difference between how Know-It-Alls and Challengers provide direction and pursue opportunities for their organization.

Diminishers operate as Know-It-Alls, assuming that their job is to know the most and to tell their organization what to do. The organization often revolves around what they know, with people wasting cycles trying to deduce what the boss thinks and how to—at least—look like they are executing accordingly. In the end, Diminishers place an artificial limit on what their organizations can accomplish. Because they are overly focused on what they know, they limit what their organization can achieve to what they themselves know how to do.

In setting direction for their organizations, Multipliers have a fundamentally different approach. Instead of knowing the answer, they play the role of the Challenger. They use their smarts to find the right opportunities for their organizations and challenge and stretch their organizations to get there. They aren't limited by what they themselves know. They push their teams beyond their own knowledge and that of the organization. As a result, they create organizations that deeply understand challenge and have the focus and energy to confront it.

The Mind of a Multiplier

What are the assumptions that lie at the heart of these different approaches? Consider our two CEOs. What caused Matt to challenge his organization in a way that allowed others to do their very best thinking and best work? And why did other people's intelligence and capability stagnate around Richard? We know that both executives are highly intelligent, with a clear vision for their organizations and a passion for their work. But if we examine their approach to setting direction, we can distinguish two different logics at work.

Deeply embedded in Richard's logic is the assumption: *I need to have all the answers.* He sees this as the essence of his job as leader. And if he doesn't know the answers, he needs to either find them himself or appear to know the answers. What does he do when he doesn't have the answer? He stalls until he can find it. He buys a book on it. He reads the operations manual. He googles the answer. He assumes his role is to know and to be the expert. It is an assumption that may have become entrenched in the years he studied expert systems.

If a leader holds the assumption that it is their role to provide the answers, and if the employees resign themselves to this mode of business, a downward Know-It-All spiral naturally follows. First, the leader provides all the answers. Second, subordinates wait for the directives they've come to expect. Third, the subordinates act on the leader's answers. Finally, the leader concludes *they would never have figured this out without me.* He or she sees evidence to support this belief and concludes: *It's obvious I need to tell others what to do.*

Matt's leadership at Gymboree follows a different logic. He uses his intellect and energy on two things: first, asking the bold questions, and second, parsing the challenge into reasonable increments so the team can build intellectual muscle and the confidence that comes from clearing progressively higher bars. His assumption seems to be that *people get smarter and stronger by being challenged.* As people embrace the challenge, both their insights and the belief grows. Soon, the impossible begins to look possible.

If leaders have to spread their intelligence across asking the questions *and* finding all the answers, they tend to ask questions they already know the answers to. Once a leader accepts that he or she doesn't have to have all the answers, he or she is free to ask much bigger, more provocative, and, frankly, more interesting questions. They can pursue things they don't know how to do.

Let's look at another Challenger in action.

The Challenger

By 1995, the Oracle Corporation was headquartered in the affluent waterfront neighborhood of Redwood Shores on the San Francisco Peninsula. Oracle had begun retooling its products for the Internet, but the business strategy was still unclear. The challenge of figuring it out would fall to Ray Lane, Oracle's president, who had joined Oracle two years earlier and had grown the US business from $571 million to $1.2 billion.

RAY'S REVOLUTION. Ray decided to gather the top 250 leaders of the company from across the globe in a series of forums to educate them on the corporate strategy and to align the leadership team behind this strategy. Ray and the other senior executives, including CEO Larry Ellison and CFO Jeff Henley, prepared their strategy presentations and gathered the first group of thirty executives. They gave their presentations and held discussions, but as the week went on, the group became more and more confused. One VP spoke for the group when he said, "We aren't clear on the strategy. We just saw a lot of Power-Point slides."

Ray and his team went back to the drawing board and did a major overhaul of their presentations. They invited another group of thirty executives. This time the feedback was different: all-out revolt. One of the executives took a risk and said, "Stop getting people together until there is a clear strategy!" The team was not buying what Ray and the rest of the team were selling.

INDEPENDENCE DAY. The senior executive team quickly regrouped at Ray's house on their first available day, the Fourth of July. They realized the global business had become more complex and diverse than they originally thought and that they couldn't build this strategy alone at corporate. So they decided to take a fundamentally different approach. Ray and the executive team had started out trying to tell others all the answers. Now they switched to sharing the fundamental questions, trends, and assumptions that were shaping their views.

When they came back together with the next forum of leaders, Ray and the other executives shared what they saw happening in the business and where they saw the world going. Ray seeded the opportunities that these trends would present for Oracle and presented a framework for a strategy—four key transformations needed in the business. And then, with this broad stroke of his brush, he stopped telling and started asking, "Are these the transformations needed in the business?" and "Which of our assumptions about the future might be wrong?"

Ray gave the group a challenge to fill in the blanks. The team would have two days to examine each of the four transformations, identify milestones, and pinpoint the implications for the business, and then pass their thinking on to the next group of leaders, who would go further. The group did exactly that, advancing the thinking of the executive team and then handing off their work to the next group of executives. The group reveled in their collective success and left the forum knowing that they had begun something big. The process continued until every SVP and VP had been involved and each group had challenged the work that had been done before them. They took their task seriously, turning the strategy upside down and sideways as they looked for holes, logic flaws, and vulnerabilities. In the end, they emerged with both a validation and a refinement of the collective thinking. And momentum was still building.

THE CONVENTION. Ray and the other executives culminated this process by convening the entire leadership team of the company. The executive team unveiled the strategic intent of the organization and the transformations needed in the business. The reaction of the global leadership team was overwhelming enthusiasm and optimism, knowing they would be making business history. The strategy was fresh and compelling, yet it was familiar to them because they had cocreated it and could see their fingerprints on it.

When the meeting was divided into regional breakouts, the scene was far from typical. Instead of a discussion about "why this won't work in Europe, the Middle East, and Africa (EMEA)," the conversation in the EMEA breakout room was almost boisterous with questions like, "What is the first step?" and "Where can we start implementing this in Germany?" The scene in the Japanese breakout room said it all. They discussed the strategy and its implications for Japan, and then, with quiet fervor, began to organize as if they were going to battle.

What was unveiled in the meeting and the breakout sessions was a manifestation and statement of the collective will of the organization. In the next four years, under Ray Lane and Larry Ellison's leadership, Oracle led the enterprise computing market and grew from $4.2 billion to $10.1 billion, more than doubling revenues.

Ray Lane began with an honest attempt to sell a strategy to the organization. But he emerged a more powerful leader when he first seeded the opportunity, then laid down the stretch challenge for the organization. By doing this, he wasn't setting the direction, he was ensuring the direction was set and operating as a Challenger.

The Three Practices of the Challenger

How does the Challenger engage the full brainpower of the organization? Among the Multipliers we studied in our research, we found three common practices. Multipliers: 1) seed the opportunity; 2) lay down a challenge; and 3) generate belief. We'll examine each in turn.

1. Seed the Opportunity

Multipliers understand that people grow through challenge. They understand that intelligence grows by being stretched and tested. So, even if the leader has a clear vision of the direction, he or she doesn't just give it to people. Multipliers don't give answers. Instead they begin a process of discovery: they provide just enough information to provoke thinking and to help people discover and see the opportunity for themselves.

We'll outline a few of the ways that Multipliers seed opportunity and begin the discovery process.

Show the Need

One of the best ways to seed an opportunity is to allow someone else to discover it themselves. When people can see the need for themselves, they develop a deep understanding of the issues, and quite often, all the leader needs to do is get out of their way and let them solve the problem.

The Bennion Center, on the University of Utah campus, was established to encourage students to engage in community service projects and activism while in college. Irene Fisher, the center's director for fourteen years, was hopeful that the students would sign up for some of the city's toughest problems.

Instead of making a speech or just selling her vision of service to the poorest members of the community, Irene invited students to take a leadership position and organize other students to work with the community. She took them downtown into the inner-city community so they could see the issues for themselves. They walked the streets and observed the plight of the homeless. They visited shelters and talked with single mothers struggling to get by. Because they saw the needs for themselves, they became passionate and curious about how to create change, and learned rapidly in the process. As their involvement grew, these student leaders assumed more and more challenging roles. She noted, "University students are pretty smart. Once they see something they start asking questions. Our students asked a lot of questions and then went to work." Irene seeded the opportunity and allowed the students to take the challenge. Irene added, "I don't see myself as a challenger per se. I think of creating the opportunity for people to see the challenge so they can respond to it."

The Bennion Center is still thriving today, built on the assumption that you don't get the most out of people if you just tell them what to do. You get full effort if you help people discover opportunity and then challenge themselves.

Challenge the Assumptions

Multipliers ask the questions that challenge the fundamental assumptions in an organization and disrupt the prevailing logic. Renowned management guru and strategy professor C. K. Prahalad was known for asking the questions that challenged the fundamental assumptions of an organization. He understood that strategy is about understanding and questioning assumptions. When working with management teams in leading corporations, C. K. had a penchant for asking the unsettling questions that rattled their assumptions and enabled them to see market opportunities and threats in a different light.

In working with the Philips corporation, a multinational manufacturing company, and after carefully interviewing each member of the executive team to uncover their core assumptions about the business and the tensions in the organization, he could see that they had an assumed invincibility in the market. C. K. formulated a plan. When he arrived at their executive strategy offsite, he began with a fictitious article he'd written that might appear in the *New York Times* forecasting a bankruptcy at Philips. He then launched the following questions: What changes in the current competitive landscape would devastate Philips's revenue stream? What if companies A and B merged? What market changes could lead to a bankruptcy? What is your game plan if it happens? The room became ominously silent. He had shaken their beliefs upon which the current business strategy was based. With the full interest of the executive team, he guided the discussion as they began to explore the answers.

Reframe Problems

Multipliers understand the power of an opportunity. As Peter Block, consulting guru and author, observed, "the most powerful work is done in response to an opportunity not in response to a problem." Multipliers analyze problems, but they also reframe them to show the opportunity presented by the challenges.

Consider how Alan G. Lafley, when he was CEO of Procter & Gamble, reframed the problems of generating revenue growth from new product R&D as part of his overall revitalization of the company.

As Larry Huston and Nabil Sakkab explain in their *Harvard Business Review* article "Connect and Develop," the "invent-it-themselves" model was no longer allowing P&G to sustain a high level of top-line growth. At $25 billion the company could still manage to do it, but beyond $50 billion it was impossible and P&G lost half of their market cap as their stock fell from $118 to $52 a share.

Rather than falling into the trap of doing more of the same, Lafley developed a new strategy of sourcing their innovation from the outside. The shift was from "not invented here" to "proudly invented elsewhere." Rather than thinking of innovation as "invention" where the R&D has to be done in your own physical labs, Lafley looked for ways to join forces with people in their supply chain whom they could partner with to innovate more rapidly.

For example, Huston and Sakkab relate, when the idea emerged to produce Pringles potato chips with pictures and words printed on the crisps themselves, P&G had to decide whether to create an end-to-end solution from scratch, or whether to find an innovative solution somewhere within their partner network. In the past, bringing a new product to market represented a two-year investment. But with Lafley's new reframe, they could see a smarter path.

In the case of Pringles, they "created a technology brief that defined the problems [they] needed to solve, and [they] circulated it throughout [their] global networks of individuals and institutions to discover if anyone in the world had a ready-made solution. It was through [their] European network that [they] discovered a small bakery in Bologna, Italy, run by a university professor who also manufactured baking equipment."[1] The professor's innovation allowed P&G to get to market in half the time and at a fraction of the cost of inventing the solutions in-house. The product was an immediate hit that led the Pringles division to enjoy double-digit growth for the next two years.

Create a Starting Point

Multipliers provide a starting point but not a complete solution. In this way, they generate more questions than answers. These questions then encourage their team to fully define the opportunity while giving them confidence that they are building on a solid foundation.

Ray Lane and Oracle's top executives created the skeleton of a strategic framework and then asked groups of senior leaders to work systematically and collaboratively to complete the whole strategy.

When a Challenger has successfully seeded an opportunity, other people can see the opportunity for themselves. And because the opportunity has been planted but is not fully grown, others are taken through a process of discovery. This process of exploration and discovery sparks intellectual curiosity and begins to generate energy for the challenge. The answers are not clear yet, so people know "there is still something for me to do," and they feel motivated to step in and be involved.

2. Lay Down a Challenge

Once an opportunity is seeded and intellectual energy is created, Multipliers establish the challenge at hand in such a way that it creates a huge stretch for an organization. While Diminishers create a huge gap between what they know and what other people know, Multipliers create a space between what people know and what they need to know, and that draws people into the challenge. They establish a compelling challenge that creates tension. People see the tension and the size of the stretch and are intrigued and, perhaps, even puzzled.

How does a Multiplier achieve this level of stretch without breaking an organization? How do you create intrigue rather than apprehension? In our research, we found that Multipliers achieve this energizing stretch in three ways. First, they extend a clear and concrete challenge. Then they ask the hard questions that need to be answered to achieve the challenge, but—most important—*they* don't answer them. They let others fill in the blanks.

Extend a Concrete Challenge

Sean Mendy is the senior director of development at Boys and Girls Clubs of the Peninsula. Sean previously oversaw the club's after-school program in East Palo Alto, California, a city that in 1992 had the highest per capita murder rate in the United States and where dropping out of high school is a norm. Sean himself faced many challenges growing up, but went on to attend and graduate from Cornell University and then earn graduate degrees from Stanford University and the University of Southern California. With a journey like Sean's, he has ample reason to tell the teens he works with what they need to do to succeed. But instead of telling, he challenges.

When Sean first met Tajianna Robinson (or Taji), she was a shy and hesitant twelve-year-old. When she reluctantly shook his outstretched hand, he stopped her and with a big smile said, "You know, there are three things you might want to do when you meet someone. First, look them in the eye. Second, give them a firm hand. Third, shake their hand up and down three full times." Taji was appalled but intrigued.

Sean continued to extend small, specific challenges to her. He asked Taji if she would take a newspaper class. She did. Then he encouraged her to write a main article for the school paper, meet regularly with a writing tutor, and learn how to write a great essay. Again, she did. Next, he encouraged her to raise the bar and compete in her school's Scholar of the Year competition. She won!

Sean extends these challenges by asking youths hard questions and then giving them the space to think and respond. As Taji put it, "He taught me to think for myself." This allows Taji and others to strengthen intellectual muscles and build the confidence they need to tackle the hardest challenges.

Early on with Taji, Sean looked her in the eye and asked, "If you could get out of this environment, what would you do?" There was a long silence. Finally Taji said, "I'd go to college." Sean responded, "What would it take for you to do that?" After several moments of reflection, her eyes lit up and she said, "I'd need to get into the right high school!" They set a goal for Taji to earn a scholarship to one of the top-tier prep schools in the surrounding area. Sean asked, "Where should we start?"

Taji led the process, but together they figured out which schools would be the best fit. They completed applications and prepared for her high school interviews. The night before one of the biggest interviews, Taji's family left her at home to do her homework while they went out for a drive. As the family pulled up to a stop sign, a gunman approached the car, firing multiple bullets into the vehicle that was transporting three small children. Taji's older cousin was shot in the back, and her six-year-old sister was shot in the leg. Nobody died, but it was traumatic in every conceivable way.

The next morning Sean suggested Taji might want to reschedule the high school interview they had planned. But through her emotions she yelled, "This is how I am going to get out of here! This is what I need to do to have the kind of life I want. And this is how I can help my family and make sure it doesn't happen again!" She wiped her tears, went to the interview, and blew away everyone she met. Tajianna was accepted to four competitive preparatory schools, earning full scholarships to each. Taji grew into a resilient, motivated, bright young teen, attended Sacred Heart, a private school in Atherton, California, and is now in college.

Out of the seventeen students in Sean's eighth-grade program, twelve have received scholarships to prestigious prep schools and the other five have entered rigorous college-track programs. Sean served as a Challenger, helping these youth raise their aspiration level and build the mental agility they would need to get and stay on a course of success.

Whether it is Matt McCauley at Gymboree extending the $2.00 challenge or Sean Mendy issuing the college-bound challenge, our research showed that Multipliers use their intelligence to make challenges concrete for others. These challenges become tangible and measurable, allowing people to assess their performance. By making a challenge real, they allow others to visualize the achievement and communicate the confidence that the organization has the collective brainpower required. This confidence is essential, because the challenge will demand that the entire organization extend itself beyond its current reach and capability.

Ask the Hard Questions

Diminishers give answers. Good leaders ask questions. Multipliers ask the really hard questions. They ask the questions that challenge people not only to think but to rethink. They ask questions so immense that people can't answer them based on their current knowledge or where they currently stand. To answer these questions, the organization must learn. Enabled by these big questions, a vacuum is created in the space between what people know and what they need to know, and a vacuum between what they can currently do and what they need to be able to do. This vacuum creates a deep tension in the organization and raises a need to reduce that tension. It is like a rubber band that is stretched to its limit. One side needs to move toward the other to reduce the tension.

Matt McCauley at Gymboree created this forward pull when he asked each member of his organization, "What is your Mission Impossible?" By establishing this tension, it became impossible to stay in the same place.

Let Others Fill In the Blanks

How do Multipliers get people to step into a challenge? They shift the burden of the thinking to others. Initially, when they establish a concrete challenge, the burden of the thinking sits with them as the leader. By asking the hard questions and inviting others to fill in the blanks, they are shifting the burden of thinking onto their people. The onus now sits with their team to understand the challenge and find a solution. In this shift, the Multiplier creates intelligence and energy around him or herself.

After assuming leadership of a new division in a large consumer electronics company in Korea, the CEO called his management team together and informed them of his goals to be number one in the market and to become a magnet company attracting top college graduates. He was clear that the trajectory for the organization would not be incremental. He had a vision of something big. He then engaged a broad array of stakeholders in analyzing how to achieve the number one position. The coalition included key executives, founding family members, and outside consultants. Assembling the coalition, he seeded the opportunity and posed the difficult questions, such as, "Why are we in this business?" and "Do we deserve to be in this business?" and "What would it take to be better than our competition?"

These questions cut to the bone of the organization and stirred up chaos. Yet he never backed down. The tension forced the team to generate answers. He asked the hard questions and then let the team fill in the blanks. As they did, he maintained a tight time frame. He said, "I don't need 100 percent answers. I need a 30 percent answer in two days. Give me a 30 percent answer so we can talk about it and decide if it makes sense for you to find a 50 percent answer. And if we get there, we'll block two months to get a 100 percent answer."

In the end there were clear answers. The process took months and was scrappy, but it built the intellectual muscle and energy the organization needed for the challenge.

Laying down a challenge means more than directing people to do it. It includes asking the hard questions that no one yet has the answers to and then backing off so that the people within the organization have the space to think through the questions, take ownership, and find the answers.

When a Multiplier has successfully laid down the challenge, people see the stretch, are intrigued, and become intellectually engaged. The burden of thinking has been shifted to the organization. This process of ownership and stretch continues to build energy by creating the intellectual muscle for the challenge.

3. Generate Belief

By seeding the opportunity and laying down a challenge, people are interested in what is possible. But this isn't enough to create movement. Multipliers generate belief—the belief that the impossible is actually possible. It isn't enough that people see and understand the stretch; they need to actually stretch themselves.

The following are a few ways we discovered that Multipliers produce this belief in their organizations.

Helicopter Down

One way Multipliers generate belief is by taking the challenge down to the ground level. K. R. Sridhar, CEO of Bloom Energy, whose vision is to produce power generators for homes and businesses at half the carbon emissions of traditional power generators, explains, "The direction needs to be improbable but not impossible. It can't just exist at 30,000 feet. It has to be at the 1,000 foot level. It is irresponsible to ask your team to do something if the CEO exposure is only at the 30,000 foot level. You have to take it down and show that it can be done. You have to show them a pathway and show why it can be done. You only need to do this once to create the belief." By "helicoptering" down to reality, Multipliers create a meaningful proof point that a bold challenge can be successfully met.

Cocreate the Plan

When people create the plan that they eventually will implement, belief in its viability will be inherently high. Led by Ray Lane in 1996, Oracle not only built a strategic intent, it also built a deep belief within the organization that Oracle could lead the Internet era. Because 250 senior leaders were given the opportunity to cocreate the corporate strategy, they understood the challenge ahead and knew what actions would be necessary to achieve it. They had built the collective will and energy needed to execute. The organization was ready to take the challenge.

Orchestrate an Early Win

Sometimes, the temptation exists for leaders to tackle too many problems all at once. Our research showed that Multipliers begin with small, early wins and use those to generate belief toward the greater stretch challenges.

Consider Nobel Prize winner Wangari Maathai, who passed away in 2011. In her words, "I was hearing many Nairobi women complain that they didn't have enough firewood, they were also complaining that they did not have enough water. 'Why not plant trees?' I asked them. And so they just started, *very, very, very small*. And before too long they started showing each other. Communities began empowering each other to plant trees for their own needs."[2]

From just seven original trees planted by Wangari on June 5, 1977, on World Environment Day, the Green Belt movement has successfully planted more than 40 million trees in Africa. And, of course, the movement goes beyond trees. Wangari has written, "Many people don't understand that the tree is just an entry point. It is an easy point. Because it is something that people understand. It is something people can do. It is not very expensive to do it. And you don't need too much technology to do it. But once we get into the community through tree planting, we deal with a lot of other issues. We deal with issues of governance, issues of human rights, issues of conflicts and peace, [and] issues of long-term resource management."

Senior leaders in corporations can generate belief about significant challenges by orchestrating small, early wins.

When the Multiplier has generated belief in what is possible, the weight shifts and the organization is willing to leave the realm of the known and venture into the unknown.

The Academy Award–winning documentary *Man on Wire* chronicles the feat of renowned high-wire artist Philippe Petit in 1974 as he walked a tightrope stretched 140 feet across the expanse between the 1,368-foot-high Twin Towers of the World Trade Center in New York City. In the movie, Petit explains the moment of truth when he stood on the edge of one tower with his back foot on the building and his front foot on the cable. "I had to make a decision of shifting my weight from one foot anchored to the building to the foot anchored on the wire. This is probably the end of my life to step on that wire! On the other hand, something I could not resist . . . called me up on that cable."

I have seen this shift of weight happen many times inside organizations. You can almost feel the energy of the organization begin to tip in a new direction. This shift happens when an individual or organization has fully embraced a challenge and has generated the belief in what is possible. It is not the Multiplier who whips up this belief. Rather, it is the challenge he or she has issued that generates this commitment. This challenge process builds the intellectual muscle, the emotional energy, and the collective intent to move forward. Multipliers orchestrate the process needed to shift the weight of an organization.

The Diminisher's Approach to Setting Direction

In contrast to Multipliers, Diminishers have a fundamentally different approach to providing direction. Instead of using their intelligence to enable people to stretch toward a future opportunity, they give directions in a way that showcases their superior knowledge. Instead of seeding an opportunity and laying out a believable challenge, Diminishers tell and test. Like the stereotypical Know-It-All, they tell people what they know, tell people how to do their jobs, and test other people's knowledge to see if they are doing it right.

TELLING WHAT THEY KNOW. Diminishers consider themselves thought leaders and readily share their knowledge; however, they rarely share it in a way that invites contribution. They tend to sell their ideas rather than learning what others know. One manager in Europe "took up all the oxygen in the room" by talking endlessly about *his ideas*. A peer said of him, "He is so busy sharing what he thinks, there is no space for anyone else." A direct report added this insight, "I have worked in the same department with him for ten years, and he has never asked me a question. Not once. Not ever. I have occasionally heard him ask a question to the universe, 'I wonder why we do X?' but even then he fills the silence with his own thoughts about the answer."

TESTING WHAT YOU KNOW. When Diminishers do actually engage others, it's no surprise that they want to verify that you understand what they know. They ask questions to make a point rather than to access greater insight or to generate collective learning. Like Richard Palmer, the founder discussed earlier, they are masters of the Gotcha question. Diminishers leave people stressed, but unstretched.

TELLING PEOPLE HOW TO DO THEIR JOBS. Rather than shift responsibility to other people, Diminishers stay in charge and tell others—in detail—how to do their jobs. They assume the senior thinker posture, giving themselves permission to generate both the questions and the answers.

One such Diminisher was Chip Maxwell, an executive producer on a major motion picture production set. Despite the fact that the director had carefully assembled a world-class team of talent, Chip was constantly interfering in the team's work, routinely bypassing the director to tell his staff exactly how to do their jobs. The director of photography abruptly resigned in the middle of filming, claiming that if Chip seemed to know how to light the shot better than he did, then maybe he could be the DP. This award-winning DP knew the number of lights needed, and he certainly knew where to put them. He also knew his talents could be better used on another film.

Diminishers often unintentionally shut down the intelligence of others. Most Diminishers have built their careers on their own expertise and have been rewarded for their superior knowledge. For many, it is not until they reach a career plateau or crisis—or the director of photography quits in the middle of filming—that they begin to recognize that their base assumptions are inaccurate and are limiting themselves and others.

A colleague of mine recently took an IQ test and received a score of 144. He was exuberant and claimed that he was just one point shy of certified genius status. No doubt he was envisioning his welcome letter from Mensa. On learning of our research, his enthusiasm became a bit dampened: "Wow. I have worked all my life to prove I am a genius, and just at the point that I can say that I am, I learn that it doesn't even matter anymore!"

Of course, this is only half right. Raw mental horsepower is still relevant. But the most powerful leaders are those who not only have this mental horsepower themselves but also know how to multiply it by accessing and stretching other people's intelligence. Consider the difference between a leader who yearns for an additional IQ point to take their IQ to 145, official Genius Level, and leaders who use their intelligence to add an IQ point to every person in their organization! What could your organization accomplish if every person became effectively "one point smarter"?

There are times when a leader is so knowledgeable and personally brilliant that it seems tempting for them to provide directives centered in what they know. However, in the end, Know-It-Alls limit what their organization can achieve to what they themselves know how to do. Under their leadership, the organization never leverages its full intelligence, and the true capacity of the organization is idled away or becomes consumed by the "fire drill" of figuring out what the boss thinks.

DIMINISHERS CREATE IDLE CYCLES. A highly intelligent vice president at a major global technology firm was accustomed to a fast-paced and demanding environment. He was a competitor in the market who never stopped challenging himself and others. However, after transferring to a division led by a classic Know-It-All, he found himself idle most of the time. He said, "I spend most of my time waiting for my boss to make decisions. In the meantime, I can't do much else. I am essentially working part-time. I'm bored, but I am enjoying taking sailing lessons!" This vice president was ready for high-speed battle but was relegated to easy sailing.

In contrast, Multipliers create rapid cycles. By playing the Challenger instead of the Know-It-All, they access more brains, get those brains working faster, and earn the full discretionary effort of their people. Once they have a clear view of latent opportunities and challenges, they understand that there are no resources worthy of waste. Under the direction of Challengers teams are able to accelerate their performance. Because the organization does not have to wait for the leader to think of it first, they can solve tougher problems at an accelerated rate. Because people understand the context, they can act for themselves rather than wait to be told or approved. Because they are encouraged to be "smarter than the leader," people can stop competing for idea validation and instead commit themselves to the challenge. And the result is that intelligence grows—individually and collectively. The collective intent built within the organization enables the whole group to break through challenges no single leader, however intelligent, could have done alone.

This understanding leads to a key question: how does someone provide direction like Matt McCauley at Gymboree or Ray Lane at Oracle? How does someone go from a Know-It-All to a Challenger?

Becoming a Challenger

Challengers start with developing their overactive imagination and a serious case of curiosity. In our research, we analyzed how Multipliers and Diminishers were rated against forty-eight leadership practices. It is not surprising that the highest-rated practice for Multipliers was Intellectual Curiosity. Multipliers create genius in others because they are fundamentally curious and spark learning in those around them. The question "why" is at the core of their thinking and takes the form of an insatiable need for deep organizational understanding. Challengers are Multipliers who ponder possibilities. They want to learn from people around them. At the heart of any challenge is intellectual curiosity: *I wonder if we could do the impossible?* When deeply rooted in a mindset of curiosity, one is ready to begin working as a Challenger. Here are several starting points.

The Starting Block

1. TAKE THE EXTREME QUESTIONS CHALLENGE. Most executives are barraged with questions, constantly responding to others seeking their opinion. The nature of the executive role makes it easy to stay rooted in answer mode and to be the boss. A bad leader will tell people what to do. A good leader will ask questions and let his or her people figure out the answers. A great leader asks the questions that focus the intelligence of their team on the right problems. The first step in this journey is to stop answering questions and begin asking them.

Several years ago I was commiserating with a colleague at work about our parenting challenges. Brian also had several small children, so he was simpatico as I lamented that I had become a bossy mom, constantly telling my kids what to do and barking orders. I detailed a typical evening at my house: "Get ready for bed. Stop that. Leave her alone. Pick up your toys. Put on your pajamas. Brush your teeth. Go back and use toothpaste this time. Story time. Get into bed. Go back to bed. No, not in my bed, *your* bed. Okay, now go to sleep."

Now, I wasn't looking for advice—this was purely recreational complaining. But Brian offered an interesting challenge. He said,

"Liz, why don't you go home tonight and try speaking to your children only in the form of questions. No statements, no directives, no orders. Just questions." I quickly countered, "But this is impossible. I'll be home by six o'clock p.m. and I can't get them to go to sleep until nine thirty. That's three and a half hours!" Brian assured me that he understood and reiterated the challenge, "No statements. Just questions." As I drove home I became more intrigued and decided I would take the challenge to the extreme. Everything I said would be a legitimate question.

I summoned strength, opened the house door, and began the experiment. Dinner and playtime were interesting. When it got close to bedtime, I looked at my watch and asked my children, "What time is it?" One responded, "It's bedtime." I continued, "What do we do to get ready for bed?" They explained, "We get our pajamas on." "Okay, who needs help?" The two-year old did, so I helped him while the girls got themselves dressed for bed. "What's next?" I asked. Their responses showed remarkable understanding of the bedtime routine and eagerness to act. Soon their teeth were brushed. "What story will we read tonight? . . . and whose turn is it to pick the story? And who is going to read it?" After story time I asked, "Who is ready for bed?" Eagerly, they said their prayers and hopped into their beds. And stayed there. And then nodded off to sleep.

I stood in the hallway in shock and wondered, *Have I just witnessed a miracle? What has happened to my children?* And, *How long have they known how to do this?*

I was intrigued by this dramatic change in our home, so I continued the experiment a couple more nights. Yes, I did return to a more balanced pattern of communication, but not before the experience had a profound and permanent shift in the way I led. When I moved out of the mode of giving the answers and started asking the questions, I discovered that my kids knew how to do a lot of things that I had been doing for them. I decided to try it at work. I began asking questions like, "What do you think might go wrong?" or "How can we solve this problem?" As I began to tell less and ask more, I found that my management team was even smarter than I had previously seen. Most of the time, they didn't need me telling them what to do; they needed me to ask an intelligent question.

I learned that the best leaders ask questions and let other people find answers.

Take the Extreme Question Challenge to shift from Know-It-All into Challenger mode. Start with 100 percent. Try it at home—you might find that your children (or housemates) are good guinea pigs and great teachers! At work, take the first step by finding a meeting that you can lead solely with questions. You might be surprised at what people around you already know. If you're concerned this extreme approach will seem abrupt or strange, let your team know you're experimenting with a new approach. While taking the Extreme Question Challenge is a useful exercise for disrupting existing patterns of behavior, it's not intended to be a permanent mode of operating. Once you've developed a greater ability and propensity to lead through questions, you can strike an appropriate balance between inquiry and advocacy, especially one that is in harmony with your national culture.

2. CREATE A STRETCH CHALLENGE. Engage your team by giving them a "mission impossible," a hard, concrete challenge that will stretch them and develop new capabilities. Identify a major challenge and start the team by getting specific. Make it an intriguing puzzle by detailing the constraints, such as, "How do we accomplish X by Y date, with only Z resources available to us?" Then stand back and let your team solve the puzzle. When leaders offer a challenge and then create a culture of belief, the organization steps up. People contribute beyond what they thought they could. Your team will likely report the experience as "exhausting but totally exhilarating" and will want to sign up for another stretch.

3. TAKE A BUS TRIP. University of Michigan professor Noel Tichy tells a story about an executive at GE who found a creative way to seed a challenge and help his organization see a need in the marketplace.[3] When Tom Tiller took over the failing appliance division at GE, the division was losing money, slashing its workforce, and hadn't released a new product in years. Tom loaded forty people from his management team onto a rented bus and headed for the Atlanta Kitchen and Bath Show. The group was to find trends and needs, and generate new product ideas that would keep the plant alive. The group developed a new line of products and turned around the division, from a staggering loss to a $10 million profit.

There are many ways to take a bus trip. Irene Fisher of the Bennion Center took people into the inner city so they could see the needs of the poor firsthand. As a corporate manager, you might visit a customer's factory floor to watch how a customer actually uses your product. You can take your team down to the local mall to watch people shop. But take that bus (or van or train) trip together. Help people see the need that must be met. Make it a learning experience that will reveal that need, create energy, and ignite a fire within your organization.

4. TAKE A MASSIVE BABY STEP. The corporate world has a plethora of terms for this: creating an early win, delivering a symbolic victory, and—the favorite—picking the low-hanging fruit. The problem is that most leaders do this in isolation. They pick a small group to run a pilot, which catches the attention of management but doesn't have the visibility to get the attention of the entire organization. Instead, do it en masse. Make it visible. Create a conference room pilot for a new technology and hold an open house. Win back an important customer through the efforts of a cross-functional task force. Get the entire organization to take a small, first step. But do it together so everyone can see the results and start to believe that something great is possible. This belief is what will shift the weight of the organization out onto that high wire.

A Good Stretch

Jimmy Carter said, "If you have a task to perform and are vitally interested in it, excited and challenged by it, then you will exert maximum energy. But in the excitement, the pain of fatigue dissipates, and the exuberance of what you hope to achieve overcomes the weariness." Our research showed that Multipliers make challenges both provocative and plausible, attracting others to join them and offer their full capability, both intellectually and emotionally. Their approach generates the collective will and stretch needed to undertake the most paramount of challenges.

Our research has shown that when people work for Diminishers, they give only half of their capability, yet they consistently report the experience to be "exhausting." In contrast, under the leadership of Multipliers, people are able to give their all—100 percent even—and describe the experience as "a bit exhausting but totally exhilarating!" Isn't it interesting that giving half our capability is exhausting, but giving our all is exhilarating? We often think burnout is a result of working too hard; more often burnout occurs when people are merely doing more of the same or when they can't see the results of their hard work. Good leaders don't just give people more work, they give them harder work—a bigger challenge that prompts deep learning and growth.

When leaders operate as challengers—telling less and asking more—they get contributions from their people that far surpass what they thought they had to give and it is this concomitant exhilaration that makes people sign up again and again. Why? Because they have been offered a deeply challenging and rewarding experience. Ask for more and you will get more. So will the people who work for you.

Chapter Four Summary

The Know-It-All Versus the Challenger

KNOW-IT-ALLS give directives that showcase how much they know. As a result they limit what their organization can achieve to what they themselves know how to do. The organization uses its energy to deduce what the boss thinks.

CHALLENGERS define opportunities that challenge people to go beyond what they know how to do. As a result they get an organization that understands the challenge and has the focus and energy to take it on.

The Three Practices of the Challenger

1. *Seed the Opportunity*
   - Show the need
   - Challenge the assumptions
   - Reframe problems
   - Create a starting point
2. *Lay Down a Challenge*
   - Extend a concrete challenge
   - Ask the hard questions
   - Let others fill in the blanks
3. *Generate Belief in What is Possible*
   - Helicopter down
   - Cocreate the plan
   - Orchestrate an early win

Becoming a Challenger

1. Take the extreme questions challenge
2. Create a stretch challenge

3. Take a bus trip
4. Take a massive baby step

Leveraging Resources

	Know-It-Alls	**Challengers**
What They Do	Give directives that showcase "their" knowledge	Define opportunities that challenge people to go beyond what they know how to do
What They Get	Distracted efforts as people vie for the attention of the boss	Collective intent toward the same overarching opportunity
	Idle cycles in the organization as people wait to be told what to do or to see if the boss will change direction again	Rapid cycles and accelerated problem solving without the initiation of the formal leader
	An organization that doesn't want to get ahead of the boss	People's discretionary effort and intellectual energy to take on the toughest organizational challenges

Unexpected Findings

1. Even when leaders have a clear view of the future, there are advantages to simply seeding opportunities.
2. Challengers have full range of motion: they can see and articulate the big thinking and ask the big questions, but they can also connect that to the specific steps needed to create movement.
3. If you ask people to take on the impossible in the right way, it can actually create more safety than if you ask for something easier.

FIVE

The Debate Maker

It is better to debate a decision without settling it
than settling a decision without debating it.

JOSEPH JOUBERT

How leaders make decisions is profoundly influenced by how they engage and leverage the resources around them. Our research has shown that Diminishers tend to make decisions solo or within a small inner circle. As a result, they not only underutilize the intelligence around them but also leave the organization spinning instead of executing. Multipliers make decisions by first engaging people in debate—not only to achieve sound decisions but also to develop collective intelligence and to ready their organizations to execute. Jonathan Akers illustrated the difference between the two approaches when he drove a high-stakes decision at a multinational software company.

Jonathan Akers had recently landed a global role as vice president in corporate planning and was eager to make an impact on the business. The company was entangled in a competitive contest over ownership of the midmarket space. Their largest competitor dominated the small business market, while they owned the enterprise data space. In search of market control and revenue growth, this company began moving downmarket while their competitor was moving up. Winning the midmarket was symbolically important, but it would take an entirely new business model to get there. Jonathan had been asked to lead the development of a new pricing model to enable them to penetrate the market. It was just the opportunity he needed to deliver a tangible success.

Eager to get it right on an issue of such strategic import, Jonathan assembled a team with all the right players, including a broad coalition of leaders from product, marketing, services, and business practices, many of whom had a deep understanding of the midmarket space. The group came together in a large conference room on the top floor of their sleek headquarters in Silicon Valley. Jonathan sat at the head of a narrow table, the logical spot where everyone could see him.

He began the conversation by laying out the challenge to the group, teeing up the issues and turning on the heat for the work of the task force. He made it clear that the CEO and the other top lieutenants of the company were expecting significant progress in the midmarket. Driven by a high-stakes mandate, people began compiling data and analysis and submitting it to Jonathan over the course of several weeks. From Jonathan's point of view, the task force was off to a great start—people were energized and engaged.

The task force had just been set in motion, but already it was beginning to spin with confusion. Jonathan had left unclear the role the task force members would play and how the recommendations and decisions would actually get made. Instead of using the brainpower inherent in the task force, Jonathan used the task force to answer questions. While he thought he was providing much-needed clarity, the participants felt they were merely an audience for his own ideas. He consumed most of the time of the task force meetings over-articulating his own biases or dropping names. Although he gathered data from each task force member quite tenaciously, none of this information was shared or discussed in the task force meetings. There was plenty of data gathered, but there was simply no debate. The meetings atrophied into opinion-based conversation—mostly Jonathan's. One task force member shared his frustration: "I came to these meetings hoping to hear from this brain trust we assembled, but all I heard was Jonathan's point of view."

Although people were led to believe they would be a critical part of the decision, they quickly realized that the task force wasn't where the decision would be made (or even recommended), nor was it a forum for debate where their individual or collective thinking would be challenged. Their suspicions turned out to be true. It appeared that the decision would be made by a select few behind closed doors. Nothing much came of their work, but they did eventually receive a sudden email from Jonathan with the subject line "Announcement of New Pricing Model" and knew the decision had been made without them.

So, instead of generating collective understanding and optimism about the midmarket, Jonathan generated disillusionment about the company's prospects for winning in this market, and he personally earned a reputation as a time waster, because instead of energizing the team, he left them enervated. The immediate impact was apparent the next time Jonathan called a task force meeting: every other chair around the huge conference room table was empty. But the more far-reaching result was that the company continued to stall in the midmarket while their competitors gained traction and market share.

This story plays far and wide in legions of other top-floor conference rooms. It is repeated because, while many leaders like Jonathan attempt the management practice of inclusion and discussion, they are still operating with an elitist view of intelligence, believing the brainpower for the organization sits with a select few. They lack a rich view of intelligence in which there are many sources of insight waiting to be more fully utilized and where intelligence develops through engagement and challenge.

A leader's ability to garner the full intelligence of the organization depends on some of his or her most deeply held assumptions.

The Decision Maker Versus the Debate Maker

Diminishers like Jonathan Akers seem to hold an assumption that *there are only a few people worth listening to.* Sometimes they state that thought out loud, like the executive who admitted to listening to only one or two people from his 4,000-person organization. But typically, such executives manifest their assumption in more subtle ways. They ask their direct reports to interview candidates for an open position, but they end up hiring the person their "star employee" favors. They say they have an open-door policy, but seem to spend a lot of time in closed-door meetings with one or two highly influential advisers. They might patronize people by asking for their opinion, but when it comes down to the high-stakes decisions, they make them privately and announce them to the organization.

Multipliers hold a very different view. They don't focus on what they know but on how to know what others know. They operate on the assumption that *with enough good minds on it, we can figure it out.* They are interested in every relevant insight people can offer. Like the executive who, late at night, after a twelve-hour debate, insisted the team listen to one more comment from a junior member of the group. That comment turned out to be the crucial insight necessary for solving the question at hand. It's no surprise that Multipliers approach decisions by bringing people together, discovering what they know, and encouraging people to challenge and stretch each other's thinking through collective dialogue and debate.

These core assumptions lie at the heart of the differences in how

Diminishers and Multipliers make decisions. By assuming there are only a few people worth listening to, Diminishers operate as Decision Makers: when the stakes are at their highest, they rely on their own knowledge or an inner circle of people to make the decision.

When Multipliers are faced with a high-stakes decision, they have a different gravity pull toward the full brainpower of their organization. In harnessing this knowledge, they play the role of the Debate Maker. They realize that not all decisions need collective input and debate, but on decisions of consequence, they lead rigorous debate that prosecutes the issues with hard facts and depersonalizes decisions. Through debate, they challenge and stretch what people know, thus making the organization smarter over time and creating the organizational will to execute the decisions made.

The Decider Versus Civic Discourse

Examining the core decision-making approach of two public servants—one a head of state and the other a head of a police force—reveals key differences in their approach to making high-stakes decisions.

Our first example is President George W. Bush, who characterized himself as "the decider." [1] And *Time* magazine [2] described him as leading the "Blink Presidency," after Malcolm Gladwell's book *Blink* about the phenomenon of making instantaneous decisions.

In an interview with *Washington Post* writer Bob Woodward, President Bush said, "I'm a gut player. I play by instincts. I don't play by the book." After writing a four-book series on the president, which included eleven hours of personal interviews with him, Woodward concluded, "I think [Bush] is impatient. I think, my summation: He doesn't like homework. And homework means reading or getting briefed or having a debate. And part of the presidency, part of governing, particularly in this area, is homework, homework, homework."

We saw the consequences of rapid, centralized decision making, which led the United States into war with Iraq in 2003. Regarding the 2007 surge in Iraq, President Bush asked tougher questions of his security team than he had with the original invasion because "Different times call for different kinds of questions."[3] But as a matter of record, he kept himself away from some of the meetings where key decisions about the surge were made, telling Woodward, "I'm not in these meetings, you'll be happy to hear, because [I've] got other things to do."

Consider another public service leader, who approached vital decision making by reaching deep into his constituent base. Arjan Mengerink is the District Police Chief Eastern Netherlands in IJsselland, Nieuwleusen, Netherlands. Before his career began, Arjan was a twenty-year-old "boy" with idealistic goals of doing something for others and making a difference. After seven years as an agent working on the streets, he was ready for the next step and signed up for a three-year training at the police academy. From there he progressed to supervisor and then to police chief at fifty-three years old.

As he advanced in his career, Mengerink was always aware of the importance of cooperating with the officers in the force. He understood that the plans devised and discussed in chambers affect colleagues who have to implement them on the streets and with the general population.

Arjan had been through a failed reorganization. He said, "The plans were brilliant, but they were conceived in a club and not discussed with the staff that had to perform them. That resulted in so much resistance that we got stuck, and we had to abandon our failed plan. That was a sour experience, but I learned how I could have dealt with the situation better the next time."

When Arjan was faced with another reorganization, he took a new approach, leaning on others in the organization for help. As he planned the new reorganization process, he invited the national police employee base to play a major role. Focused on how he could engage employees in the process, he organized sessions and invited one hundred employees from a cross-section of the organization—from lawyer to secretary and police chief to agent—so that everyone could contribute his or her own professional knowledge. During these sessions, his team presented ideas on the reorganization process, and encouraged the police employees to voice their agreement, shoot down, and debate, bringing their different perspectives to the table.

By setting up debate sessions with a cross-section of the employee base, Arjan found that their plans were better thought out, and also that the process ensured that the people became co-owners. Rather than a plan being imposed on them, the police employees cocreated it, refined it, and in the end believed in it. He found that they also then conveyed their belief in the plan to others.

These two approaches capture the essence of the difference between Decision Makers and Debate Makers. One makes fast decisions that leave others in the dark, debating amongst themselves and trying to understand the rationale behind the decision. The other leader facilitates a debate before deciding, and in the process builds a team that can take intelligent action.

The Debate Maker

Lutz Ziob, the executive at Microsoft highlighted earlier, approaches decision making in his organization with both the mind and the practices of a Debate Maker. When Lutz took over the education business at Microsoft in 2003, it was a traditional education business that delivered five-day instructor-led classes through corporate training partners. But it was falling short of its goals for revenue and reach.

Lutz faced a double whammy: the organization urgently needed to return to positive and profitable revenue growth, and at the same time, it needed to greatly extend its reach to ensure as many customers and potential customers as possible had a command of Microsoft's technology. As general manager of the Microsoft Learning Business, Lutz needed to decide if they should look for this revenue and reach within the current base of corporate training partners or if they should pursue a bold—and potentially risky—new approach in the academic sector.

Lutz, who speaks with a softened German accent, has that rare combination of passion and reserve. He is a veteran of the technology education business, with a masterful command of both the strategy and the details of running his business. His team is diverse, precisely because he has recruited them to be. Several are longtime Microsoft staffers. Others have deep experience with education at other global technology firms. Several are new to their current role, because they are in stretch assignments outside their usual domain and functional expertise.

After fifteen minutes with Lutz, you can tell he is quite capable of making these decisions himself based on his vast knowledge. And, given the stakes, many executives would have felt the pull to do so. But Lutz has a bias for debate and a conviction that the more vital the decision, the more rigorous and inclusive the decision-making process should be. So he set out to engage his leadership team with the challenge at hand.

He gathered his team and teed up the issue with big questions: Should they refocus their entire business on the academic market, distributing education through the schools instead of through corporate training providers? Should they risk their current business model to potentially achieve significantly higher reach? He gave the team their assignments. They would meet in a couple of weeks on Orcas Island near Microsoft's HQ in Redmond, Washington. They were to bring all the information they could gather and come with views about the academic market space.

Gathered on Orcas Island, the team had the usual off-site

environment—a great physical location, pens and flip charts, a big, open, light conference room—but more important, they had been given permission to think! Because everyone was prepared, Lutz could quickly frame the issue and launch right into the challenge: "As you know, the entire $300 million education business we are in has been based on a potentially outdated model. The decision we face is whether to cling to this business model or introduce a totally new model that would push the education out of the corporate classroom space and into academics where we would reach students much earlier in their careers."

He set broad parameters for the debates. He insisted, "I expect your best thinking here. Everyone should feel not only welcome to speak up, but an obligation to speak up. You can expect us to be thorough. We will be prosecuting assumptions and asking ourselves the tough questions." Then he officially launched the first of several debates.

He sparked the debate through a series of bold questions: "Should we be in the academic space?" and "What would success require?" After each question, he let the team jump in and allowed free debate to proceed.

When the discussion was beginning to reach a settling point, he pushed harder, asking people to switch sides and argue against their previously stated position—"Chris, switch sides with Raza. Raza, you've been for this idea, you now argue against it. Chris, you now argue for it." They would switch roles, which felt awkward for a moment or two, but soon they'd begin to pound the issues from the other vantage point. Or, to broaden people's perspectives, he asked his people to assume roles outside of their functional area. Lutz persisted, "Teresa, you've been offering an international perspective on this, now look at it with a domestic hat on." And "Lee Anne, you've been looking at the technical issues. I want you to debate this from the marketing perspective." The team stepped away from their positions and a new set of sparks erupted. Lutz loved to stir up controversy and would become noticeably disappointed if the debate wasn't charged and the sparks flying.

The team listened passionately to the rich and different perspectives. They challenged one another's assumptions and, often, their own. They happily dropped the polite professionalism that typifies so many corporate meetings and took on the challenges with an almost ferocious appetite. This was a high-stakes approach to a high-stakes decision.

In the end, the organization decided that they would pursue the academic market, and they spent the next two years repivoting the business around students and academia. The business expanded their reach from 1,500 corporate training partners to 4,700 academic partners—three times the scale—in just two years. It is currently set to become the biggest reach driver of their now-profitable business.

Lutz did not leave debate to chance. He knew that while creating a debate is easy, creating a rigorous debate requires a deliberate approach.

The Three Practices of the Debate Maker

In our research we found that Multipliers did three specific things very differently from Diminishers when it came to decision making. While Diminishers raise issues, dominate discussions, and force decisions, Multipliers: 1) frame the issues; 2) spark the debate; and 3) drive sound decisions. Let us examine each of these in more detail.

1. Frame the Issue

Our research has shown that the secret to a great decision is what the leader does before the debate starts. They prepare the organization for discussion and debate by forming the right questions and the right team. Then they frame the issues and process in a way that everyone can contribute. In framing an issue, there are four parts to a well-crafted frame:

- ➤ **THE QUESTION:** What is the decision to be made? What are we choosing between?
- ➤ **THE WHY:** Why is this an important question to answer? Why does the decision warrant collective input and debate? What happens if it is not addressed?
- ➤ **THE WHO:** Who will be involved in making the decision? Who will give input?
- ➤ **THE HOW:** How will the final decision be made? Will it be made by majority rule? Consensus? Or will you (or someone else) make the final decision after others provide input and recommendations?

A great debate begins with an important, provocative question— not just any question but the right question. Tim Brown, chief executive and president of IDEO, the famously innovative global design consultancy firm, said:

As leaders, probably the most important role we can play is asking the right questions and focusing on the right problems. It's very easy in business to get sucked into being reactive to the problems and questions that are right in front of you. It doesn't matter how creative you are as a leader, it doesn't matter how good the answers you come up with. If you're focusing on the wrong questions, you're not really providing the leadership you should.[4]

Tim Brown also went on to say, "The right questions aren't just kind of lying around on the ground to be picked up and asked."[5] The work of the Multiplier is to find the right issue and formulate the right question, so others can find the answers.

A common mistake is attempting to debate a topic rather than a question. The most productive debates are in answer to a well-defined question, one with clear, often mutually exclusive options. For example, a weak debate question is: Where should we cut expenses? A stronger debate question would be: Should we cut funding for project A or project B?

Once the issue is framed, the leader resists the temptation to jump in, where there is fire for the deed, and begin the debate. Instead, they wisely give people time to prepare and assemble their thinking, knowing the extra space will serve to strengthen the thinking and remove emotion from the discussion. They not only frame the issue but also delineate each person's assignment. Often this assignment includes coming with a clearly thought-through point of view and evidence to support it. Interestingly enough, we find that teams come to the soundest decisions when people come in having established a clear opening position, rather than starting from a neutral position.

When Lutz Ziob engaged his team in the vital decision described above, he clearly framed the issue: Should they refocus their entire business on the academic market, distributing education through the schools instead of through corporate training providers? He explained why this decision was vital to their ability to expand their reach and educate as many potential users as possible. He outlined the process and gave each member of his team two weeks to prepare, asking them to come with a point of view and information to inform the decision.

When a leader has framed the issues well, the rest of the team knows where to focus. They know what's in bounds, and they know what is out of bounds. This framing operates much like the surgical drape used in most medical procedures. Imagine you are sitting atop the gurney in pre-op while the nursing staff prepares you for knee surgery. You are poked and prepped, checked and rechecked, and handed numerous forms to sign. Then the nurse hands you a big, black Sharpie marker and asks you to write NO on the wrong knee and YES just below the knee to be operated on. While you might find this disconcerting at first, you realize that you will soon be fully anesthetized and happily write your final instruction to your surgeon. Once in the operating room, another nurse places a thin, blue surgical drape over the designated knee, blocking off everything except that knee, visible through the five-inch square opening in the middle of the drape. The surgical team sees only an impersonal knee that needs a new anterior cruciate ligament. Freed from distraction and contamination, the surgical team is ready to work. When a leader has clearly framed an issue (clarifying the question, rationale, and process) and allowed people to prepare, the team is ready for debate.

When a decision is high-stakes, Debate Makers require everyone's best thinking. They know people will do their best thinking if the issues are framed well and defined, and if the questions of the debate are clear. They know that the debate will be richest if it is based in facts, not opinions, and that it takes foresight to gather the right information.

Because they take time to prepare and frame the issue, Multipliers are able to leverage more capability from their people than their Diminisher counterparts. Multipliers ensure that people don't waste their brainpower and enthusiasm "spinning" on tangential issues. By framing the debate in terms of key questions within a clear context, they are able to foster motivation and readiness and help elicit 100 percent from their people. Multipliers love debate, and they debate with a purpose. They know what they want out of the debate and what they want out of the people involved. Multipliers aren't just debaters; they are Debate Makers.

2. Spark the Debate

After framing of the issue, Multipliers spark the debate. Through our research and coaching work with executives, I have observed four elements of a great debate. A great debate is:

➤ **ENGAGING:** The question is compelling and important to everyone in attendance.

➤ **COMPREHENSIVE:** The right information is shared to generate a holistic and collective understanding of the issues at hand.

➤ **FACT BASED:** The debate is deeply rooted in fact, not opinion.

➤ **EDUCATIONAL:** People leave the debate more focused on what they learned than on who won or lost.

How do you lead this type of debate? There are two key elements that couple and form the yin and the yang of great debate. The first is to create safety. The second is to demand rigor. Multipliers do both.

The Yin: Create Safety for Best Thinking

How do Multipliers create a safe climate for people's best thinking?

They do it by removing fear. They remove the factors that cause people to doubt themselves or their ideas and the fear that causes people to hold back. One senior manager we interviewed told us about his current boss, "Amit has strong opinions but he lets the discussion happen *before* he expresses that opinion." And further, "You know where you stand with Amit. He maintains a balance of respect but is also brutally honest if something doesn't make sense. I've never gotten into trouble telling my manager what I think."

Another executive we've worked with knew that she had a reputation for being smart and strong-willed, and that she could be intimidating. A direct report has noticed a recent change in her: "When the group is debating an issue, Jennifer makes it a point to hold her views until the end. She gives a chance for each member of her executive team to express his or her views before she adds her own."

Multipliers create safety, but they also maintain pressure for a reality-based, rigorous debate. Multipliers make sure everyone is wearing a seat belt because they are about to put their foot on the accelerator.

The Yang: Demand Rigor

How do Multipliers demand rigor?

They ask the questions that challenge conventional thinking. They ask the questions that unearth the assumptions that are holding the organization back. They ask the questions that cause the team to think harder and to dig deeper. They ask for evidence. According to one of his management team members, Jim Barksdale, former CEO of Netscape, was well-known for saying, "If you don't have any facts, we'll just use my opinion." Debate Makers aren't overly swayed by opinion and emotional arguments; they continue to ask for evidence, including evidence that might suggest new or alternative points of view.

When the senior management team of a European online distribution company met to discuss whether to add a new feature to their online store, there was strong support among the team for the idea. But the CEO wasn't satisfied with intuition and wanted to inject more rigor into their collective thinking. He asked the senior executive team whether the new feature would actually drive higher sales. At first there were opinions, but the CEO wanted data and wanted to know what the facts proved. The executive team began to dig into the facts in a summary analysis. Again the CEO dug deeper. He asked the group to go country by country, poring over the data to look for an answer to the questions.

As one executive who was present said, "Nobody got away with their own opinions." The group wrestled with the issue until they finally concluded that they didn't have enough information yet to make a clear decision, and they identified what additional data they needed. This company's leader kept the debate going by demanding rigor and sound decision making.

Sue Siegel, when she was president of Affymetrix, led the company through a moment-of-truth decision in 2001 by using the power of facts and openness to harness the full brainpower of the organization.

Affymetrix produced microarray technologies that allow scientists to analyze complex genetic information. The company had been public for three years and had grown steadily to 800 employees. Sue received some troubling news from customers that there were some problems with the GeneChip microarrays that could potentially render inaccurate results, but only for a minor portion of its applications. As president, she would have to make one of the toughest decisions that the company would face in the next several years: should they recall the product?

Sue was a veteran executive in the life-sciences industry and had deep knowledge of the underlying technology and issues. But instead of relying solely on her own understanding of the situation, she went beyond the management hierarchy and reached deep into the organization for data and for insight. She went straight to the people who understood the issues and let them know she needed their input.

She then convened a larger forum of several layers and management. She framed the magnitude of the issue and the potential impact to the company. Product development cycles in biotech tend to be long, and fixes can't be made overnight. For a young company, this was a decision with far-reaching consequences, and the answer was far from clear. Either way, they would live with the consequences for years to come. She laid out a couple of scenarios and then began asking questions, ensuring that the group thought through the decision from every angle: "What is the impact for our customers? . . . What is our legal obligation? . . . What is the financial impact?" Sue asked for data and recommendations. The group debated for two arduous days, then Sue asked the management team to weigh in, and then they made the decision to recall the product. The next day, she boarded a plane to present at the Goldman Sachs financial conference in Laguna Niguel, California, attended by more than a thousand analysts, shareholders, and industry experts, to tell them about their mistake and their decision.

The product recall was a financial setback for the young organization, adversely impacting market cap for two quarters and sending it from Wall Street darling to leper overnight. However, with the company staff behind the decision, they were able to execute the decision with conviction and explain it to their customers and to the market. This allowed them to rebound quickly to regain their market position and exceed their market cap. In fact, the product recall became a turning point in building deep customer relationships and respect for employee input that would become the hallmark of the company. In the four years that Sue led the company following the product recall, Affymetrix continued to grow sales and beat expectations for both revenue and earnings.

Sue Siegel led this organization successfully through one of its toughest decisions, because instead of turning inward, she reached out and utilized the full intelligence of the organization to make a decision that was grounded in full disclosure and fact, and in the best interest of their customers.

Debate Makers pursue all sides of the issue. When the group moves too quickly toward agreement, Multipliers often step back and ask someone to argue the other point of view. Or they might make the argument themselves. They make sure all the rocks are turned over. Recall how Lutz Ziob sparked rigorous thinking during debate. After early consensus began to form, he would jump back in to stir things up, creating new bits of unresolved controversy. Next came "the switch." After asking people to come prepared with an opening position, he asked them to drop their position and argue from the exact opposite point of view. Imagine the effect this has on a team. By arguing from the opposite, or a different point of view, the individuals 1) see the issues from another person's perspective, developing deeper empathy and understanding, 2) have to argue against themselves, surfacing the problems and pitfalls in their opening position, 3) find new alternatives that elicit the best ideas from the competing options, and 4) separate themselves from a position. When the final decision is reached, it no longer has an owner or advocate. The group owns the final position.

The following chart summarizes some of the practices Debate Makers use to create safety while also demanding rigor:

Create Safety for Best Thinking (The Yin)	Demand Rigor (The Yang)
• Share their view last after hearing other people's views	• Ask the hard questions
• Encourage others to take an opposing stand	• Challenge the underlying assumptions
• Encourage all points of view	• Look for evidence in the data
• Focus on the facts	• Look at the issue from multiple perspectives
• Depersonalize the issues and keep it unemotional	• Attack the issues, not the people
• Look beyond organizational hierarchy and job titles	• Ask "why" repeatedly until the root cause is unearthed
	• Equally debate both sides of the issue

3. Drive a Sound Decision

Multipliers may relish a great debate, but they pursue debate with a clear end: a sound decision. They ensure this in three ways. First, they reclarify the decision-making process. Second, they make the decision or explicitly delegate it to someone else to decide. And third, they communicate the decision and the rationale behind it.

Reclarify the Decision-Making Process

After the issue has been debated, Multipliers let people know the next step in the decision-making process. They summarize the key ideas and outcomes of the debate, and they let people know what to expect next. They address such questions as:

➤ Are we making the decision right now or do we need more information?
➤ Is this a team decision or will the leader make the final call?
➤ If it is a team decision, how will we resolve any differing views?
➤ Has anything that has surfaced in the debate altered the decision-making process?

One executive we studied was strong on closure: "Allison says who is going to make the decision and when. People aren't left in limbo wondering how the decision will be made."

Multipliers let people know what will be done with their thinking and their work. With this sense of closure, people around them are assured that their discretionary effort won't be wasted, and they are likely to give 100 percent the next time. In this way Multipliers get full contribution not just once but over and over again.

Make the Decision

Although Multipliers know how to generate and leverage collective thinking, they are not necessarily consensus-oriented leaders. At times, they may seek the full consensus of the group; however, our research shows that they are equally comfortable making the final decision.

One manager responsible for emerging markets within a global technology firm said of her leader, "Chris prefers collective decisions and consensus, but he's practical and he'll either make the final decision for speed or defer to someone else because it is clearly within that person's domain."

Communicate the Decision and Rationale

One of the benefits of purposeful, rigorous debate is the business case and momentum it builds to execute the decision. As people debate an issue thoroughly, they develop a deep understanding of the underlying problems and opportunities and the imperatives for change. They put their fingerprint on the decision. Because they achieved a collective understanding, they are capable of executing collectively.

Lutz often held his organization's debates in a conference room they came to call the Theater. The Theater looked like any other conference room, with a large table that the key players sat at during the debates. However, the room had twice as many chairs set up around the perimeter of the room, because these debates were open to anyone in the organization. Anyone interested in the issue could come and listen. The team called it the Theater because it was like a surgical theater in a teaching hospital. As people watched these debates, they came to a better understanding of the issues. When decisions were reached, there were people at all levels of the organization ready to execute. With this model of transparent decision making, communicating the decision and the rationale is easy because the organization is already prepared to move forward.

The Theater not only helped employees in this organization understand and prepare to execute the decision at hand; like medical students learning to perform surgery, they were also learning what was expected of them when they were called to the table to a debate on another issue.

The Diminisher's Approach to Debate

Instead of looking out broadly into their organization for intelligence, Diminishers tend to make decisions quickly, either based solely on their own opinions or with input from a close inner circle.

Then people begin to spin and speculate and get distracted from enthusiastically carrying the decisions out.

In sharp contrast to the Theater of the executive above, one Diminisher I worked with held meetings in his office in a two-circle format. Seated at a small, round table was his equally small inner circle, who would discuss the issue and make the decisions. But around the perimeter of the room was a collection of silent people standing and taking notes. After participating in this strange meeting format, I couldn't help but ask one of these voiceless individuals standing on the outer edge about the role of this silent body. She said, "Oh, we don't ever participate in these decisions and we certainly don't get a 'seat at the table.' We're just here to take notes so our SVP doesn't have to tell us what to do later." This was less of a surgical theater and more of a lecture auditorium.

Instead of framing issues for debate and decisions, Diminishers tend to raise issues abruptly, then dominate the discussion before forcing a decision.

RAISE ISSUES. When a problem surfaces, Diminishers bring issues or decisions to people's attention, but they don't necessarily frame them in a way that allows others to easily contribute. When they raise the issue, they focus on the "what" rather than on the "how" or the "why" of a decision. One CIO routinely raised a variety of distracting issues at his weekly staff meetings. One of his directors explained, "Once he came in and raised the issue of ergonomically sound keyboards and then went on about them for an hour. He is intense and intelligent, but all over the place. He makes a millimeter of progress in a million directions."

DOMINATE THE DISCUSSION. When issues get discussed or debated, Diminishers tend to dominate the discussion with their own ideas. They are debaters, not Debate Makers. Looking back at Jonathan Akers, where did he fall short? He gathered the right players and he gathered the data. But he never sparked a debate. Instead he dominated the discussions with his opinions and shut down the intelligence—and drive—of the players he had assembled.

FORCE THE DECISION. Rather than driving a sound decision, Diminishers tend to force a decision, either by relying heavily on their own opinion or by shortcutting rigorous debate. As one executive said in an attempt to drive closure after dominating the discussion during a task force meeting, "I think we're all in agreement that we should centralize this function on a global level." The group looked bewildered, knowing that this was not the shared opinion of the group. One brave woman broke the silence and responded with, "No, Joe, we have heard your opinion, but we don't have agreement."

What is the impact to the organization of the Diminisher's approach to decision making? At first glance, it appears that Diminishers make efficient decisions. However, because their approach only utilizes the intelligence of a small number of people and ignores the rigor of debate, the broader organization is left in the dark, not understanding the decision or the assumptions and facts upon which it is based. Lacking clarity, people turn to debating the soundness of a decision—"spinning" it rather than executing it.

This spin phenomenon is one of the reasons Diminishers create resource drain rather than resource leverage. Decision Makers don't use the full complement of talent, intelligence, and information available to them. This capacity sits idle in their organization. To counteract this, they continue to ask for more resources, wondering why they aren't more productive.

By contrast, Multipliers not only engage the best thinking of the resources around them; they use debate to stretch the thinking of the individuals and the team. While decisions are debated vigorously, real facts and issues surface, forcing people to listen and learn. As a result, Multipliers get full capability out of their current resources and they stretch and increase the capacity of the organization to take on the next challenge.

Becoming a Debate Maker

What drives a Debate Maker? How does someone learn to lead debate like Lutz at Microsoft Learning or Sue Siegel at Affymetrix? And how does someone go from being a Decision Maker to a Debate Maker?

Our research and experience coaching executives reveals that leaders can move along the Diminisher–Multiplier continuum. But it requires more than just adding some new leadership practices. It often requires a fundamental shift in the assumptions of the leader. Often this shift happens when a leader begins to view his or her role differently. It can happen when leaders see that their greatest contribution lies in asking the questions that produce the most rigorous thinking and answers.

Several years ago I volunteered to be a discussion leader for a Junior Great Books program at an elementary school. It seemed like a simple volunteer job. The assignment was straightforward: lead a discussion of a group of third-grade students on a piece of great youth literature. The goal was clear: have them dig deep into the story for meaning and debate it with their peers. Despite my protesting that I knew how to facilitate discussion, I was sent to a one-day training workshop to learn a technique called "shared inquiry."[6] What I found was a simple but powerful technique for leading debate.

There are three rules in shared inquiry:

1. **THE DISCUSSION LEADER** only asks questions. This means that the leader isn't allowed to answer his or her questions or give his or her interpretation of the story's meaning. This keeps the students from relying on the leader's answers.

2. **THE STUDENTS** must supply evidence to support their theories. If the student thinks that Jack went up the beanstalk a third time to prove his invincibility, he or she is required to identify a passage (or more than one) in the text that supports this idea.

3. **EVERYONE** participates. The role of the leader is to make sure everyone gets airtime. Often the leader needs to restrain stronger voices and proactively call on the more timid voices.

As discussion leader, it was liberating to ask the questions but not give the answers. In fact, I found it strangely powerful. And when the students spouted off their views and interpretations of the story, it was thrilling to look them straight in the eye and say, "Do you have any evidence to support that claim?" Initially, they looked terrified. But they quickly learned that the cost of an opinion was evidence. As they gained experience, they learned to respond quickly. They would assert an opinion, and then I would insist (with my best intimidating look), "Show me your evidence." They would scurry to locate the exact place in the text that supported their claim and cite it with conviction. And because everyone was called on, every student learned to state their views and support their ideas with data.

This experience cemented my belief that there is a process and a formula for great debate.

The Starting Block

MAKE A DEBATE. Identify an important decision that would best be made with rigorous thinking and collective intelligence. Frame the issue, prepare the team, and lead the debate . . . not with forceful ideas, but with a sound process that encourages people to weigh in before having to buy in.

Try debating like a third-grade student with these three requests:

1. **ASK THE HARD QUESTION.** Ask the question that will get at the core of the issue and the decision. Ask the question that will confront underlying assumptions. Pose the question to your team and then stop. Instead of following up with your views, ask for theirs.

2. **ASK FOR EVIDENCE.** When someone offers an opinion, don't let it rest on anecdote. Ask for the evidence. Look for more than one data point. Ask them to identify a cluster of data or a trend. Make it a norm so people come into debates armed with the data—an entire box if necessary.

3. **ASK EVERYONE.** Reach beyond the dominant voices to gather in and hear all views and all data. You might find that the softer voices belong to the analytical minds who are often most familiar with and objective about the data. You may not need to literally ask everyone, but be sure to ask enough people to invite diverse thinking.

To drive further rigor into the conversation, you might try a fourth ask:

4. **ASK PEOPLE TO SWITCH POSITIONS.** Invite people to consider the issue from another point of view. It will reduce personal attachment and increase collective ownership.

As you rethink your role as a leader, you will come to see that your greatest contribution might depend on your ability to ask the right question, not have the right answer. You will see that all great thinking starts with a provocative question and a rich debate, whether it is in the mind of one person or an entire community.

Discussion, Dissent, and Debate

Hubert H. Humphrey, America's vice president under Lyndon B. Johnson, captured the essential principle of how Multipliers make decisions when he said: "Freedom is hammered out on the anvil of discussion, dissent, and debate." Our research showed that it is this discussion, dissent, and debate that also hammer out sound decisions.

When leaders play the role of decision maker, they not only carry the burden of making the right decision, they also are left to carry it through to completion. With only a select few understanding the real issues, this can be a heavy burden. But when a leader engages the team in making the most vital of decisions, they distribute this load. Informed by collective intelligence, better, more thoughtful decisions are made. Having thought through and fought through the issues, the team builds strength and puts their full weight behind the decisions. Through discussion, dissent, and debate they've generated collective willpower and the commitment to see this decision through, solving the intended problems with precision and potency. As Margaret Mead famously said, "Never doubt that a small group of thoughtful, committed citizens can change the world; indeed, it's the only thing that ever has."

Too many leaders exhaust themselves trying to garner buy-in across the myriad of stakeholders in their community. Instead of building support, their work often builds resentment as people reluctantly surrender to the inevitable. Reverse this cycle by investing your energy up front. Let people weigh in, and they will give you their buy-in.

Chapter Five Summary

The Decision Maker Versus the Debate Maker

DECISION MAKERS decide efficiently with a small inner circle, but they leave the broader organization in the dark to debate the soundness of the decision instead of executing it.

DEBATE MAKERS engage people in debating the issues up front, which leads to sound decisions that people understand and can execute efficiently.

The Three Practices of the Debate Maker

1. *Frame the Issue*
   - Define the question
   - Form the team
   - Assemble the data
   - Frame the decision
2. *Spark the Debate*
   - Create safety for best thinking
   - Demand rigor
3. *Drive a Sound Decision*
   - Reclarify the decision-making process
   - Make the decision
   - Communicate the decision and rationale

Becoming a Debate Maker

Make a debate with four asks: 1) Ask the hard question, 2) ask for evidence, 3) ask everyone, 4) ask people to switch.

Leveraging Resources

	Decision Makers	Debate Makers
What They Do	Engage a select inner circle in the decision-making process	Access a wide spectrum of thinking in a rigorous debate before making decisions
What They Get	Underutilization of the bulk of their resources, while a select few are overworked	High utilization of the bulk of their resources
	A lack of information from those closest to the action, resulting in poorer decisions	Real information they need to make sound decisions
	Too many resources thrown at those who don't have the understanding they need to execute the decisions effectively	Efficient execution with lower resource levels because they have built a deep understanding of the issues, which readies the organization to execute

Unexpected Findings

1. As a leader, you can have a very strong opinion but also facilitate debate that creates room for other people's views. Data is the key.
2. Debate Makers are equally comfortable being the decision maker in the end. They are not only consensus-driven leaders.
3. Rigorous debate doesn't break down a team; it builds the team and makes it stronger.

SIX

The Investor

If you want to build a ship, don't drum up the men to
gather wood, divide the work and give orders. Instead,
teach them to yearn for the vast and endless sea.

ANTOINE DE SAINT-EXUPÉRY

It is after midnight at the McKinsey office in Seoul, South Korea. The
lights are out, except in one conference room occupied by a project
team that is two days away from a critical presentation to one of the
firm's biggest clients in Asia. The team is led by Hyunjee, a sharp,
highly regarded project leader. Joining them this night is Jae Choi,
one of McKinsey's partners based in Seoul. Jae knows the team has a
critical deadline and, as is typical, is meeting with the team to guide,
challenge, and shape the thinking as they build the first major presentation of their findings to the client.

The project leader, Hyunjee, is at the whiteboard. She and the
team are retesting the storyline with some new facts that surfaced
during the past week. The team is struggling to integrate the findings
into the overarching message about the client's business transforma-

tion. Jae listens carefully and asks a lot of questions, as he is known for doing.

It becomes clear that the team is stuck. The team leader is systematically working this tough problem but looks at Jae with a look that signals *I could use a little help here!* Jae has been on countless numbers of these projects and has stood in the project leader's shoes many times. He can see a storyline that the team, who has been buried in the details, has not yet considered.

Jae offers a few thoughts for the team to discuss, standing up to take the whiteboard marker from the team leader. Heading to the board, he begins to list several emerging themes, encouraging the team to view the facts from a different angle. The group is thrilled to have the fresh perspective, and excited voices are now engaged in testing, pushing, and building on the ideas despite the late hour. With new insights coming from the renewed discussions, Jae can now visualize the new presentation flow in his mind. He feels a familiar comfort up at the whiteboard. The desire to drive the team toward completion is alluring. He is tempted to lay it all out for the team so they can all go home and get some rest. The consultant in Jae tells him to go on and finish the job and complete the storyline himself. But the leader in Jae signals restraint. He stops sketching and turns to the project leader, checking to see if she is comfortable with the new direction. Seeing the smile on her face, Jae says, "Okay . . . looks like we've got a new line of thinking to run with. Let's see what you can do with this." He then hands the pen back to Hyunjee, who resumes command of the process and leads the team to build an outstanding presentation for the client.

Surely it was tempting for Jae to jump in, rescue the struggling team, and drive the presentation to completion himself. He would have felt like a hero (and probably a few years younger, too). And it was tempting for the team to let him do it, given the late hour. But Jae's proclivity to invest in people and their development won out. Jae reflected on the leader's role: "You can jump in and teach and coach, but then you have to give the pen back. When you give that pen back, your people know they are still in charge."

When something is off the rails, do you take over or do you invest? When you take the pen to add your ideas, do you give it back? Or does it stay in your pocket?

Multipliers invest in the success of others. They may jump in to teach and share their ideas, but they always return to accountability.

When leaders fail to return ownership, they create dependent organizations. This is the way of the Diminisher. They jump in, save the day, and deliver results through their personal involvement. When leaders return the pen, they cement accountability for action where it should be. This creates organizations that are free from the nagging need of the leader's rescue.

Multipliers enable others to operate independently by giving other people ownership of results and investing in their success. Multipliers can't always be present to perform emergency rescues, so they ensure that people on their teams are self-sufficient and can operate without their direct presence.

Thus far the book has explored why Multipliers make people smarter and more capable in their presence. Now I ask you to consider a different question: What happens when the Multiplier isn't there? What happens to people when the sunlight of the Multiplier isn't shining in their part of the world?

This chapter addresses this most curious question: How do Multipliers create organizations that act intelligently and achieve results without their direct involvement?

The Micromanager Versus the Investor

Multipliers operate as Investors. They invest by infusing others with the resources and ownership they need to produce results independent of the leader. It isn't just benevolence. They invest, and they expect results.

Forever Strong

Larry Gelwix stood on the side of the rugby pitch, watching his high school team practice. He thought back to the first team he had coached to the national championships. He remembered them being up before dawn, training together. Larry said under his breath, "Well, that was then."

The team in front of him was good, to be sure. They were learning the game, but he noticed they didn't have the physical stamina of previous teams. Larry felt stuck. It wasn't like he hadn't tried. He reminded them at practice all the time. They would nod their heads, but then they didn't do it.

He could cancel practices and hold fitness training in its place, but that put the skill level of the team at risk. He could yell at them, but that would only work for a day or two. Larry leaned over to an associate coach and said, "We need to turn this over to the captains!"

The next day, Larry stood up, walked quickly to the chalkboard, and drew a line from one side of the board to the other. He said, "We have six weeks left until the finals, and it takes a pretty good athlete six or seven weeks to build the endurance he needs." The coaches and captains were listening to every word. He continued, "If we figure this out now, we can win the nationals. If we can't, we'll be running on empty."

He gave them the low-down: "There are two options: the coaches can keep trying to figure something out or you as the captains can take ownership for finding a solution. What should we do?"

There was a pause. Then the captain of the backs said, "We'll take it on."

Larry said, "Right now I own this challenge. Once you take it on, you'll own it completely. We'll expect an update from you two weeks from today, but we won't bug the team at all."

There was silent agreement in the look that passed between the captains, then the captain of the forwards stood up and went to the board. He turned to Larry, who had sat down with the other coaches, and said, "Okay, we have a few questions." Larry and the coaches,stayed and answered questions about what types of fitness training produced speed, agility, and endurance until eventually the coaches were excused and the four captains, all in their teens, took a turn figuring it out, standing in a semicircle around the chalkboard.

The solution they implemented was to divide the team into small groups of four to six people, each with its own leader. The captains would keep the subgroup leaders accountable, and the leaders would keep the players accountable. The smaller groups met before or after school for fitness training for weeks, and the team soon became one of the fittest in the thirty-four years Larry had coached the team. They went undefeated all season and won the national championship.

How would a micromanaging coach have approached the same problem? We don't need to wonder.

Calling Every Play

Marcus Dolan shouted across the school at John Kimball, "Get over here!" Marcus was a muscle-head coach who wanted to micromanage every aspect of his team. He yelled at one of his team captains, "Don't ever hold a practice without me or you'll be off this team. You've probably already messed everyone up."

Not surprisingly, John didn't try that again, and little by little, he and the other players slowly stopped taking initiative entirely. Playing for Marcus meant you did what he said without question. The endless laps at practice just had to be done. Even in the games, he called every play for every player. The team was so focused and dependent on Marcus, they couldn't think intelligently or adapt rapidly to changes on the field. They lost every game. Marcus took a group of players that had begun with a sense of ownership for the team and micromanaged it out of them. Interestingly, *Sports Illustrated* later elected Marcus Dolan the most losing coach in high school sports history.

More interesting still, eight of his players eventually left the team and went to play for Larry Gelwix. In fact, they were on the team described earlier that woke before dawn to practice and the same team that led Highland to its first national championship.

Running onto the Field

Why is it that when the stakes are high, many managers jump in and take over? I've watched hundreds of youth soccer games, and I have to admit that I find myself watching the coaches more than the players (one of the curses of genius watching). I've seen a lot of very frustrated coaches during those games when the team is down and playing horribly. I've seen crazy arm waving, copious shouting, occasional tantrums on the sidelines. But I've never once seen a coach run out onto the field, steal the ball away from a player, drive down the field, and score. Yet each one of these coaches had the skills required to score the game-winning goal. And I'm sure a few have been tempted to do it.

So why don't they? Beyond the obvious reason that it is against the rules, it simply isn't their role. Their job is to coach, and their players' job is to play. What perhaps isn't so obvious is why, when the stakes are high, many managers in organizations don't hesitate to run onto the playing field, steal away the ball, and score the winning goal. Managers jump in because in their organization it isn't illegal, and many can't resist the temptation. Consider two such examples that occur every day in workplaces.

- ➤ The sales manager who doesn't see fast enough progress in winning an important prospective client and jumps into the sales process, trying to win the deal himself.
- ➤ The marketing vice president who watches one of her people stumble as he presents the new product go-to-

market plan to the CEO. When the CEO fires tough
questions at him, the marketing VP leaps in and not only
answers the tough questions but finishes the presentation.

You might ask yourself: How would I coach if I could never step
out on the playing field? How would I lead if I couldn't jump in and
take over? How would I respond to a performance gap if I were a
Multiplier?

Multipliers understand that their role is to invest, to teach, and to
coach, and they keep the accountability for the play with the players.
By doing so, they create organizations that can win without them on
the field.

Let's now explore the discipline of the Investor and how Multipliers create organizations that can perform and win, not only without
them on the field but long after their direct influence has ended.

The Investor

Ela Bhatt (known as Elaben) is a slight seventy-eight-year-old Indian
woman, soft-spoken to the point of seeming at first a bit fragile. She
lives in the simplest two-bedroom bungalow, with her bed doubling
as a desk chair. She grew up listening to her teachers speak of India's
struggle for independence and her parents tell stories of her grand-
father who joined the twenty-four-day Salt March from Mohandas K.
Gandhi's ashram in Ahmedabad to the Arabian Sea to make salt, in
symbolic defiance of British law.

In order to gain firsthand experience of rural poverty, Elaben
went to live in the villages of India and saw for herself that the political independence gained from British rule was not enough. Economic independence would be the next victory. In the villages she
saw both the vibrancy and the struggle of the self-employed seam-
stresses, street vendors, and construction workers and in response

founded the Self-Employed Women's Association (SEWA) in 1972, which gradually became a significant union in the region.

It would have been easy for Elaben to be elected general secretary of SEWA every three years, as dictated by law, forever. In this way she could have owned the organization's agenda indefinitely and just assigned tasks to everyone else. SEWA, after all, was her creation. It had evolved slowly in her mind and it would have been understandable, if not expected, for her to remain its formal leader in perpetuity.

Yet Elaben insisted on turning over the responsibility of running SEWA to new and younger leadership. She personally invested the time and energy into educating members about the democratic process and encouraged everyone to gain the political literacy needed to step up and run for one of the open positions.

In a fascinating embodiment of SEWA's mission and management philosophy, Jyoti Macwan, who enrolled as member of SEWA as a poor, Guajarati-speaking, cigarette-rolling worker, went on to become the English-speaking general secretary for SEWA. In this role, she has led the union, which at the most recent election involved 1.2 million people. Jyoti could have spent her work years figuring out how to survive from day to day, but because of Elaben's leadership, she has used her intellect solving complex problems that reach across international boundaries and affect more than 1 million women like herself. She recently stood shoulder to shoulder with Elaben and US Secretary of State Hillary Clinton as they answered questions at a press conference.

Jyoti's story is just the beginning. If you look at the second generation of chief executives of all the SEWA organizations, they all first worked under Elaben's tutelage. Each was given greater and greater ownership as they matured into capable managers. Every time Elaben established an institution, she invested in the future leaders and stepped away from the operational management. Each time, the succession was handled so gracefully that she could leave with the confidence that her presence would still be felt even when she is elsewhere, investing her energy in establishing another institution. The SEWA union was followed by a bank (created from four thousand women each depositing ten rupees[1]), and this has been followed by the Gujarat Mahila Housing SEWA Trust, the Gujarat State Mahila SEWA Cooperative Federation, SEWA Insurance, SEWA Academy, Homenet South Asia, and many others.

Elaben continues to invest in building leaders and organizations so they can operate independently of her. Her influence is like that of a parental figure or wise elder who gives guidance when people ask for it, support when she is needed. Her approach to management is the outgrowth of her simple motto: "A leader is someone who helps others lead." Today Elaben serves as a member of The Elders, an international nongovernmental organization of public figures noted as elder statesmen, peace activists, and human rights advocates, who were brought together by Nelson Mandela in 2007.

How does a leader like Elaben create other leaders who can assume ownership and deliver on the mission of the organization themselves? We find answers in the three practices of the Investor.

The Three Practices of the Investor

As we studied the unique way Multipliers drive results, I found the practices remarkably similar to another world I know—a world driven by intellectual assets and investment multiples, where technology and business leaders develop other leaders in search of growth and returns and the creation of wealth.

This is a world whose nerve center is just a mile from my house. On Sand Hill Road in Menlo Park, California, home to Silicon Valley's venture capital community, multimillion-dollar investment decisions are made many times daily. Venture capital firms scour industries looking to invest in emerging technologies and young companies destined to become the industry leaders of the future.

When a venture firm places its bet and invests a round of funding, it draws up a term sheet to govern the deal. Of particular interest to all parties is the specification of ownership levels. These ownership levels outline relative ownership for the business (post-investment) and dictate expectations for leadership and for accountability. Simply put, the term sheet lets the parties know who is in charge.

Once ownership of the new company is established, the venture firm cuts a check and the investment of resources begins. This funding provides the financial resources to secure capital, intellectual property, and the human resources to fuel the business. But the value isn't limited to the financial resources. The real value often emerges from the insight and coaching the start-up company receives from the senior partners at the venture firm—men and women who have grown businesses, incubated technology, and often managed very large companies themselves. They not only invest the capital of the fund, they invest their know-how into these nascent companies. They coach the CEO, they lend their Rolodex to assist with business development and sales, and they work with the management team to ensure financial targets can be met.

After infusing capital and know-how, the venture partners look for expected returns. The returns in the marketplace may be years away (or may never materialize), but they watch for key milestones. The accountability is clear. If the company produces expected results, a second or third round of funding is likely. Otherwise the company is left to make it on its own or die on the vine.

Similarly, in their role as Investors, Multipliers define ownership up front and let other people know what is within their charge and what they are expected to build. They invest in the genius of others in a similar way. They teach and coach. They back people up, infusing the resources they need to be successful and to be independent.

And Multipliers complete the same investment cycle as they demand accountability from others. They understand that this accountability isn't ruthless. It is the draw that creates such extraordinary growth of intelligence and capability in others.

We'll look at each of these three steps in turn: 1) defining ownership; 2) investing resources; and 3) holding people accountable.

1. Defining Ownership

Investors begin this cycle by establishing ownership up front. They see intelligence and capability in the people around them, and they put them in charge.

Name the Lead

When John Chambers, then CEO of Cisco, hired his first vice president, Doug Allred, into the company, he gave the new VP of customer support control and made sure their respective roles were clear: "Doug, when it comes to how we run this area of the company—you get 51 percent of the vote (and you're 100 percent responsible for the result). Keep me in the loop, and consult with me as you go." Weeks later, when Doug was updating John on progress, John responded with, "I knew you'd surprise me on the upside." And it wasn't just Doug who received majority voting rights. John gives "51 percent of the vote" to every member of his management in their respective areas of accountability.

If your boss had told you that you owned 51 percent of the vote, how would you operate? Would you second-guess yourself and run all decisions by him? Or would you swing in the opposite direction and make decisions without consulting him? You probably would do neither. Most likely, you would consult your boss on important decisions to get a second opinion, while for the smaller stuff, you might be wise to ignore him or her as needed to get your job done.

Giving someone 51 percent of the vote and full ownership creates certainty and builds confidence. It enables them to stop second-guessing and start getting second opinions. Clarifying the role that you will play as a leader actually gives people more owner-ship, not less. They then understand the nature of your involvement and when and how you will invest in their success. Most important, they understand that they hold the majority ownership position and that success or failure hinges on their efforts.

Give Ownership for the End Goal

A management team is assembled for an off-site meeting to plan an important acquisition for their business. They kick off their work with a simple but powerful management exercise called the Big Pic-ture.[2] The team divides into nine pairs, and each pair is given a one-inch square from a photo of a famous modern painting. Each team is tasked with creating a reproduction and enlargement of its piece of the picture. In other words, each team is given a little piece of a bigger picture. The goal for the team is to bring all the enlargements together to form a unified replica of the original painting. The result should be a painting that is technically accurate and flows together seamlessly. The challenge is that no pair has seen the "big picture."

I hope you can visualize the scene. Each pair, energized by the challenge, studies their one-inch square and begins to replicate it onto the large piece of paper in front of them. They dive into the task, make sketches, and soon color erupts everywhere. When the time allotted for the first phase of work expires, they turn their attention to neighboring colleagues. They begin to connect the pieces and notice that the painting isn't coming together very well. The lines don't match up. The colors don't blend. Their creation is like a Franken-painting.

The session leader reminds them that their job is to optimize the whole, not their individual piece. They start to pay attention to the bigger picture. They rework their sections, focusing on integration and blending, although it is far too late to create a seamless product. The team delivers the big picture, but it remains a patchwork only moderately resembling the original artwork.

When people are given ownership for only a piece of something larger, they tend to optimize that portion, limiting their thinking to this immediate domain. When people are given ownership for the whole, they stretch their thinking and challenge themselves to go beyond their scope.

Stretch the Role

We consistently find that Multipliers get twice the capability from their people that Diminishers do. And time after time, people tell us that Multipliers got not only 100 percent of their skills and know-how but 120 percent, or even more. Multipliers do get more than 100 percent because people grow under the watch of a Multiplier. One way that Multipliers incite this growth is by asking people to stretch and do something they've never done before.

Consider these three individuals:

Eleanor Schaffner Mosh was a champion who needed a bigger cause. As the marketing director for the small IT (information technology) practice within Booz Allen Hamilton in 1988, she ran basic demand-generation programs. But she suddenly found herself with a really big job when BAH decided to turn over the reins of the IT practice to a different partner, who was intent on transforming the function. Within months she was organizing a corporate-wide kick-off event to launch the vision for the IT practice. Next she convened a forum of the top CIOs in the world. When she found herself sitting next to the CEO of Booz Allen Hamilton during one of the meetings, she confidently explained to him why the IT industry and the IT practice inside their firm was going to change the world. She later said, "I wasn't afraid of anything or anyone. We knew what we were doing and we felt like we could do anything."

Mike Hagan was ready to take on the world, but he literally needed a passport. He worked as the director of sales operations for the billion-dollar US sales division of a multinational company. His job was to make sure the sales force complied with company policy. When the president of the sales division wanted to globalize and grow the business, he tapped Mike to figure this out. One day Mike was the policy police, writing tickets for sales administration offenders. The next day he was the architect of sales operations and policy for the entire global business. Initially Mike protested, citing his inexperience with global operations, and he confessed that he didn't even have a current passport. His protests were ignored. The president told him that he was smart and would surely figure this out. And he did. The experience was grueling but invigorating. Mike reflected, "I was given an opportunity to do something I had never done before. In fact, no one had ever done it." The job was huge, but Mike grew into it as predicted.

Polly Sumner was a powerhouse waiting to be unleashed. When a new president joined Oracle, he noticed this channel sales manager's strategic savvy and drive and asked her to assume a vice president role, running alliances and strategic partnerships. In time, Polly was right in the middle of a very messy high-stakes conflict. The management team could not agree on how quickly Oracle would release new versions of its database code to its applications partner (and competitor) SAP. Polly escalated the issue to her new boss, who responded, "This is a complex issue, and probably beyond the scope of your role, but you should be the one to lead the resolution." Polly went right to the people who could fix the problem. She found herself brokering a conversation between the billionaire founders and CEOs, Hasso Plattner of SAP and Larry Ellison of Oracle, in a meeting held at Larry's favorite Japanese teahouse. The issue was resolved to their mutual satisfaction and Polly was a superstar.

These three individuals all worked for the same boss, just in different settings. Who was the common denominator in this equation? It was Ray Lane, known for challenging his team and for exacting every ounce of their capability. When we asked people why they gave Ray so much, their answers revealed a consistent story: he asked them to go outside their comfort zones. He could spot smarts in others and gave people a chance to stretch well beyond their current capabilities. He gave them ownership, not at the level of their current capability, but always one—and occasionally two—levels up.

When Investors stretch the role, they stretch the person in it. This bigger role creates a vacuum that must be filled.

2. Investing Resources

The moment Investors establish an ownership position, they step in and begin investing. They protect their investment by infusing the knowledge and resources the person will need to successfully deliver on their accountability.

Teach and Coach

When Jae Choi at McKinsey inserted himself into the discussion with the project team, it wasn't to show-and-tell what he knows. He "grabbed the pen" so he could teach and coach. It is a simple and vital distinction: Diminishers tell you what they know; Multipliers help you learn what you need to know. Jae is not only a business leader but also an avid teacher who looks for the teachable moments when a team is spinning or has suffered a setback. That's when minds are most open and hungry, and he knows how to contribute a relevant insight or ask just the right question to move the group forward.

K. R. Sridhar, CEO of Bloom Energy, who has been described several times in previous chapters, is another masterful teacher. K. R.'s teaching doesn't occur in a classroom or in a corporate training center; he has to "coach" right in the middle of a tough game and in the face of very real problems. When the team is wrestling with a technical setback, K. R. engages not with a solution but with a thought-provoking question. He'll ask, "What do we know about what doesn't work?" and "What assumptions led us to these outcomes?" and "What risks do we face now that need to be mitigated?" His team pursues these questions in turn, unearthing their individual knowledge and building a collective body of intelligence.

K. R. says, "You are teaching by helping your team solve real problems. Even if you know the solution, you don't offer it. If you do, you've lost the teaching moment. It has to be Socratic. You ask the question and tease out the answer."

Although K. R. focuses on immediate problems, his investment in these teaching moments returns far more than just solutions to these problems. When leaders teach, they invest in their people's ability to solve and avoid problems in the future. This is one of the most powerful ways that Multipliers build intelligence around them.

Provide Backup

When you think of investing intellectual capital in your direct reports, it is easy to assume that you are the one who needs to provide the capital. But this limits the investment options to what you know and what you have time and energy to invest. Additionally, when you are the sole investor, your presence can be overpowering and your attempts to help can be more disruptive than beneficial, especially when the stakes are high.

When people are stretched and working above their current capability level, they are bound to trip up or take false steps. These situations are ripe for Diminishers, especially well-meaning managers prone to rescuing struggling employees. How can a manager intervene without usurping control? A wise Multiplier ensures there's a safety net in place—a planned backup, someone the employee can go to for advice on how to recover gracefully. It should be no surprise that the best safety nets are not managers; very few people enjoy falling on their backs and getting rescued by their bosses. Typically, the best people to provide this layer of support are colleagues who can offer guidance without undertones of judgment and disappointment. Instead of jumping in, the Investor provides a backup.

When leaders define clear ownership and invest in others, they have sown the seeds of success and earned the right to hold people accountable.

3. Holding People Accountable

In working with hundreds of business executives, there is something I've noticed about the finest of these leaders. They all appear to have slanted tables in their offices. Sure, the desk they sit at (with their computer and phone) is perfectly flat. But their meeting table has a distinct slant to it. Perhaps you may not have noticed it, but surely you have seen how accountability for action rolls from their side of the table down to other people—and often to you. It may look flat to the unsuspecting eye, but if you placed a marble on one side, that marble would surely roll right off the opposite end! These leaders have a natural leaning to give accountability to others and keep it there. When their people push problems over to the manager's side of the table, by the end of the conversation, those problems slide right back to where they came from. The leader helps, offers suggestions, asks great questions, and may highlight or escalate a critical issue, but the accountability slides back and rests with their staff. Their tables slant in the direction of other people.

One senior executive I worked for carried a small leather note-book with him in every meeting. Strangely, he never took meeting notes in it. But in every meeting, he was mentally present and fully engaged, listened intently, and offered carefully dispensed insight. During these meetings, I would furiously take notes, making care-ful notation of my action items, and others did the same. On rare occasions, I would see him write a single note. These occasions were reserved for when he alone was accountable for an action. This was the slanted desk in action. This leader knew how to keep the account-ability with his people. He was fully engaged, but he did not take over. And because he assumed accountability with careful restraint, when he wrote an action down in his little leather book, you could be sure it would get done, without delay.

Give It Back

Investors get involved in other people's work, but they continually give back leadership and accountability.

John Wookey is an executive vice president of industry applications at Salesforce, a veteran in the applications software business, and a Multiplier who builds organizations with know-how. He knows that delivering software on time and with quality isn't a hands-off job. But he sees a clear distinction between micromanaging and being involved in the work people are doing.

One of the breeding grounds for micromanagement in the software development business is the user interface review meeting. A typical software application has about 250 screens whose usability can make or break the product in the marketplace, so most executives are keenly interested in getting this right. By the end of a user interface review meeting, the micromanaging development executive will have seized the pen, sprung to the whiteboard, and redesigned the screens himself in front of the group as an impressive show of his design savvy.

John has seen his former peers and bosses do this countless times, but he makes the investment instead. When John sees problems in the screens, he makes suggestions, discusses options and trade-offs, and then asks the team to go back to their "lab" and figure it out. John says, "I give people feedback as guidance rather than an order because I assume that someone who has been working on something full-time, for many weeks, has insight into it that I won't have after a few minutes." John does offer his insights, gained from decades of building business applications, and reminds his team to think about what real users need from the software. He keeps his guidance focused on what they all can do to build a product they can take pride in.

John does jump in, but, like the partner at McKinsey in Seoul, he hands the pen back. By doing so, he signals that he is interested and engaged, but not the one in charge. He gives it back, and the accountability for designing and building a great product stays with the other person, who incidentally is also built up in the process.

Michael Clarke, the president of infrastructure at Flextronics, has a clever little two-step process for giving accountability back to people in a way that encourages their continued intellectual contribution. He listens to a presentation or an idea with interest, and then with a wry smile and a thick Yorkshire accent, says, "Hey, that is good thinking." So he begins by praising the edge of great thinking. Then he affirms their ownership of the business problem at hand by saying, "I'd love to know whether we should invest in X or Y. I mean, you're smart. You can figure this out." These words are heard again and again by his team: "You're smart. You figure it out." Their ideas are validated and the onus for solving the issue is back with them.

Expect Complete Work

It was the summer of 1987, and I had just landed the internship of my dreams. I would be working for Kerry Patterson, a former professor of organizational behavior at the business school that I attended, who was now running a management training company in Southern California.

Kerry was known for his brilliant and slightly demented mind. Kerry is what happens when you pack an Einstein-size brain into a Danny DeVito–size body. Everyone wanted to work for Kerry, but I managed to get the job through some combination of faculty recommendation and advanced Jedi mind tricks. I eagerly drove to Southern California to work and study under his mentorship.

As in most internships, I did an assortment of odd jobs. I created training content and did computer work and even handled a few stray legal issues. But my favorite job was editing anything that Kerry wrote. Sometimes it was a training manual, sometimes it was a speech, but my job was always to edit and find and fix mistakes. On this particular day, I was editing a marketing brochure that Kerry had written. I did the usual routine. I found and fixed typos and grammar errors. I rewrote a few sentences that were awkward. Then I stumbled on a particularly troublesome tangle of words. I tried a couple of times to rewrite the sentences, but I couldn't think of anything better than what Kerry had written, and it was too big a mess for me to fix. I figured Kerry, with his great big brain, would know best what to do, so I labeled it as awkward by noting the standard editorial term, AWK, in the margin.

About an hour after I returned the document to Kerry's desk, he returned from a meeting to find my edits. I heard him marching down the hall toward my office, and his pace indicated that he wasn't coming to thank me. He burst across the threshold and marched right up to my desk. Feeling somewhat worried, I sat up straight getting ready for whatever Kerry was going to throw at me. Without so much as a hello, he dropped the document in front of me with a dramatic thump, looked me straight in the eye, and said, "Don't ever give me an A-W-K without an F-I-X!" With a twinkle in his eye, the consummate teacher turned and left my office. Point taken. I worked a little harder, applied a little more brainpower, and fixed the awkward sentences. I snuck back into Kerry's office and returned the new edit to his desk.

Kerry continued to teach and to write prolifically, and is the author of four best-selling books (*Crucial Conversations, Crucial Confrontations, Influencer,* and *Change Anything*). I completed the internship, finished business school, and then made my way in the corporate world having learned from Kerry one of the most important professional lessons: Never give someone an A-W-K without an F-I-X. Don't just identify the problem; find a solution.

Throughout my management career, I've told this story to dozens of people, perhaps hundreds. I've shared it with virtually every person who worked on my team and dropped a problem on my desk without an attached solution. I passed along, "Don't give me an A-W-K without an F-I-X!"

When we ask for the F-I-X, we give people an opportunity to complete their thinking and their work. We encourage them to stretch and exercise intellectual muscles that might otherwise atrophy in the presence of other smart, capable people. Multipliers never do anything for their people that their people can do for themselves.

Respect Natural Consequences

Several years ago, our family took a vacation to Maui, Hawaii. We parked ourselves on the beach at the very end of Ka'anapali, at the base of Black Rock point. It is a beautiful beach, but at that spot the ocean confronts the huge rock jutting out of the beach, and the surf can be rough. My then three-year-old, Christian, was fascinated by the ocean and kept straying out of the baby waves and into the dangerous surf. The scene is familiar to every parent. He would venture out too far, then I would go fetch him back, get down at eye level, and tell him about the power of the ocean and why it was too dangerous for him to go out so far. He would resume playing, forget my teaching, and venture out again. We repeated the cycle several times.

I decided it was time for him to learn the lesson from Mother Nature instead of from Mom. I watched for a midsize wave to come toward shore. I selected one that would give him a good topple but wouldn't sweep him off to Japan. Instead of pulling him back in as the wave approached, I let him venture out. And rather than grabbing his arm and lifting him out of the water, I simply stood by his side. Several parents nearby looked alarmed as they saw the wave coming. One tried to get my attention by giving me that "bad mother" look. I assured him I was on duty but as more of a teacher than a lifeguard. The wave came in and instantly dragged Christian under the surf and tossed him around several times. After he'd had a good tumble, I pulled my toddler back up to safety. Once he caught his breath and spit out the sand, we had a talk about the power of the ocean. This time he seemed to understand, and now stayed closer to shore. He continues to love the ocean, is an avid surfer, and displays a respect for the power of nature.

Nature teaches best. When we let nature take its course and allow people to experience the natural consequences of their actions, they learn most rapidly and most profoundly. When we protect people from experiencing the natural ramifications of their actions, we stunt their learning. Real intelligence gets developed through experimentation and by trial and error.

Allowing consequences to have their effect allows natural forces to inform intelligent action. It communicates that the manager believes people are smart enough to figure things out. People become more independent because they feel they own their actions, as well as the results or consequences of those actions. Investors want their investments to be successful, but they know they can't intervene and alter natural market forces. By providing the possibility to fail, these leaders give others the freedom and the motivation to grow and succeed. Elaben Bhatt captured this well when she said, "There are risks in every action. Every success has the seed of some failure."

Multipliers have a core belief that *people are smart and will figure things out.* So it makes sense that they operate as Investors, giving ownership that keeps rolling back to other people. They invest the resources they need to grow a business and the people in it. They engage personally, offering their insight and guidance, but they remember to "give the pen back" when they are done so people remain accountable to deliver on the expected returns.

Through investing in others, Multipliers generate independence in others. They create organizations that can sustain performance without their direct involvement. When the organization is truly autonomous, these leaders have earned the right to step away. When they leave, they leave a legacy.

The Diminisher's Approach to Execution

The Diminisher operates from a very different assumption: *People will never be able to figure it out without me.* They believe if they don't dive into the details and follow up, other people won't deliver. These assumptions breed dependency among people, as full ownership is never offered to them. Diminishers assign piecemeal tasks, then jump in, believing that other people cannot make it work without them.

Unfortunately, in the end, these assumptions are often proven true because people become disabled and dependent on the Diminisher for answers, for approval, and to integrate the pieces together. When this happens, Diminishers look outward, asking themselves only, *Why are people always letting me down?* When Diminishers eventually leave an organization, things fall apart. Things crumble because the leader has held the operation together with micromanagement and sweat equity.

Consider the private equity investor in Brazil who stifled his entire organization with his micromanagement. Celso is extraordinarily smart and considered by his colleagues to be a financial genius. He was a superior analyst and a rock star of a stock trader. But his control-freak management style hampered his ability to build great companies. Unfortunately, as the head of a private equity firm, his job was exactly that: to build companies.

In staff meetings, his staff rarely got through their reports on prospective investments or portfolio companies before he interrupted with his pithy analysis. Sure, he'd make a few great points, but it discouraged other people from thinking. His signature remark was, "I can't believe you haven't figured this out."

Celso tracked performance of their portfolio companies with second-by-second monitoring and arranged to receive all company sales reports on his cell phone. When sales dipped off target, he'd call the CEO at random hours of the night and start screaming. Whatever the situation, Celso was the first to respond. Like Pavlov's dog, there was no delay between stimulus and response. When he found a problem, he'd jump in immediately and try to fix it himself.

Over time, Celso's micromanagement created a sharp division inside the organization. Most of his colleagues would lie low, knowing that he eventually would do things himself. As much of the talent retreated, he compensated by hiring aggressive graduates of elite colleges who didn't have enough experience to expect a different type of leadership. The organization began to look a lot like Celso over time and resembled an alpha-male annual convention with a revolving door. Like many Diminishers, Celso's micromanagement stifled the intelligence within an organization chock-full of really smart people.

Let's look at the ways in which Diminishers cripple the capability of their people and create dependent organizations.

MAINTAIN OWNERSHIP. The approach of the Micromanager is well captured in a comment made by a staff member of a prominent professor: "I can't make any decisions. I don't have lead in my pencil until Dr. Yang says that I do." Diminishers don't trust others to figure it out for themselves, so they maintain ownership. When they delegate, they dole out piecemeal tasks but not real responsibility. They give people just a piece of the puzzle. It is no wonder that people have a hard time putting the puzzle together without them.

Eva Wiesel is smart and energetic and, most unfortunately for her team, decidedly a morning person. As operations manager in a manufacturing plant, each day she'd come to work with a fresh set of ideas for her management team. She would plan out the day on her commute in to work, arrive at the plant, walk through the door, and begin dropping by her people's office to let them know exactly what she wanted them to do that day. Some days it was more of the same, but other days the tasks took them in entirely new directions. Her people noticed the pattern and began a simple coping routine. Every day about 8:00 a.m., they began lining up in the hallway that led from the lobby to their office area. With pads of paper and coffee in hand, they waited for her to burst in and deliver their "marching orders" for the day. It was just easier for everyone to wait to be told what to do.

No doubt, Eva thought she was a great leader who was delegating and communicating clearly to her team. In reality, Eva was a Micromanager who did all the thinking for her team and hoarded the ownership of the work.

JUMP IN AND OUT. Micromanagers hand over work to others, but they take it back the moment problems arise. They get lured in like a fish to the shiny objects on a fisherman's line. Emergent problems and big hurdles are irresistible bait for Diminishers. They see these shiny objects and are attracted. They are fascinated by the intellectual challenge to solve the problem. They are lured by the attention and kudos they get for saving the day. And they're hooked on the feeling of importance as people become dependent on them and their brilliance to deliver results. They love to be lured in, and the diminishing impact on their people is set.

The problem is that they don't just get lured in and stay there. They come in and out. An issue gets onto the radar screen of senior management, and suddenly they are all over it. They spring in and then when the fun is over, they spring back out. They are bungee bosses.

Garth Yamamoto is the chief marketing officer for a consumer products company. Garth has two modes: one is "all over it" and the other is "completely absent." When his team is working on an issue with CEO visibility, he jumps in, takes over, and delivers the work straight to his boss, a highly mercurial leader. When the CEO isn't involved, Garth is nowhere to be seen. His people struggle to get his attention on the less visible but equally critical projects that form the backbone of the business.

When these leaders bungee in and out of their own organization, they create dependency and disengagement. When they strike at random, they produce disruptive chaos.

TAKE IT BACK. I was twenty-five years old and six months into my first management job. It was 7:30 p.m., as I sat at my desk at 500 Oracle Parkway, Oracle's main office tower. The halls were dark and all my staff had gone home for the night. Everyone was home but me. I was still busy, trying to close out my "to dos" for the day, many of which had emerged during the course of the workday as one little crisis after another landed on my desk. I came up from my absorption in my work and thought, *Why am I still doing so much of the work? I've delegated. Why does it all come back to me?* People were bringing me their problems, and I would take them back.

At this realization, I became irritated at my team for dumping the problems on me and for not doing their jobs. Then, alone in a dark office, I had the epiphany: I wasn't doing *my* job. As a manager, my job was no longer about me. It was my responsibility to manage the work, not do the work. I had been solving problems like some overzealous superhero, when I was really supposed to help other people solve problems. My job was to flow the work to my team and keep it there. It is an embarrassingly simple idea, but for me, as a newly promoted manager, it was a startling realization.

In my executive coaching, I am frequently surprised at how many senior leaders and even executives haven't discovered this simple lesson. When managers take it back, not only do they end up doing all the work but they rob others of the opportunity to use and extend their own intelligence. They stunt the growth of intelligence around them. They begin to slide down the slippery slope of the Accidental Diminisher.

Whether accidental or not, Diminishers are costly to organizations. They might be superstars themselves, but they quickly become the boundary factor that limits the growth of their organizations. The cost of the Micromanager is that organizations cannot grow beyond them and struggle to leverage the other intellect inside the organization.

Micromanagers don't use the full complement of talent, intelligence, and resourcefulness available to them, so these capacities sit idle in their organizations. To counteract this, they continue to ask the organization for more resources, wondering why people aren't more productive and are always letting them down.

In contrast to this, Investors not only engage people through clearly delegating responsibilities to them, they extend assignments that stretch the thinking and capability of the individuals and the team. They grow the assets in their portfolio. As a result, they get full leverage out of their current resources and they stretch and increase the capacity of the organization to take on the next responsibility.

The Serial Multiplier

After seven hours of conversation in a studio apartment next to one of Mumbai's slums, Narayana Murthy and six of his friends agreed to a vision for a software firm in Bangalore that they hoped would do two things. First, persuade their wives to each contribute $250 as seed money. Second, garner respect around the world. They accomplished both.

Their investment of intellectual energy and financial capital turned out to be very sound, as Mr. Murthy led Infosys Technologies from its tiny beginnings to become the first Indian company to be listed on the NASDAQ, with a valuation of $10 billion. Murthy helped his team reach beyond their dreams, encouraged India's entrepreneurs to believe in themselves, and gave a face to the new India.

He became a revered name inside and outside the company (*The Economist* ranked him among the ten most-admired global business leaders in 2005[3]) and could have easily stayed at the top and enjoyed the fame and power of his exalted position.

Instead, on his sixtieth birthday, Narayana Murthy stepped aside as CEO. No crisis triggered the move and there had been no power play to topple him. The move was the extension of a deliberate plan. He had spent years investing in the other cofounders so they could operate independently of him. Consistent with his plan, he handed the role of CEO over to one of the other cofounders, Nandan Nilekani, and Murthy stayed on as nonexecutive chairman and chief mentor of the company, a role he has performed for ten years. Infosys has continued to grow its market value—$32 billion as of November 2016.

Asked at the World Economic Forum in Davos, Switzerland, why he chose that role for himself, Murthy said his primary role as a leader was to ensure successive generations of leaders. When asked what drives him to invest in this way, he said, without hesitation, "The reward for winning a pinball game is to get a chance to play the next one." In other words, he doesn't crave the spotlight of being a CEO as much as he hungers to freely invest again elsewhere. While some CEOs are addicted to praise, this leader is addicted to growing other people. A Multiplier to his core, he recognized that his greatest value was not in his intelligence but in how he invested his intelligence in others.

And now, in his second career, he has again been investing in the growth of others, just with a much broader sphere of influence. Free from the operational management responsibilities at Infosys, Murthy has gone on to invest in governments and institutions around the world, including Thailand and the United Nations, and educational entities like Cornell University, the Wharton School of Business, and Singapore Management University. He has the ear of the prime minister of India and is making a case to him to invest in the next generation. In his words, "We have to put young people in charge of these massive educational initiatives." And his investor approach to management has established a pattern at Infosys.

When leaders like Narayana Murthy invest in the development of other leaders, they earn the right to step away without jeopardizing the performance of the organization. The Investor not only reaps these rewards but is now available to repeat the investment cycle elsewhere.

Much like a serial entrepreneur who builds one successful company after another, these leaders can become Serial Multipliers. Of course, doing so requires the leader to break free of the addiction to praise that entraps many senior leaders and instead become addicted to growth—growth of the business and growth of the people around them. Serial Multipliers grow intelligence. This intelligence isn't ephemeral, fleeing when the Multiplier is no longer by their side. It is real, and it is sustainable, which is what allows the Multiplier to replicate the effect again and again.

Becoming an Investor

To become a Serial Multiplier (or serial entrepreneur), you have to have a starting point and a first success to begin the positively addictive cycle. Here are four strategies for becoming an Investor.

The Starting Block

1. GIVE 51 PERCENT OF THE VOTE. When you delegate, you probably let people know what you are expecting of them. Take this to the next level and let people know that they (not you) are in charge and accountable. Tell them how you will stay engaged and support them, but that they remain in charge. Give them a number to make it concrete. For example, tell them they have 51 percent of the vote and that you have only 49 percent. Or be bold and make it a 75/25 split.

Give them charge of something that requires them to stretch beyond their current capabilities. Start with ownership for the current scope of their role, and then take it up one level. Look for ways to uplevel their responsibility and give them a job that they aren't yet fully qualified for.

2. LET NATURE TAKE ITS COURSE. Nature is the most powerful teacher. We can easily forget this when consequences are artificially imposed on us. But we remember and learn deeply when we experience the natural consequences of our actions. Letting nature teach is hard, because our managerial performance instincts kick in. We want to ensure that our team delivers successfully. The good news is that you don't need to let a major project fail. Find the "smaller waves" that will provide natural teaching moments, without catastrophic outcomes. To let nature teach, try these steps:

1. **LET IT HAPPEN.** Don't jump in and fix an assignment so it doesn't fail. Don't take over a meeting because someone isn't handling it well. Let the person experience a degree of failure.

2. **TALK ABOUT IT.** Be available to help someone learn from the failure. Be standing by after a failed meeting or lost sales deal to help them get up, brush off the sand, and talk about what happened. Ask great questions and avoid the ever-diminishing "I told you so."

3. **FOCUS ON NEXT TIME.** Help them find a way to be successful next time. Give them a way out and a path forward. If they've just botched an important sales call, ask them how they'll handle a similar situation with another customer in their pipeline.

Not only are there natural consequences to our mistakes, there are natural consequences to good decisions. Allow people to experience the full force of their successes. Step out of the way, give them credit, and let them reap the full benefits of their victories.

3. ASK FOR THE F-I-X. Many people are promoted into management positions because they are natural problem solvers. So, when someone brings you a problem, it is only natural for you to want to fix it. And chances are, people will expect you to because you so often do. In that split second before you respond, recall Kerry Patterson marching into the office of his intern and demanding she do more than just point out awkward sentences. Ask for people to complete the thought process and provide a fix. Use simple questions such as these:

- ➤ What solution(s) do you see to this problem?
- ➤ How would you propose we solve this?
- ➤ What would you like to do to fix this?

Most important, don't assume responsibility for fixing the problem. Put the problem back on their desk and encourage them to stretch further. When someone brings you an A-W-K, ask for an F-I-X.

4. GIVE IT BACK. When someone is stuck and asks you for your opinion, it can be hard not to take over. For some, the tendency to take over is so great that they sit on their hands, afraid to speak out lest it turn into a hostile takeover. When you see your team members struggling, offer help, but have an exit plan. A conversation can happen anywhere—in a conference room, one-on-one in your office, during a spontaneous meeting in the hallway. Regardless of the venue, visualize the point in the conversation when you symbolically give the pen back. Imagine yourself at the whiteboard, adding a few ideas to the collective thinking on the board. You finish your thought and then hand the pen back. This gesture lets your colleagues know they are still in the lead and are accountable to finish the job.

Here are some statements that signal that you are handing back the pen:

- ➤ I'm happy to help think this through, but I'm still looking to you to lead this going forward.

➤ You are still the lead on this.

➤ I'm here to back you up. What do you need from me as you lead this?

Each of the above is a simple entry point. But done repetitively these actions can instigate the Multiplier effect inside your organization.

The Multiplier Effect

When Multipliers invest resources and confidence in other people and give them the ownership of their success, they uncover the vast intelligence and capability that lies within. Muhammad Yunus, 2006 Nobel laureate and father of the microcredit movement, said, "Each person has tremendous potential. She or he alone can influence the lives of others within the communities, nations, within and beyond her or his own time."

Multipliers invest in others in a way that builds independence to allow others to apply their full intelligence to the work at hand, and also to expand their scope and influence. The independence they create in others also allows the Investor to reinvest over and over, becoming a Serial Multiplier. The math is simple but powerful. The immediate Multiplier effect is that Multipliers get, on average, twice the capability from someone they lead. When extrapolated across an average organization of average size, approximately fifty people, that's the equivalent of adding an additional fifty people. Repeated over potentially ten different leadership roles over the course of a career, that is an additional five hundred people.

Multipliers continually double the size of their workforce for free. This 2× return in perpetuity for leading like a Multiplier makes a compelling business case, even to the most discerning investors on Sand Hill Road.

Chapter Six Summary

The Micromanager Versus the Investor

MICROMANAGERS manage every detail in a way that creates dependence on the leader and their presence for the organization to perform.

INVESTORS give other people the investment and ownership they need to produce results independent of the leader.

The Three Practices of the Investor

1. *Define Ownership*
   - Name the lead
   - Give ownership for the end goal
   - Stretch the role
2. *Invest Resources*
   - Teach and coach
   - Provide backup
3. *Hold People Accountable*
   - Give it back
   - Expect complete work
   - Respect natural consequences

Becoming an Investor

1. Give 51 percent of the vote
2. Let nature take its course
3. Ask for the F-I-X
4. Give it back

Leveraging Resources

	Micromanagers	Investors
What They Do	Manage every detail of the work to ensure it is completed the way they would do it	Give other people the ownership for results and invest in their success
What They Get	People who wait to be told what to do	People who take initiative and anticipate challenges
	People who hold back because they expect to be interrupted and told what to do instead	People who are fully focused on achieving results
	Free riders who wait for the boss to swoop in and save them	People who can get ahead of the boss in solving problems
	People who try to "work" their bosses and make sophisticated excuses	People who respond to the natural forces around them

Unexpected Findings

1. Multipliers do get involved in the operational details, but they keep the ownership with other people.
2. Multipliers are rated 42 percent higher at delivering world-class results than their Diminisher counterparts.[4]

SEVEN

The Accidental Diminisher

We judge others by their doings,
but ourselves by our intentions.

EDWARD WIGGLESWORTH

While it may seem that the Diminishers described in previous chapters were tyrannical bullies and know-it-alls, it turned out that they actually weren't all jerks, and some were really good people. While the narcissistic leaders grab the headlines, the vast majority of diminishing happening inside our workplaces is done by the Accidental Diminisher—managers with the best of intentions, good people who think they are doing a good job leading.

How might we, with the very best intentions, be having a diminishing impact on the people we lead? Can people be hindered by our honest attempts to help, teach, or lead by example?

A high school was facing a critical application deadline that would determine its ranking and status as a "blue ribbon" school, and the responsibility fell on Sally, a veteran principal. She loved analytical work and was drawn to anything that involved data, spreadsheets, and synthesis. She dove into the briefing documents to get a thorough understanding of the analysis that would need to be done. Realizing that the project was significant and needed a lot of further analysis, she decided to get her assistant principal involved.

Marcus was relatively new to his role (and to spreadsheet work), but he was smart, thorough, and insightful. She decided to hand the data analysis over to him, giving him full ownership. Sally wanted him to be successful, so she carefully planned the handoff. She met with him, reviewed the report specifications with him, told him he would be in charge, and laid out clear expectations for what needed to be done.

Sally then began working on other elements of the report and waited for Marcus to send the data analysis to her. When he hadn't sent it two days later, she suspected he was struggling and wanted to help him, so she sent him more instructions and suggested some categories to use for analyzing the data. Again, she didn't hear much from him. She stopped by his desk to see if he had finished it. He hadn't.

Knowing how conscientious Marcus was, Sally assumed he needed more help. She sat down, offered her support, and asked, "How can I be of help to you with this analysis?" When she didn't get a concrete response, she began offering suggestions. "Would it help if I gave you a quick tutorial on how to use the statistics functions in Excel? Or perhaps we can sit down together and go through the data elements?" Strangely, he didn't bite at any of the offers.

Sally was growing frustrated. Clearly Marcus needed help, but she couldn't figure out how to help him. Sally was about to offer to do the first set of analysis with him, but he started to speak before she could. Sally stopped talking and gave him her full attention, thrilled to finally learn what help he needed from her. He began tentatively, holding back how irritated he was by her deluge of offers to help, but he grew more confident and finally was able to say, "Sally, I think I could use . . . just a little less help from you."

Sally sheepishly acknowledged his message, backed off, and gave him the space he needed to figure it out on his own. He did figure it out, and the analysis from this smart, conscientious assistant principal became a vital component of the report that once again earned the school blue ribbon status.

Despite the best intentions, this leader had become an Accidental Diminisher. While her intent was to help, her help was a hindrance. What happens when a manager is too quick with ideas and too swift with action? Or too supportive and helpful? Or just enthusiastic or optimistic? Surely these can be character virtues—the kind taught in business school or Sunday school. Indeed they are, but many popular management practices can lead us, subtly but surely, down the slippery slope to becoming an Accidental Diminisher.

The Accidental Diminisher

We all have Accidental Diminisher moments. The secret to the Multiplier effect is knowing what your vulnerabilities are, spotting them in action, and turning these situations into Multiplier moments. Let me share a few of the ways that really well-intentioned leaders end up having a diminishing impact on the people around them. As you consider each, you might ask yourself, What is my vulnerability? How might my best intentions be shutting down good ideas and smart people?

Idea Guy

This type of leader is a creative, innovative thinker who loves an idea-rich environment. He is a veritable fountain of ideas. Ideas bubble up for him 24/7, so he bursts into the office brimming with new ideas to share with colleagues. This leader doesn't necessarily think his ideas are superior. He simply believes that the more he tosses around his ideas, the more he will spark ideas in others.

But what actually happens around an Idea Guy? The ideas he tosses out seem compelling, so his team begins to chase them. But as soon as they begin to make progress on yesterday's idea, the next day brings a new idea du jour. The team makes ephemeral progress on multiple fronts. The great chase becomes a standstill as they realize that they always end up back at square one—*so why not just stay there*? As they learn to stop acting on the leader's ideas, they also stop trying to come up with their own ideas. After all, if they actually need a new idea, they can just wait for the fountain to spew.

It is easy to get idea lazy around people who are idea rich.

Always On

This dynamic, charismatic leader exudes energy; he or she is always engaged, always present, and always has something to say. These are the leaders with a big personality that can fill a room. They assume that their energy is contagious, like a virus to be caught by anyone in their presence.

But, like the common cold, this leader can be draining—she enervates rather than energizes the people around her. As she expands, like a gas consuming all the available oxygen, others suffocate; most find her just plain exhausting. Soon people avoid making eye contact or having encounters with her, thinking, I just don't have the energy right now. And all too often around this leader, thinking introverts are suppressed while action-oriented extroverts dominate.

We know what the Always On leader does to others—we've all seen it and felt it—but what do others end up doing to this type of leader? Well, what do you do to the human being who lacks an "off" switch? If you can't find a dimmer switch, you simply turn her off inside your head. You put her in the background; she becomes white noise. Her endless spray of speech becomes muffled and sometimes completely unheard by the people she leads. The Always On leader thinks she is playing big, but actually she becomes small, and she makes everyone around her small, too. Energy isn't contagious, but attitude and confidence in others are.

When the leader is always on, everyone else is always off.

Rescuer

He is a good manager and a decent person, the type of leader who doesn't like to see people struggle, make avoidable mistakes, or fail. At the first sign of distress, he jumps in and helps. Occasionally, he swoops in with a big, heroic rescue. More often than not, he simply lends a hand, resolves a problem, and helps people across the finish line. Incidentally, we find that this is the most common way leaders accidentally diminish.

The intention of the Rescuer is noble. He wants to see other people be successful; he desires to protect the reputation of the people who work for him, but because he interrupts a natural performance cycle, he starves people of the vital learning they need to be successful. When a manager helps too soon and too often, people around him become dependent and helpless. Instead of feeling successful, employees experience frustration and depleted confidence when they fail to cross the finish line.

Yes, there are times when employees appear to appreciate the help, yet the behavior is nonetheless diminishing—while they may feel relief, they haven't grown or even fully utilized the intelligence they have. Furthermore, when the Rescuer intervenes, he can create a vexing and all too pervasive performance disconnect, by depriving people of the feedback that comes from the natural consequences of mistakes. While the manager sees failure and a gap they have to step in and close, employees often see success. You can hardly blame the employees for this delusion; after all, their work always crosses the finish line on time, because they are helped by the invisible hand of the Rescuer.

As leaders, sometimes we are most helpful when we don't help.

Pacesetter

This is the achievement-oriented leader who leads by example. To build momentum, she personally sets the standard for performance and for exemplifying the values of the organization (such as quality, customer service, innovation, etc.). She takes the lead, sets the pace, and expects that the people around her will notice, follow, and, of course, catch up. For example, a manager might wish to send a strong message that customer service is a top priority, so she increases the time she spends in the field, traveling to customer sites, meeting with key clients, and writing up and distributing trip reports. Her intention is to send a signal that her organization should be actively listening for the voice of the customer.

What actually happens when the leader speeds out ahead? Do others pick up the pace or do they fall behind? The effect is subtle. The leader is half right: people do take notice. They catch on, but they rarely catch up. Instead of increasing their own pace, they most often assume the role of spectator, watching the Pacesetter do her thing. While she is expecting her staff to speed up, they are actually slowing down or sitting down. Instead of initiating customer contact themselves, they assume this is an executive role and sit back and read the reports. Or perhaps, recognizing the widening gap between the Pacesetter and themselves, they simply give up.

I've seen this dynamic many times in the workplace but have learned it most poignantly in a footrace against an eight-year-old. For most of his second-grade year of school, my son Joshua insisted we race to the bus stop each day. Like any good parent, I understood the purpose of these races to be that of encouraging his budding love of sport and competition, so I made sure to let him win or to make it a close, rousing competition.

But every now and then I would forget. I, too, love to run and enjoy the feeling of turning it on and crossing the finish line first (or maybe just not last). Joshua is my youngest child and at this point he was the only child I could still beat on foot. Fueled by some sudden vain ambition (i.e., midlife crisis), occasionally I would take off running at full speed and easily beat him to the bus stop. Catching my breath and looking back, I would see that he had stopped running and was now walking. This seemed strange because he loved to race! As he walked closer, the look on his face was a muddle of disappointment and disapproval. When he arrived at the bus stop, he would shrug his shoulders and say indifferently, "We weren't racing that time." Every time I lost my head and raced out in front, creating a gap too big for him to close, the same scene ensued. He had learned that when he couldn't keep up, it was best to just let me win.

As leaders, sometimes the faster we run, the slower others walk. When leaders set the pace, they are more likely to create spectators than followers.

Rapid Responder

What about the leader who is quick to take action? This is the leader who prizes agility and fast turnaround. He takes responsibility and is "on it"—he is quick to respond, troubleshoot problems, and make fast microdecisions. Most of us work with some sort of rapid responder. He sees a problem; he solves it. He sees a bear; he shoots it. Emails don't last long in his in-box. He opens, reads, and resolves immediately. His intent is noble, of course. He wants an agile organization that pounces on problems and responds rapidly to stakeholders.

But instead of agility, the Rapid Responder tends to generate low-grade apathy. Even the best employees are slow to respond when they know that someone else is already "on it." Consider what happens when an urgent email hits an employee's in-box. She opens the email and recognizes its importance. She sees that her boss is copied on it, but the issue falls in her area of responsibility, so she jumps on it. She rereads it carefully and thoughtfully contemplates the options. She realizes that she needs more information and consults a colleague. When the employee returns to draft her reply, she notices she has new mail and gets that sinking feeling that her boss may have already responded in the interim. And of course he has. Not wanting to get out of synch, she just lets it go. When this happens frequently enough, employees learn to just let the boss deal with the issue—even when the issue at hand was actually theirs to handle. Not only is the Rapid Responder the first one and the only one to respond, this boss is the only one growing.

The Rapid Responder can create activity traffic jams across his organization. Because he responds to problems and questions quickly, he releases a lot of decisions into the workflow of his team. The roads become flooded with decisions and as those decisions prompt an excess of action, people move at a crawl, and soon it is full-fledged gridlock.

The leader reacts quickly, but the people around him tend to react slowly, if at all.

Optimist

This positive, can-do manager always sees possibilities and believes that most problems can be tackled with hard work and the right mindset. She has read the research on the power of positive thinking and the incredible mental and physical benefits of optimism. She is a "glass half full" kind of person.

The Optimist isn't necessarily a cheerleader; she just focuses on what is possible and believes that the people around her (herself included) *are smart and can figure it out*. So how could this possibly be diminishing?

A colleague and I were in the middle of a high-stakes research project where we had a small window of opportunity to write an article for a prestigious academic publication. To pull this off, we needed to complete some complex analysis, do a round of additional research, and actually write the article, all while working on several other projects and operating on a thin budget.

After years of experience in the corporate world, where a given week involved juggling knives, pulling rabbits out of hats, and rubbing two nickels together to pay for it all, to me this seemed feasible and an interesting challenge. I enthusiastically attacked the project, providing leadership along the way to my more junior colleague.

At one critical meeting, he turned to me and said, "Liz, I need you to stop saying that!"

"Saying what?" I asked.

He replied, "'How hard can it be?'"

I looked puzzled. He explained, "You say that all the time: 'How hard can it be? We can do this. After all, how hard can it be?'"

I could see his point emerging. While I was working for Oracle, a rapidly growing company, I had been thrown into management at the tender age of twenty-four and faced a steady onslaught of challenges for which I was untrained and underprepared. These formative experiences taught me that a team of smart, driven people could do almost anything. I learned to say to myself, *I can do this. After all, how hard can it really be?* This attitude (termed a "growth mindset" by Dr. Carol Dweck)[1] had worked beautifully for me and many of my colleagues over the years.

My current colleague's voice reeled me back from my reflection: "Yes, *that* is what I need you to stop saying."

"But why?" I probed. He paused and looked me straight in the eye and said, "Because what we are doing *is actually* really hard." After another deliberate pause he continued, "And I need you to acknowledge that."

He wasn't opposed to the idea that it was doable; he simply wanted me to acknowledge the challenge and recognize his struggle. He didn't want me glossing over the challenge with my optimism. Having heard his sincere message, I looked at him squarely and acknowledged, "Yes, what we are doing is hard. It is really, really difficult. I suppose I just meant that we are very capable, and I'm confident we'll figure it out." I could see the tension lifting. I assured him that I would do my best to stop saying "that thing." Meanwhile, in the back of my mind I told myself, Sure, I can stop saying that. After all, *how hard can it be?*

Is it possible that a can-do attitude that worked so well for you in a previous role might be working against you as a leader? When you play the role of the optimist, you undervalue the struggle the team is experiencing and the hard-fought learning and work. Your staff may wonder if you have lost your tether to reality. Or, worse, you might be sending an unintentional message that mistakes and failure are not an option; after all, *how hard can it be*?

When the leader sees only the upside, others can become pre-occupied with the downside.

Protector

It's easy for a well-intended manager to fall into the "mama bear" trap and become the Protector who shields his or her staff, buffering people from the hazards of corporate life, the way the grizzly female protects her offspring from predators. Whereas the Rescuer saves the day after problems arise, the aim of the Protector is simply to keep his people safe and unscathed—not even seeing the problems. He worries that if team members get entangled in ugly politics, they might be eaten alive, so he fights off bullies and shields his staff from nasty internal politics.

Often managers have a better understanding of the darker forces that exist inside the organization, and they assume that this is their burden to bear. The Protector worries that if his people are exposed to the harsh reality, they might become tainted or disillusioned and decide to leave for greener pastures. So, he keeps his staff out of the most contentious meetings with senior executives, knowing these encounters can be career limiting. He shields people from the brutal facts and steers his team clear of danger and creates a seemingly safe haven, a happy valley where his people can flourish. While certainly there are situations when wise managers should shield their team, it can become a dangerous practice itself.

Unfortunately, the "mama bear" can prevent staff from learning from hardship and taking full accountability. It is a misguided attempt to manufacture safety. We know that Multipliers create intellectual safety (where people are free to express their ideas), but they don't shield people from reality, and they don't necessarily remove obstacles for people. In fact, with the assumption that *people are smart and will figure it out*, a Multiplier is inclined to expose people to such toxins and challenges, hoping that they will build resistance and strength.

If the leader continually protects people from danger, they never learn to fend for themselves.

Strategist

The Strategist is the big thinker who casts a compelling vision of the future. She shows the team a better place, a destination worth striving for, and she sells it with evangelical zeal. The Strategist thinks she is generating energy and the momentum needed to escape the gravitational pull of the status quo. Certainly, a wise leader knows how crucial it is to provide the big picture, the context, the "why" behind what the team is doing. And it is.

But sometimes a strategic, visionary leader can go too far and be too prescriptive. She might not be leaving enough space for others to think through the challenges themselves and generate the intellectual muscle needed to make a vision a reality. People can spend their time second-guessing what the boss wants rather than finding answers themselves. Instead of running with it, people climb up the mountaintop to seek guidance from the guru. This leader would generate more movement by seeding a challenge rather than selling a big vision.

If you've built a reputation as a big thinker, don't be surprised if people save the big thinking for you.

Perfectionist

We all know the leader with perfectionist tendencies: he appreciates excellence and loves the feeling of getting something perfect. He goes beyond setting a high standard for others to follow (as does the Pacesetter) and wants everyone around him to have the satisfaction of getting it just exactly right. So, he offers helpful critiques and points out little mistakes and flaws, the way a home owner might use blue construction tape to mark the slightest imperfections in a home improvement project—a drip of paint here, a stray exposed nailhead there—so the builder can fix the mistakes, work down the punch list, and enjoy pride of craftsmanship.

While he is offering these suggestions for improvement, he is envisioning a masterpiece in the making, an A+ grade on an important assignment. He knows that excellence doesn't come in one fell swoop, but in back-and-forth iteration. But, while he see an A+ in progress, others see nothing but red marks and blue tape all over their work. They see blood and loss and can easily become disengaged and disheartened.

Sometimes a 90 percent solution executed with 100 percent ownership is better than getting it 100 percent right with a disengaged team.

The above examples show just a few of the ways that well-intentioned leaders can have a diminishing effect. As you read the various Accidental Diminisher profiles above, surely some resonated, giving you a sharp insight or maybe even a pang of guilt. The question isn't which one of the above is your vulnerability; the real question is, "How do you discover your areas of vulnerability?" You can bring this vague suspicion into sharper focus by taking our online quiz, "Are You an Accidental Diminisher?" at www.multipliersbooks .com. This three-minute quiz provides additional structure to help you self-assess and analyze your potentially diminishing habits.

Are You an Accidental Diminisher?

I should clarify: having any of the above-described tendencies does not make you a Diminisher; it simply increases the likelihood that you will have a diminishing impact. That's the good news. The bad news is that when you have a diminishing impact, you are likely to be completely unaware of it and probably the last to know. As a leader, how do you know whether you are having a diminishing effect, despite having the best intentions? How do you increase your self-awareness? Formulating and recording your own insights is a reasonable first step, but you'll learn more by asking the people you lead to share *their* insights.

Several years ago I was teaching a Multipliers workshop in Abu Dhabi, in the United Arab Emirates. The room was full of men in the beautiful white robes and headpieces known as kanduras. I was on high alert, knowing the ideas were perhaps unconventional and that the way I was teaching was probably violating cultural norms. But the group was delightfully engaged and enjoying the session.

I asked each person to write down one way he or she might be accidentally diminishing. They did. I then asked them to share their insight with their colleagues at the table. They hesitated for a moment but then did. This was a huge relief, so I sat down to collect my thoughts. A couple minutes later, I looked up and noticed that the exercise was not proceeding as planned. There was a swirl of white kanduras, and I could see that people were getting up and moving around. Immediately I assumed that the participants were opting out of the exercise and conducting other business instead. Concerned, I moved closer to observe and then asked Khalid, a warm and perceptive Emirati national, to help me understand what was happening. He responded, "We were sharing our own observations, but then we realized we really should be asking our colleagues to tell us how we are accidentally diminishing. We are moving into new groups, so we can get feedback from the people we work with most closely." I watched in fascination as individuals moved energetically around the room, scurrying to find a small group or partner who could give them honest feedback.

This leadership team understood that self-awareness as a leader comes from understanding the perspectives of those we lead and serve, those who are the "customers" of our leadership. Our learning can start with our own insight, but it can't end there.

As you seek to get feedback from others, you can use a 360-degree assessment to get unfiltered feedback (see www.multipliersbooks .com), but you can also do it the old-fashioned way—by asking good, honest, face-to-face questions. Here are some questions you might use to elicit this feedback:

➤ How might I be shutting down the ideas and actions of others, despite having the best of intentions?
➤ What am I inadvertently doing that might be having a diminishing impact on others?
➤ How might my intentions be interpreted differently by others? What messages might my actions actually be conveying?
➤ What could I do differently?

Hazel Jackson, cofounder and CEO of a consultancy in Dubai, includes this question in each of the performance check-ins with her employees: How might I be diminishing you? Then she listens and adjusts. You can get feedback through a formal tool or through a casual conversation or a regular check-in. Either way, what is critical is that you get new information to raise your self-awareness and recalibrate your approach. To become intentional Multipliers, we must understand how our best intentions can be translated and received differently by others.

Leading with Intention

Leading with intention starts with understanding how our natural tendencies can take us down the wrong path—how great habits and seemingly strong leadership traits can go awry and become our vulnerability.

John C. Maxwell, the leadership author, coach, and speaker, is an undeniable leadership genius. His 105 books, including thirteen bestsellers, have sold more than 26 million copies. Not only does he teach leadership, he is a dedicated practitioner as well. He has built five successful companies and has personally mentored hundreds, if not thousands, of other leaders.

When John first heard the idea of leader-as-Multiplier, it struck a chord with him. Every one of the ideals and practices of Multipliers resonated with what he had practiced as a leader. However, the idea of the Accidental Diminisher gave him pause. An avid learner, as he listened to the Diminisher qualities, he recognized he had all of those, too, and he realized that some of his natural strengths might be having a negative effect on his team. John identified his blind spots and diminishing tendencies, especially as Pacesetter, Optimist, and Rescuer.

John set a one-year goal to adjust his intentions and resist his diminishing effects as a leader. He started by better understanding how his best intentions as a leader might be accidentally diminishing his team and sought feedback from his inner circle, particularly from Mark Cole, the CEO who runs his five companies. The conversation was made possible by the trust they had built over many years of working and growing together. Mark and others helped John see that, while he was often needed to hit home runs for the team, he didn't need to go to bat for his players as often as he had been doing. John, a sports fan, could see his vulnerability. He believes that everything rises and falls on leadership, so it is hard for him to stand back and let one of his players strike out. He started to use an idea he got from Glen Jackson, cofounder of Jackson-Spalding. In baseball, a 3–2 count is called a "full count," meaning that just one more strike will cause the player to strike out and have no more opportunities to get on base and score. John said, "When the count is 3 and 2, my natural tendency is to step in and take the last swing."

John and his team developed a code. When a project seemed to be in jeopardy, Mark or another trusted colleague would say, "The count is still 3 and 1." The message was clear—the team member was indeed struggling but was not yet in danger of striking out. John could stand back a little longer.

For example, one of John's leaders started creating a new business line. That's not unusual, because John is very entrepreneurial, and so is his team. However, this particular business wasn't right for John. It didn't fit his vision. John's natural inclination would have been to jump in and address the issue. Instead, he allowed Mark Cole to address it the way he wanted to. John backed off and allowed Mark to take leadership on the issue, and he worked it out effectively.

John realized that when he held back, it didn't express indifference but rather a vote of confidence in his player at bat. Mark said, "John allowed me to handle it with my solution and in my timing. It actually worked out very well and gave me greater credibility with the leader. And we were able to get that leader's area back on track."

Later, John reflected, "Learning about Diminishers and working on my own diminishing tendencies has been one of the most important things I've done for my growth in the last year." This leader who has developed millions of other leaders is able to do so because he never stops developing himself.

To lead on purpose, we must understand how we diminish by accident. How might you be accidentally diminishing? How can you see what you alone can't see?

Even the best leaders have blind spots. Once you identify yours, you can work with your team to develop a set of signals and workarounds. Having a set of common signals will help you spot and avoid Diminisher bait; the workarounds will then help you turn these would-be diminishing episodes into Multiplier moments.

The following chart offers strategies to develop these new practices. You might try one of the Multiplier Experiments found in appendix E. Or you might try a simple workaround that you can use in the moment. These include abiding by a simple rule of thumb like *Wait twenty-four hours before replying to emails if you want others to respond* or creating a filter like *If you don't want anyone to take action on this idea, don't share it yet.* As one aspiring Multiplier said, "I can't control the ideas that pop into my head, but I can control the ones that come out of my mouth."

Do Less and Challenge More

Becoming a Multiplier often starts with becoming less of a Diminisher. And this usually means doing less: less talking, less responding, less convincing, and less rescuing of others who need to struggle and learn for themselves. By doing less, we can become more of a Multiplier.

Doing less to achieve more is one of many examples where counterintuition is more instructive than intuition. When no one else is speaking up, the compelling inclination is to jump in and fill the void, but we become a Multiplier when we learn to hold back and allow silence to draw others in. When we feel the need to be big, let it be a signal that we need to be small and dispense our views in small but intense doses. And when our instincts tell us to help more, we might need to help less.

Becoming a Multiplier requires us to understand how our most noble intentions can have a diminishing effect, sometimes deeply so. American theologian Reinhold Niebuhr said, "All human sin seems so much worse in its consequences than in its intentions." Likewise, while leaders view their own leadership through the lens of their positive intentions, their staff perceives that same behavior only by its negative consequences. By learning to do less and challenge more, we can transform ourselves from Accidental Diminisher to Intentional Multiplier.

MINIMIZING YOUR ACCIDENTAL DIMINISHER TENDENCIES

TENDENCIES	INTENTIONS & OUTCOMES	SIMPLE WORKAROUNDS	LEARNING EXPERIMENTS
IDEA GUY	**Intention:** For their ideas to stimulate ideas in others. **Outcome:** They overwhelm others, who shut down or spend time chasing the idea du jour.	**Create a Holding Tank.** Before sharing new ideas, stop and ask yourself if you want the people who work for you to take action now. If not, hold off sharing and save it for later.	Extreme Questions Make a Debate
ALWAYS ON	**Intention:** To create infectious energy and share their point of view. **Outcome:** They consume all the space, and others tune them out.	**Say it Just Once.** Instead of repeating yourself for emphasis, try saying things once, and create a reason for others to chime in and build on the idea. Set expectations for others to speak up.	Play Fewer Chips Give 51% of the Vote
RESCUER	**Intention:** To ensure people are successful and protect their reputation. **Outcome:** People become dependent, which weakens their reputation.	**Ask for Their "F-I-X."** When someone brings you a problem or signals a need for help, remind yourself that he or she probably already has a solution. Ask, "How do you think we should solve it?"	Make Space for Mistakes Give It Back
PACESETTER	**Intention:** To set a high standard for quality or pace. **Outcome:** Others become spectators or give up when they can't keep up.	**Stay Within Sight.** If you have a tendency to pull out ahead, remind yourself to stay within sight, so people don't give up or get lost. Stay within a distance that someone could catch up.	Give 51% of the Vote
RAPID RESPONDER	**Intention:** To keep their organization moving fast. **Outcome:** Their organization moves slowly because of the traffic jam of too many decisions or changes.	**Set a Mandatory Waiting Period.** Wait 24 hours (or however many) before responding to any email that falls into someone else's job. Give that person the right of first response.	Extreme Questions Make a Debate

TENDENCIES	INTENTIONS & OUTCOMES	SIMPLE WORKAROUNDS	LEARNING EXPERIMENTS
OPTIMIST	**Intention:** To create belief that the team can do it. **Outcome:** People wonder if they appreciate the struggle and the possibility of failure.	**Signal the Struggle.** Before offering your boundless enthusiasm, start by acknowledging how hard the work is. Let people know, "What I am asking you to do is hard. Success isn't guaranteed."	Make Space for Mistakes Talk Up Your Mistakes
PROTECTOR	**Intention:** To keep people safe from political forces in the organization. **Outcome:** People don't learn to fend for themselves.	**Expose and Inoculate.** Expose your team members to harsh realities in small doses, so they can learn from their mistakes and develop strength.	Make Space for Mistakes
STRATEGIST	**Intention:** To create a compelling reason to move beyond the status quo. **Outcome:** People defer up and second-guess the boss rather than finding answers.	**Don't Complete the Puzzle.** As you paint a picture of the future, leave sections for your team to complete. Frame the puzzle by establishing the WHY and the WHAT, but let your team fill in the HOW.	Lay a Concrete Challenge Ask the Questions
PERFECTIONIST	**Intention:** To help people produce outstanding work they are proud of. **Outcome:** People feel criticized, become disheartened, and stop trying.	**Define the Standards.** Define the standards of excellence up front. Let people know what "outstanding" looks like and define the criteria for completeness. Ask people to self-assess by the standards.	Make Space for Mistakes Give 51% of the Vote

SEE APPENDIX E FOR LEARNING EXPERIMENTS

Chapter Seven Summary

The Accidental Diminisher

ACCIDENTAL DIMINISHERS are managers who, despite the very best of intentions, have a diminishing impact on the people they lead.

Accidental Diminisher Profiles

Idea Guy: Creative, innovative thinkers who think they are stimulating ideas in others

Always On: Dynamic, charismatic leaders who think their energy is infectious

Rescuer: Empathetic leaders who are quick to help when they see people struggling

Pacesetter: Achievement-oriented leaders who lead by example and expect others to notice and follow

Rapid Responder: Leaders who are quick to take action believing that they are building an agile, action-oriented team

Optimist: Positive, can-do leaders who think their belief in people will inspire them to new heights

Protector: Vigilant leaders who shield people from problems to keep them safe

Strategist: Big thinkers who cast a compelling vision thinking they are showing people a better place and providing the big picture

Perfectionist: Leaders who strive for excellence and manage the fine details to help others produce superior work

Decreasing your Accidental Diminisher Tendencies

- Seek feedback
- Lead with intention
- Practice the workarounds and learning experiments found in appendix E, "Multiplier Experiments"
- Do less and challenge more

CHAPTER EIGHT

Dealing with Diminishers

However vast the darkness,
we must supply our own light.

STANLEY KUBRICK

Sean Heritage is a cryptologic warfare officer in the US Navy. He attended the US Naval Academy and earned graduate degrees from Johns Hopkins University and the Naval War College. He is representative of a growing class of military leaders who are not just brilliant commanders but also innovative thinkers, fierce learners, and collaborative leaders.

After a tour serving as commanding officer, Heritage was assigned to a joint command under the leadership of a colonel in the US Air Force. Commander Heritage's immediate senior wasn't just from a different branch of the military; he operated with a very different leadership style. This colonel apparently never learned that a leader's responsibility is to inspire others to accomplish the "what," not to dictate a specific "how." He told people exactly what to do and showed visible disappointment when subordinates took another approach, even when they delivered the desired outcome. While Commander Heritage and the rest of the team poured their hearts and souls into their work, the colonel found ways to deliver consistently destructive criticism. After months of cutting remarks from his superior and his own stymied attempts to make progress, Commander Heritage finally hit a wall—quite literally, he punched a wall in the colonel's office. After he collected himself and apologized for his unprofessional behavior, the sting of the wall still hurt, but it was nothing compared to the dull ache of knowing he was stationed at this post for two more years. He felt stuck and helpless and even contemplated leaving the navy.

Commander Heritage turned to his peers for guidance. Their response was affirming: "Don't quit on us. You are our beacon of hope, our ray of light." Commander Heritage sought additional guidance from his trusted Personal Board of Directors (PBOD), a group of senior mentors he consulted with regularly. His PBOD gave him a forum to vent and the opportunity to learn from their wisdom, and Commander Heritage began to reorient himself. Instead of complaining about the leader he didn't have, he would be the leader his team deserved and attempt to inspire the colonel to do the same. To address his disappointing reality, he started pretending a bit more. He played the "as if" game, operating as if his boss were more of a Multiplier. Instead of keeping his superior officer out of his operation, he brought him in. He wanted the colonel to see the energy of the team, so he invited him to witness the party himself. Rather than criticize the work transpiring in his absence, the colonel began cocreating a movement that was shaped in his presence. Sean reflected, "We were on the same ship and on the same course, but we were now moving faster."

Heritage began making fun at work a more visible priority and spent time developing the leadership skills of his peers and juniors. And, yes, he shared an abstract of this book, held discussions with his team, and even created a "culture club" for those who wanted to help create a more collaborative work environment. He reinforced all attempts at Multiplier leadership with the people around him, and all along the chain of command. He didn't wait for perfect behavior; he celebrated anything in the right direction, even attempts that were wobbly at first. He said, "If you want to change the culture, you have to be like Wayne Gretzky, the ice hockey legend, and 'skate to where the puck is heading.' " Focusing on what happened to be in his control, he decorated his workspace, introducing a new piece of art each week. As a way to share his personality and lighten up the mood, he brought in some happy, hopeful pieces—graphic illustrations with titles such as *Making Ideas Happen* and *Stay Amazing*—which became affectionately known as the "Wall of Optimism."

Two months later, the colonel removed his second in command and asked Heritage to serve in that role. This appointment served for the entire team as a visible validation of Commander Heritage's leadership style and the culture they were now building together. A year later, when the colonel retired, he spoke at length during his retirement ceremony about Sean's influence on him as a leader. Soon after, the four-star admiral leading US Cyber Command at the National Security Agency asked Commander Heritage, artwork and all, to join him in the front office and serve as his executive assistant. As Sean shifted his focus from confronting to constructing, he found greater purpose as a leader; he was no longer a victim of poor leadership but a respected leader who was shaping the future.

Sometimes, the best way out of a diminishing situation is to multiply up. When stuck under a Diminisher, what's your best strategy? It is tempting to hit a wall and confront your Diminisher; it is equally tempting to fall back and comply. But there is a third, more productive, alternative: multiply your way out.

Too many well-intended mangers are stuck beneath diminishing leaders. They aspire to lead by bringing out the best in others but find themselves being sucked down a Diminisher's vortex. I often hear the following said in frustration: "I want to be a Multiplier leader, but my boss is a total Diminisher, so I can't." Or, as one group of South African managers put it, "We've all heard about Multipliers, but what the [bleep] do we do about the Diminishers around here?"

How do you work for someone who is sucking the life out of you, slowly draining your energy? How can you possibly bring out the best in others when your boss brings out the worst in you? The research my team and I conducted, interviewing dozens of professionals and surveying hundreds more, showed that the five most prevalent reactions to Diminishers are: 1) confront them, 2) avoid them, 3) quit, 4) comply and lie low, and 5) ignore the diminishing behavior. My research also showed that the five least effective strategies in dealing with Diminishers are: 1) confront them, 2) avoid them, 3) comply and lie low, 4) convince them you are right, and 5) take HR action. In other words, the most popular strategies for dealing with Diminishers are also the least effective.[1]

However, we shouldn't be surprised that strategies for dealing with Diminishers are faulty and feckless. After all, that's the point—we aren't at our best around Diminishers. The anxiety they invoke triggers our brain's amygdala (our emotional brain), which reacts faster and hijacks our neocortex (our rational brain), which leads to irrational actions and destructivity.[2] When powers of reasoning are threatened, it follows that judgment and coping strategies for dealing with Diminishers are vulnerable as well. Dealing with Diminishers is difficult and requires our best thinking.

This chapter is for those of you stuck under diminishing leaders; it's intended to supply you with proven strategies to help you respond at your best. If you are fortunate enough to be surrounded by Multipliers, skip this chapter and proceed to the final chapter, "Becoming a Multiplier."

This chapter's message is simple: you *can* be a Multiplier while working for a Diminisher. With the right mindset and a set of smart tactics, you can minimize the diminishing effect. There are no templates, just sound ideas that must be executed with discretion and savvy. While leading like a Multiplier might be management science, dealing with Diminishers is an art form. But done thoughtfully and persistently, you might even find that you become immune to the effects of diminishing leaders. Ultimately, you might join the ranks of those I call Invincibles—people who continue to work using their highest capacity and offer their greatest intelligence, despite being surrounded by diminishing behaviors.

The Death Spiral Versus the Growth Cycle

Being diminished, especially chronically, is both stressful and exhausting. Although people react to being diminished in a myriad of ways, there are a couple of knee-jerk responses. As Dieter, a corporate middle manager from Europe, observed, "It is easier to align with the Diminisher and feast on the misfortune of other colleagues than it is to fight the battle and get eaten too." It's also easier to return a set of diminishing actions with a diminishing response. Unfortunately, this only perpetuates the problem.

Consider the following picture of the "spiral of despair." Your boss is a micromanager—he controls, dictates, and obsesses over the minutest details of your work. In public and on the surface, you respectfully acquiesce to his directives and inquisitions, but in private, with the professional mask off, you feel disrespected, untrusted, unseen, and undervalued. We feel that our most basic sense of self-determination has been denied.

When we sense we've been wronged or wrongly judged, our natural instinct is to be judgmental in return. So we criticize. We stop listening and become dismissive of their input. We want the diminishing to stop, so we exclude the Diminisher, keeping the boss at arm's length or further if we can. Or, if we've been made to feel like we can't do anything right, we cease trying or tune out.

But the death spiral does not end there, with merely disaffected relationships, because the diminishing tends to increase. When bosses sense that their power is being threatened or their ideas not heard, they tend to respond with even greater force, typically doubling down on their point of view. When denied access to details, micromanagers become nervous, even suspicious. Sensing that something is amiss, they interfere more, determinedly forcing themselves into discussions and decisions. Now there is a standoff—not between a Diminisher and a victim but rather, between two Diminishers—the original micromanaging boss and the newly minted Diminisher, who is now bringing out the worst in the boss.

As depicted in the chart below, the spiral continues: they prescribe, we withdraw; they decree, we give up; and once again they conclude that the only way to get something done is to be all over us. The research that I have conducted indicates this extended spin cycle lasts, on average, 22 months, which is 85 percent of the average duration of time the survey respondents worked with the person.

THE DIMINISHING DEATH SPIRAL

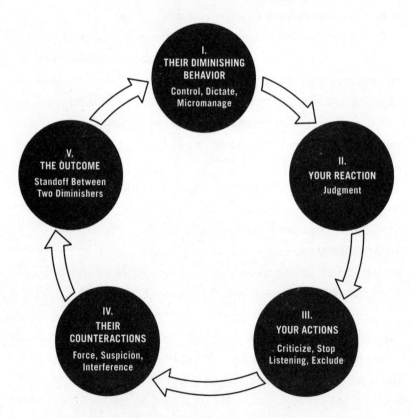

This scenario is, unfortunately, all too common. It is impossible to diminish someone out of being a Diminisher. The best way out of a diminishing death spiral is through multiplication—using the logic of multiplication and leading like a Multiplier yourself.

Let's look at how changing your response can break the cycle of diminishing. Say you work for a micromanaging tyrant. What if, instead of responding with criticism and avoidance, you respond with intellectual curiosity, a hallmark of Multiplier leaders? True intellectual curiosity is a deep and persistent desire to know or understand. While we hope that curiosity does not "kill the cat," as the adage goes, we know that it can kill conflict. What if you took his perspective and asked questions like: Why is he worried? What does he need from me to feel confident and in control of his business? Or, simply, What causes an otherwise decent human being to act like a Diminisher?

As you ask these questions and build empathy for his concerns and reality, you might listen in order to understand the source of tension. With ego set aside, you might even find yourself noticing and appreciating his strengths or feeling less angry, and with this insight, you can then work in a more cooperative spirit that smooths ruffled feathers and makes everyone less defensive.

As you respond differently, your Diminisher is likely to respond differently as well. Feeling more respected, he is apt, in turn, to extend more respect. The same process works in building (or rebuilding) trust.[3] When you demonstrate understanding of his expectations, the diminishing manager is more likely to back off and allow more space to breathe and room to maneuver. He might even show more appreciation for your work. As depicted in the chart below, the diminishing death cycle breaks, and confrontation or tepid compliance is replaced with cooperation—not between a Diminisher and an employee, but between a more elastic Diminisher and a Multiplier, one who brings out the best in everyone, including a pain-in-the-backside boss.

BREAKING THE DIMINISHING DEATH SPIRAL

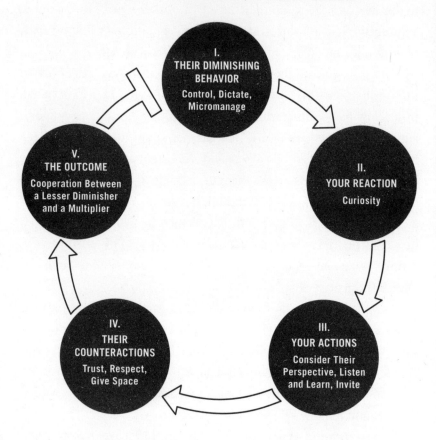

Let me clarify further, for those of you thinking, *You don't under-stand my boss; this person is a hardened, lifelong, textbook Diminisher and isn't going to change.* Changing your response, no matter how enlightened you become, isn't guaranteed to change a Diminisher, but it will turn down the volume on the Perfectionism, the Rescu-ing, Pacesetting, and other diminishing practices, allowing you more space to think and work.

Cycle Breakers

When dealing with a Diminisher, you can hope—dream even—that this person will become a Multiplier, and perhaps she will. Or you can choose to be the Multiplier yourself. Most great accomplishments require a great leader—but the leader may not always be the boss. Sure, no one likes having to be "the adult" to an incapable parent, but we all crave being allowed to work at our best.

Here we offer strategies to break the cycle of diminishing and mitigate the havoc of less-than-wonderful bosses and toxic colleagues. These tactics were suggested by my research as well as my own experience in the workplace and flow from a set of fundamental principles about the nature of humans at work.

1. **IT'S NOT NECESSARILY ABOUT YOU.** Although you are the one feeling the pain, your actions aren't necessarily the root cause. The Diminisher's behavior is more likely a function of the pressure they feel from above or the residual effects of ineffectual role models from their past. But, at the same time, it is entirely possible that your reactions to the Diminisher are inflaming the situation.

2. **DIMINISHING ISN'T INEVITABLE.** When dealing with a controlling boss, we have more control than we might think. We choose how much legitimacy we grant to a Diminisher's views; we choose whether or not we embrace lowered expectations for ourselves; we choose how she makes us feel. Those are choices. So, too, we can choose to maintain high expectations for ourselves, and our own analysis and evaluation of our contribution can help us to stand up to Diminishers in healthy and helpful ways. The diminishing may continue, but we can mitigate its destructive effect.

3. **YOU CAN LEAD YOUR LEADER.** Very few managers will ever know you as well as you do. Therefore, if you want someone to

utilize you at your best, you will need to guide them. You can be your own agent and advocate for your capabilities and defend yourself from well-meaning but overbearing management.

From my initial research, it was obvious that Diminishers were getting a reduced level of capability from others. But it wasn't until more research, after I'd heard from thousands of people who were stuck working for Diminishers, that I fully understood the deep crater carved by these leaders. People who are shut down, limited, and bullied at work feel the toxic effects seep into all aspects of their lives. People consistently reported experiencing increased stress, reduced confidence, low energy, depression, poor health, general unhappiness, and more. And the collateral damage doesn't stop there; if not addressed, diminishing usually intensifies. The majority of individuals also reported that they carried stress home and became angry and irritable, complained more, and withdrew socially.

Among the hundreds of comments in our study, there were two that especially struck me. One person wrote, "I doubted I could do anything right, and I doubted that anything I had done had been right. I felt like I was a disappointment to my family, my friends, and my coworkers. I unfriended most everyone on Facebook/Google+, had massive depressive episodes, and even contemplated ending my life." The other heart-wrenching story was from someone who said that the stress and self-doubt got so bad, "I couldn't even take care of my dog."

The strategies offered below are intended to improve your reactions to Diminishers, relieve stress, neutralize immediate problems, and halt the downward spiral. They are basic survival strategies—self-defense to help you work with the more entrenched, hardened Diminishers and to help minimize the magnitude of their sting. None of these strategies will immediately transform the Diminisher into a Multiplier leader (nor ever be able to solve deep psychological problems). What these strategies can do, when played well, is to greatly decrease the diminishing effect a person is having on you and allow your ideas to be heard, buying you some valuable thinking time and enabling you to play bigger.

All of these strategies work off the core assumptions that *It's not necessarily about you, Diminishing isn't inevitable,* and *You can lead your leader.* On Level 1 are defensive moves to enable you to deflect diminishing actions. On Level 2 you'll find proactive strategies, offense plays to aid your forward progress. Level 3 gives coaching strategies for you to help the Accidental Diminisher become more of a Multiplier.

It will be worth your while to try the strategies on Levels 1 and 2 before going on to Level 3. You might think of the three levels as loosely following a "research and development" timetable where you don't want to rush the new product to the market without performing due diligence. Though most people wish to start at Level 3, few find themselves with permission to coach before they've invested time in strengthening their own game skills.

Level 1: Defenses Against the Dark
Arts of Diminishing Managers

1. TURN DOWN THE VOLUME. A colleague of mine was once described as "a dog that barks at everything," meaning that she was overly reactive to potential threats and didn't differentiate between serious attacks and passing annoyances. My research showed that people who cope best with Diminishers don't bark at every disturbance. They've learned what to ignore. They don't avoid the Diminisher or pretend the problem doesn't exist; they merely tune out some of the interference. They choose to turn down the volume, reducing the Diminisher's intrusion into their head and the other person's consumption of their life and psychic energy.

When we are being nitpicked and undermined, we tend to turn inward and question ourselves. It's easy to assume that the Diminisher doesn't value our contribution; however, in reality, they probably just value their own contribution more. Instead of reading too much into a situation, we can zoom out and take a broader perspective.

When Jackie,[4] a talented HR executive, took a senior management role at a hot start-up company, she was expecting both challenge and adventure. What she hadn't anticipated was that her biggest challenge would be working for an unpredictable CEO who flip-flopped on critical decisions and intruded into every situation in order to dominate. Jackie felt continually frustrated with her boss and contemplated leaving. After several agonizing months, she decided that she would neither take it personally nor let the situation define her. She stepped back, took inventory of her life values, and realized, "the worst thing that can happen to me is getting fired, and, in the grand scheme of things, that's not the worst thing that can happen to me." With her diminishing boss in perspective, she did what she could to create a positive environment. She didn't roll over and play dead, and she didn't let the situation kill her joy.

Ignoring a negative situation typically requires an active choice. This is how Glenn Pethel, a sage education leader from Georgia, has learned to manage through frequent brushes with uncooperative colleagues. After these contentious encounters, his close associates would ask him why he wasn't upset. Pethel, who speaks with a gentle, southern charm, would reply, "Because I don't want to be. Something caused this person to behave this way, and it wasn't necessarily me. Do I like it? No. But it's not going to dip from my bucket."

As when dealing with teenagers, a smart parent knows to ignore a lot of noise and negative stimulus. You need to continually remind yourself, *It isn't me, and it isn't forever.* Ignoring a persistently defeating and deafening message is a big task. But it becomes easier to filter it out when you turn down the volume of diminishing messages and turn up the volume for other, more enabling, voices—your own, as well as those of supportive leaders and colleagues.

2. STRENGTHEN OTHER CONNECTIONS. Building on the idea above, we can reduce the effects of the Diminisher by increasing our connections to different people and work. In other words, if you can't get inside the Diminisher's trust circle, build other circles of influence.

When Chuck, now a director at a large accounting firm, was a project manager, he worked several levels under one of the firm's tyrannical partners, who created a tense environment, gave erratic feedback, and led people around in circles. Chuck couldn't figure out how to please this partner or make progress, and he was spending most of his time editing and reworking documents based on this partner's random feedback. Feeling stuck and miserable, he wallowed for a couple of months while he contemplated a complete career change. After some therapeutic venting with his colleagues, his immediate manager gave him some good advice: "Quit whining. Do something about it or leave."

He realized that he wasn't going to change the tyrannical partner, but he could change his perspective. He divided his day into chunks in order to minimize the time he spent responding to the plethora of comments from the partner. Instead of trying to perfect the work, he made it directionally correct and then passed it to the partner, knowing that another iteration was inevitable. He didn't avoid the partner, but he began spending much less time fending off diminishing feedback. He spent his newly freed up time with clients and in benchmarking work with other colleagues, both of which he found fulfilling. His confidence returned, and he even mustered the courage to send an email to the partner providing feedback on the ineffectiveness of their work process. The partner offered only a mild apology, but taking action felt empowering to Chuck. The lesson he learned was simple: Don't let your domineering boss dominate your day.

Like Chuck, the individuals who most effectively deal with Diminishers take steps to broaden their support base and strengthen other relationships, much like a torn ligament requires the strengthening of proximal muscles. A petty officer in the US Navy described it this way: "When I find myself dealing with a bad leader, I still take their orders, but I latch on to another leader that I trust, someone who can give me an alternative point of view, especially about myself."

When you find yourself weakened by an overbearing or undermining colleague, invest elsewhere, in places where you can build collateral strength. Create an internal or external advisory board—a group of trusted colleagues or mentors who can guide you as you navigate a difficult relationship. Find a safe sounding board—colleagues where you can test your ideas and sanity-check your work. (Make sure, though, that this does not become merely a place to vent or an echo chamber for your current thinking.) Build a cheering squad—people who know your real capabilities and can give you a useful second opinion and a healthy new perspective on yourself. Their alternative view will remind you that you are smart and will figure it out. Lastly, develop a career network—supporters who will help you advance when your boss isn't actively advocating for you.

3. RETREAT AND REGROUP. It is never wise to go head-to-head with a headstrong person, especially the boss. My research showed that a frontal attack, such as trying to prove the merits of one's ideas, only accelerated the death spiral (you might recall that confrontation is the most used yet least effective approach). Even when you win, the victories are usually pyrrhic.

When facing an impasse, try regrouping and resetting your aspiration—instead of attempting to win, just stay in the game. A former executive at Apple Inc. shared her strategy for pitching ideas to Steve Jobs. She knew there was little chance of prevailing once Steve became agitated or opinionated. Rather than argue her points, she listened, acknowledging his point of view. She then asked for time to think through his ideas and come back with a plan. While she regrouped, Steve became less entrenched. When she returned a few days later with a plan that incorporated the best of both their ideas, she found a receptive audience, and the plan advanced. While some people like to argue more than others, everyone likes to hear that someone is seriously considering their opinions. When you retreat and regroup, you give the Diminisher a way out as well—an opportunity to gracefully rethink an issue and to save face.

4. SEND THE RIGHT SIGNALS. The primary cause of micromanaging (the most prevalent form of diminishing) is concern that something won't get completed fully or correctly. As one Diminisher said, "I only become a micromanager when I think it won't get done." You can ward off this form of diminishing by providing delivery assurance. When you deliver the goods as promised, you earn the Diminisher's trust. As Stephen M. R. Covey says, "Trust, once lost can indeed be rebuilt."[5] Trust gets built in layers, brick by brick. Each brick is a win, a small success that tells the Diminisher that this person will make them look good. And the positive cycle continues: every time you deliver, you earn the opportunity to ask for the space and support you need to do your best work.

Our recent research showed that there is a greater risk of extreme diminishing when the two individuals have dissimilar personality types or processing styles. For example, a manager with a Myers-Briggs Type Indicator Judging style (methodical and results oriented) is more likely to diminish an employee with a Perceiving style (flexible and good at multitasking) than an employee with the same style as his own.

To counter this dynamic, employees can send signals that keep their manager's inner Diminisher from leaking out. Heidi, a marketing executive with a high Judging style, said, "People on my team who are Ps [Perceiving] just don't send me the signals I need to feel confident. I need them to do more than tell me, 'things are in good shape.' I need them to give me updates without being asked and say something more like, 'we've hit each milestone, and we will be ready to go by 8 a.m. tomorrow.'" Conversely, individuals with a Judging style might need to demonstrate flexibility and let their Perceiving boss know that they are open to new possibilities. They might need to say, "We have a plan, but we are open to last-minute changes." In either case, you can earn more space by determining what is important to the Diminisher and then send signals that it is also important to you.

5. ASSERT YOUR CAPABILITY. Megan Lambert, an extremely bright business consultant, was working as a volunteer in a meditation community that she belonged to. Megan was to coordinate an event for members of their meditation community but fell behind when she got caught up with several urgent work projects. The volunteer leader, who was also a friend of Megan's, was "all over her" and began treating Megan like she was suddenly incapable, texting frequently to check on her progress. After several frustrating days, Megan could feel herself becoming halfhearted and lazy in her role, and she knew she needed to reverse this cycle. An avid practitioner of Multiplier leadership, Megan said to her friend-colleague, "Hey, let's play a game. For three days, I want you to believe that I'm amazing at this job. Just pretend I'm totally competent." Her friend agreed, and stepped back. Megan stepped up and began fulfilling her volunteer responsibilities wholeheartedly again.

Sometimes you need to tell an overly helpful manager or colleague that you don't need help. If you've ever tried to help a three-year-old do something that the child could do alone (like put on a coat or carry a plate), you know exactly how the child will react. With a mix of conviction and outrage, the child will say, "No. I can do it by myself!" As the child asserts her independence, the adult remembers that the child is maturing and every day more capable than the day before. Similarly, it is easy for corporate managers to overlook the growth of the people they lead. However, by the time we enter the adult workplace, our inner three-year-old has been socialized out. Instead of pushing back against micromanaging bosses, we tend to let them step in when we could otherwise handle it ourselves.

The next time a diminishing boss or colleague tries to do something for you that you can do independently, try reminding the person that you can do it yourself. There's no need to throw a tantrum; just announce and assert your capability. For example, you might say, "I appreciate the help, and I think I can handle this one," or "Can I try this by myself and come to you if I get stuck?"

When asking for some breathing room, a little humor goes a long way, especially with the Accidental Diminisher. Ben Putterman, a longtime and dear colleague of mine, had a delightfully direct way of letting me know when I was micromanaging. If I was overly involved or prescriptive in a meeting, he would wait until we left the room and then he would yank at an imaginary rope around his neck, start gasping for air, and pretend to eek out, "Hey boss, you could probably loosen the choke chain a bit." We'd laugh, and more important, I'd get the hint, back off, and let him lead.

If your boss doesn't have a sense of humor (incidentally, humor is the trait most negatively correlated with Diminishers), just play it straight. A simple If-Then statement works, such as, "If you give me the meeting topics in advance, then I'll come prepared with ideas" or "If you let me run the meeting, then I'll make sure we fully resolve the problem." Whether your tone is lighthearted or serious, asserting one's capability is best done with humility and respect, especially in cultures that value respect for authority. Lastly, when you assert your capability and someone gives you space, be prepared to deliver your finest thinking and work in return.

6. ASK FOR PERFORMANCE INTEL. It's hard to be brilliant if you lack critical information. In particular, people generally need two types of information to achieve top performance. The first is clear direction—What is the target, and why is it important? Diminishers often become so preoccupied with telling people how to shoot that they forget to first establish the target. When a Diminisher becomes immediately prescriptive, you can ask them to back up and provide more context and direction.

When Kevin Grigsby, an organizational development expert in academic medicine and science, got off the phone with an overly directive physician leader, he faced a dilemma. The leader had been very clear what he wanted Kevin to do and specified the exact technique he wanted him to use. But Kevin knew that if he simply followed the doctor's orders, the situation wouldn't improve. So, instead of blindly taking the prescription, he elevated the conversation by asking, "Can you tell me more about what you want as an outcome? What are you trying to accomplish?" After listening and acknowledging the desired impact, he asked, "Are you okay if I take a different route to get there?" The leader hesitated momentarily and said, "Sure, as long as you get the same impact." The next time someone gives you a statement of work, ask to begin with a problem definition instead.

The second type of critical information is performance feedback: Am I actually hitting the target? When someone is missing the target, Diminishers tend to reiterate how to do it, rather than give information that would help the person to adjust their technique or their aim. When faced with a deluge of criticism, ask for feedback instead. The term *feedback* often carries the connotation of criticism or judgment; however, technically speaking, feedback is simply information to help recalibrate something. For example, a thermostat takes periodic readings to determine if the room temperature is warmer or cooler than the established target. This information is then used to raise or lower the temperature. If you are receiving too much criticism but not enough critical performance intel, ask for it. Try asking, "What should I be doing more of? Less of?" And, if you want to be on target more often, request feedback at more frequent intervals.

7. SHOP FOR A NEW BOSS. If you are in a diminishing environment, you have to ask yourself if this is the right place for you. If you are being forced into a small box where you can't grow, you might need to take the hermit crab's approach and find a bigger home where you can grow. It is probably not surprising that quitting your job is by far the most effective defense against Diminishers. (Unfortunately, against some diminishing managers, it is the only reasonable defense.)

Of course, for many people quitting isn't an option. But if you do quit, don't just swap one bad manager for another. Instead of simply searching for a new job, go shopping for your next boss. You'll be living with this decision for years, so, just as you would when making any major purchase, get information first. Ask good questions and then watch for evidence of Multiplier leadership. Pay attention to their talk-to-listen ratio. Listen to how they talk about their team. Do they mention people's brilliance or do they list their duties? How much ownership do team members have? How do decisions get made? Check reviews and see what former employees say. There are a number of websites that provide transparency into the actual inner workings of a company and its management culture.[6] You might also try before you buy and work initially as an independent contractor or consultant. If this isn't feasible, ask to sit in on a team meeting or participate on a conference call to better understand how the team works. For further guidance, see the Multiplier Experiment "Shopping for a New Boss" in appendix E.

As you seek to ward off Diminishing actions, a couple of caveats are in order. First, all of the above strategies are defensive moves that minimize the reductive effects of Diminishers. Deploying any of the above strategies need not be big conversations (other than quitting your job); they are little adjustments, part of your day-to-day interaction, that help you remain whole and work at your best. They are meant to project your strengths, not expose the Diminisher's weaknesses. These strategies aren't likely to change the leader, but they can certainly alter the dynamic.

Second, remember that if you are constantly surrounded by Diminishers, at some point you have to ask yourself, "Is it me?" You might be taking things too personally, reading malice into otherwise well-intended criticism or even looking for insults in compliments. It might be time to see your Diminishers as Accidental Diminishers, leaders with good intentions. Or you may have to admit that you are diminishing in the other direction—upward. The remedy in all cases is the same: be a Multiplier, down, out, and up.

Level 2: Multiplying Up

Many corporate managers have experience as Multipliers "down" to their direct reports and staff, but fewer are Multipliers "out" to their peers or "up" to their bosses. Our analysis of the Multipliers 360 assessment[7] has shown that, on average, managers are utilizing approximately 76 percent of the intelligence of their direct reports and only 62 percent of their peers and 66 percent of their supervisors. Yet my research has also shown that people can serve as Multipliers from any direction, even upward to a diminishing supervisor.

Here's why: Diminishers want to be valued for their intelligence and ideas; in fact, many are desperate for it. On the other hand, Multipliers enjoy finding other people's genius and engaging it. In many ways, Diminishers need Multipliers. It may not be a match made in heaven, but it is a strategy to help you escape a hellish experience, because when you bring out the best in your boss, you help create the conditions under which you can work at your best. When Diminishers feel smart, valued, heard, included, and trusted, they extend more trust in return. Essentially, by being a Multiplier to your boss, you'll create your own Multiplier environment, a place where you can thrive, not just survive.

The following are several ways you can be a Multiplier to those above you in the organization or to diminishing colleagues at your side. They aren't meant as defenses against the raving, tyrannical Diminishers; rather, these are offense plays, intended to help you move your contribution forward, especially with Accidental Diminishers, the otherwise good people who fail at being good bosses.

1. EXPLOIT YOUR BOSS'S STRENGTHS. Instead of trying to change your boss, focus on trying to better utilize his or her knowledge and skills in service of the work you're leading. You don't need to cede ownership; just make sure to use his or her capabilities at key junctures and in ways they can be most helpful. If she has a critical eye, could you use her to help diagnose an underlying problem in a project? Or, if he's a big-picture thinker, could you have him share his vision to help win over a key customer?

Ron, a senior executive at Apple Inc. widely regarded for his own creative genius, was asked to build a new, highly strategic business for Apple. He could have let Steve Jobs, the company's notoriously hands-on CEO, dictate the details of the project, or he could have tried to keep Jobs from interfering in the process. Instead, Ron sought out Job's special insight at critical development points. He took the product design to him and openly asked, "How can we make this even better?" Jobs, whose native genius had been invoked, responded not with criticism but by rattling off numerous ideas for turning good features into great ones. Ron allowed his team to do their best work, and then used the strengths of his boss to take it to the next level. Even if you don't work for a genius like Steve Jobs, you can use the same technique.

2. GIVE THEM A USER'S GUIDE. If you are one of the fortunate few, you have a manager who is perceptive and takes note of your native genius—the thing you do easily and freely. If, on the other hand, you are among the underutilized majority, you needn't sit idle, waiting to be discovered. You can broadcast your capabilities and help your colleagues pick up the signal. Or you can simply tell people what you are good at and how you can be best used.

Think of it like giving someone a user's guide to you. A good manual tells you what the product is designed to do and how best to use it. Let's say you're considering buying a cordless reciprocating saw. The guide would indicate that the saw can cut through a variety of materials—wood, plastic, and metal—and could be used to cut wood studs, tree branches, PVC, metal pipe, and even nails. The promotional literature might also indicate that it's especially handy for demolition and for working in hard-to-reach spots.

Likewise, you can give someone a user's manual to you. What are you good at? What do you do naturally, without much effort, and what do you do freely, without being coerced or incentivized? Think of this as the thing you were built to do. For example, your brilliance might be fixing broken processes—you find the source of the derailment and get things back on track. Once you've figured out your genius, give it a name, like "troubleshooting," (or even a superhero name like the Process Surgeon) and then outline a number of ways that your genius can be put to work. For example, you could help your department get a late project delivered on time, win back a troubled account, or lead a cross-team task force to reduce bureaucracy. Once you've got your "guide" together, discuss these ideas with your boss or the person who can cast you in these roles.

If you want to work at your highest point of contribution, you need to let people know your value. Remember, getting to develop your natural brilliance at work is a true privilege, so don't play the prima donna. Just because you know your native genius doesn't mean you are excused from the parts of your work that feel foreign or involve quotidian tasks.

3. LISTEN TO LEARN. Even if you find yourself stuck working for a Diminisher, figure out what this person can teach you and how he or she can still help you succeed. A common mistake people make in interacting with Diminisher bosses is dismissing their criticism too quickly. In my years in senior management at Oracle, I watched numerous people present to Larry Ellison, the company's brilliant and relentless

CEO. Those who struggled (and barely survived) got into intellectual standoffs with him. Those who thrived shared their ideas with confidence, backed them up with data, but then stopped to really listen to Larry's reactions. They didn't do this to placate him or merely to find a better angle for selling their idea. They listened to learn. One of Larry's executive staff said, "Too many people don't take the opportunity to really see what Larry can teach them."

Instead of going into battle, look for common ground. Glenn Pethel, the education administrator mentioned earlier, is a master at working across divides and building bridges. Perhaps there is something about going to war that helps one learn diplomacy. As a young man in the late 1960s, he served as a soldier in the Vietnam War and learned there his most important lessons on leadership. He discovered that in the dark of the night, when you are exposed and afraid, you learn to see differently. You look beyond outward appearances and differences—be they race, religion, circumstance, or status—to truly see people and know them for who they really are. Even shrouded in darkness, you can learn to trust and find common purpose. This profound experience helped him to see beyond diminishing behavior to discover ways to work together, even with very difficult people.

Pethel offered this advice: "Diminishers want to be heard. They want to know that the ideas that they put forth are really good ideas. If you start by acknowledging their worth and that their ideas do have merit, you've got a good beginning." But, Pethel does more than just listen; he makes sure the person knows he is *genuinely* listening. He faces them and asks, "Do you mind if I take some notes? I like to go back and think about what you said." He then summarizes what he's heard and looks for mutual agreement. In the process, the other person becomes less of a Diminisher and more of a partner.

Instead of dissenting the next time your boss shifts into Diminisher mode, ask questions that help your boss weigh both the upsides and downsides of her ideas. Ask about her fundamental objectives.

You might even take the Extreme Questions challenge and keep asking sincere questions until you truly understand the boss's point of view. Once you are clear on what she really wants, you can talk through alternative ways to help meet the objective.

When Shaw, the director of customer success for his company, took a fourteen-day "dealing with Diminishers" challenge, he decided to focus on listening to learn with his micromanaging boss, with whom he seldom agreed. Shaw noted, "When I asked questions, I found out we were actually on the same page more often that I had thought. I had been shutting her out and making assumptions too early."

Wahiba, a sales manager in Tunisia, took the same fourteen-day challenge with her hypertalkative boss and said, "When my boss discovered that I listened carefully and took notes, she was more supportive, less nervous, and we had a constructive discussion. And, when I listened without interrupting, my boss shared critical information my team needed."

4. ADMIT YOUR MISTAKES. You'll remember that at the core of Diminisher logic is the belief that *people aren't going to figure it out without me*. Nothing fuels this cycle like the unrepentant mistake. When an employee makes a mistake and hides their misdeeds, it leaves the manager to question both their capability and their judgment and to assume the mistake will be repeated. This can place the manager on a trajectory to be overly prescriptive or to intervene at the first hint of an error.

Consider breaking this cycle by talking frankly about your mishaps and sharing what you've learned, both from successes and failures. The conversation quickly shifts from blame and cover-up to recovery. When you transmit what you learned, you earn the space you need to get it right the next time. Instead of a Micromanager, your boss becomes more of an Investor—giving you ownership and the accountability that goes with it. But not only do you earn more space for yourself, you create space for others to share their mistakes also—maybe even your boss. A boss sharing his or her own mistakes! That could liberate an entire team and create a culture where experimentation and innovative risk taking are legitimized.

So, don't wait for your boss to hold a "screwup of the week" conversation where people can confess and laugh off their mistakes. Set the tone by readily admitting your mistakes, sharing your learning, and letting the boss know that you're smarter each time. Doing so will reinforce a core Multiplier belief that *people are smart and can learn from their mistakes and figure it out.*

5. SIGN UP FOR A STRETCH. Managers can get stuck in the routine of giving people additional work, somehow thinking that more work equates to more growth opportunity. But doing the same thing over and over, faster and faster, does not develop your skills (unless you happen to be a knife juggler). The rest of us grow and learn by doing something hard, something we haven't done before, something we don't yet know how to do. A good Multiplier would define an opportunity that causes you to stretch; but just because your boss hasn't asked you to take on a new challenge doesn't mean you can't volunteer.

Send signals that you are ready to tackle a challenge that is a size too big. Let your boss know that you are willing to do something uncomfortable. But be careful: indicating a willingness to take on a new challenge can easily be misconstrued as a request for a promotion or new job. Most managers don't have an endless supply of promotions to dole out, and their defenses flare when employees come looking for "bigger jobs." Most managers do have a heap of challenges that they might be willing to share. We are suggesting that instead of unilaterally seizing control of a bigger job, you show willingness to work beyond the scope of your current one. You might extend your skills to a new domain or staple yourself to a problem outside your immediate job description. Or simply ask your manager what work you can take off her plate. Start small and prove yourself. Instead of pining for an illusive promotion, construct a new challenge and show your boss how it might lead to more.

6. INVITE THEM TO THE PARTY. Instead of keeping the Diminisher out of your business, trying bringing them in. When someone is wreaking havoc on us and others, our instinct tells us to keep that person away, to hold the enemy at bay. Diminishers, when blocked, typically work even more aggressively to insert themselves. Keeping the Diminisher on the other side of the door can weaken an entire team. As discussed in chapter 7, "The Accidental Diminisher," when we attempt to protect people from harsh forces, we leave them disconnected from reality and render them incapable of fending for themselves.

Rather than having your party crashed, what if you invited the Diminisher to join the fun? This is, perhaps, the most revolutionary strategy for multiplying up. What if you shared more data, invited them to meetings, and asked them to weigh in on important issues? They might torment you and make your life miserable (though, if that's the case, they are probably already doing so). What if, instead of barely tolerating them, you invited them along? Your transparency is likely to signal that all is well and that you have nothing to hide. You might even find that they enjoy the interaction and really feel good about working with you. One middle manager made a point of including an otherwise diminishing, interfering senior executive in a critical project. Although she could have run the meetings without him, she included him on the agenda, asking him to kick off the meeting, set the context, and then turn it over to her. At the end of the project he remarked, "When I work with you, I feel like we can do anything."

Sharing your space doesn't mean giving free rein. By initiating interaction, you can maintain more control over how the boss contributes, thus minimizing the dreaded bungee-boss dynamic. For example, when you invite them to a meeting, you can suggest what role you'd like them to play and specify when you would like them to chime in. Or, when you submit a document for review, point out specific questions you'd like them to address. In this way, you focus their energy and steer their contribution to where it is most valuable or, perhaps, simply to where it is least damaging.

While multiplying up is a great way to break a diminishing cycle, it's not limited to working with Diminishers; it works in 360 degrees, with everyone around you. It is the hallmark of the Invincible Contributor—the individual who is undeterred by otherwise diminishing superiors or depleting colleagues and who steadily performs at his or her highest level no matter what.

Level 3: Inspiring Multiplier Leadership in Others

A natural consequence of embracing Multiplier leadership is the desire to aid others in becoming Multipliers—especially if the other person happens to be our boss and we feel their dulling effects on a daily basis. And, with the best intentions, we set out to help others grow as leaders. But often it is with the noblest intentions that we do the greatest damage. No matter how just the cause, we cannot diminish someone into being a Multiplier.

People cannot change others, only themselves. And change will occur only if an individual recognizes the problem of their own volition and has a deep desire (and incentive) to change their mode of operation. How do you help leaders: 1) to recognize the collateral damage left in their wake, and 2) to find a better way of leading? How do you help the Accidental Diminisher become a more intentional Multiplier? Here are a few strategies that raise awareness and incentivize leaders to make the shift.

1. ASSUME POSITIVE INTENT. Few Diminishers are willing to engage in a conversation about their diminishing ways. However, most managers are eager to explore their good intentions. If you begin by assuming that your colleague has positive intent, it will not only help you interpret their actions in the most flattering light, it will provide a shared goal. Standing on common ground, you can help your colleague see that they are not getting what they seek. For example, to your Rapid Responder colleague, you might say, "I know you want to create a responsive team, but when you are so quick to respond, other people don't get a chance to. If you were slower to action, other people would be faster."

2. ADDRESS ONE ISSUE AT A TIME. As we've seen, those who work with Diminishers feel worn down and burdened. But if we unwisely unload all our frustrations, the Diminisher will only feel attacked and retreat to what they know how to do best—shut down ideas that are not their own. Instead, introduce one small idea at a time.

3. CELEBRATE PROGRESS. When training a dolphin, the animal trainer doesn't wait until the dolphin jumps twenty feet out of the water and does a flip (the end goal of the training) before giving the dolphin a bucket of fish. All behavior in the right direction is rewarded with fish or other positive reinforcement. Likewise, if you want to help someone lead in new ways, recognize and appreciate every attempt in the right direction, even the smallest acts of good leadership.

While it is easy to see diminishing in others, it is most important to see it in ourselves. Most of us have an inner Diminisher that may be triggered during times of stress or crisis. Like a recessive gene that carries a predisposition for a certain illnesses, the gene can lie dormant until environmental conditions trigger the illness and you present symptoms. Your biggest opportunity to inspire Multiplier leadership might be in learning to recognize your own Diminisher traits and convert these conditions into Multiplier moments.

Or perhaps your breakthrough will come as you realize that you can be a better leader than your boss. There is a hidden assumption in many organizations that people are not expected, or even allowed, to outlead their bosses. The layers of the org chart appear to form a glass ceiling that caps leadership effectiveness. Given the extraordinary results that Multipliers achieve through others, I believe one can lead like a Multiplier in a Diminisher environment. Give yourself permission to be better than your boss. And then watch the organization take notice.

Supply Your Own Light

Being underutilized or actively diminished can be a difficult, dark time in one's career. The gloom can spread across other facets of your life and feel all-consuming. It is easy to succumb to the fate of the unseen worker and fade away; or to join in the diminishing and respond with your own disapproval, disregard, and disengagement; or to keep quiet and hope that your diminishing boss changes.

Or, you can be a cycle breaker. You can break the downward spiral of diminishing leaders by better asserting your capabilities or by becoming the leader that you wish you had. In our research process, the biggest regret people expressed is that they didn't take action sooner.

Dr. Martin Luther King Jr. famously said:

The ultimate weakness of violence is that it is a descending spiral, begetting the very thing it seeks to destroy. Instead of diminishing evil, it multiplies it. . . . Returning violence for violence multiplies violence, adding deeper darkness to a night already devoid of stars. Darkness cannot drive out darkness: only light can do that.

When dealing with Diminishers, we may need to be the light that cuts through the dark. In modern organizations, leadership does not only come from the top; it radiates from the middle and ascends from the bottom. When you are trapped working for a Diminisher, sometimes the only way out is up—multiplying up. Because the only Diminisher you can change into a Multiplier is yourself.

Chapter Eight Summary

Dealing with Diminishers

You *can* be a Multiplier while working for a Diminisher.

Breaking the Cycle of Diminishing

1. It's not necessarily about you
2. Diminishing isn't inevitable
3. You can lead your leader

Dealing with Diminisher Strategies

Level 1: Defenses Against the Dark Arts of Diminishing Managers

Basic survival strategies intended to improve your reactions to Diminishers, relieve stress, neutralize immediate problems, and halt the downward spiral.

1. Turn down the volume
2. Strengthen other connections
3. Retreat and regroup
4. Send the right signals
5. Assert your capability
6. Ask for performance intel
7. Shop for a new boss

Level 2: Multiplying Up

Offense plays to help you be a Multiplier to those above you in the organization or to diminishing colleagues at your side, especially Accidental Diminishers.

1. Exploit your boss's strengths
2. Give them a user's guide

3. Listen to learn
4. Admit your mistakes
5. Sign up for a stretch
6. Invite them to the party

Level 3: Inspiring Multiplier Leadership in Others
Strategies that raise awareness and encourage leaders to make the shift from Accidental Diminisher to a more intentional Multiplier.

1. Assume positive intent
2. Address one issue at a time
3. Celebrate progress

CHAPTER 9

Becoming a Multiplier

When I let go of what I am,
I become what I might be.

LAO TZU

Bill Campbell, former CEO of Intuit, began his career more than thirty years ago as a college football coach at an Ivy League university. As a coach he was smart, aggressive, and hard-hitting. When he was recruited into the consumer technology business, he operated in much the same way. When he was a young marketing manager at Kodak, he would take over and rewrite the sales leaders' business plans if he saw them failing. While working under detail-oriented John Scully at Apple Computer, Bill became the ultimate Micromanager. He burrowed into every detail in the business and directed every decision and action. He said, "I drove everyone nuts. I was a real Diminisher. Believe me, I made every decision, and I pushed everyone around. I was really bad."

Confessions of a Diminisher

Bill recalls one of his worst moments. During an important staff meeting, a member of his management team asked a simple question. Bill, annoyed at the uninformed manager, turned to him, and sharply replied (replete with unprintable colorful language), "That's the dumbest question I have ever heard." The room went silent. Bill continued the meeting, uninterrupted by any other annoying questions. Over the next few weeks, he noticed that most everyone stopped asking him questions. He had dismantled the group's curiosity.

While CEO at Claris, his hard-hitting leadership continued. A close colleague came to him and confided, "Hey, Bill, we all came here because we liked working for you at the last company. But you are back to your old ways. You are pushing everyone around and making all the decisions."

Bill knew she was right. And this wasn't the only near-mutiny. Two months into starting another company, a member of his management team approached him and said, "I am here representing the whole group. If you don't let us do our jobs, we are going to regret coming here. We don't want to leave, but we need to be able to do our jobs." Bill knew he was calling in plays at fourth down with one yard to go. He was hurting his company and jeopardizing his team of exceptionally smart players. And he wasn't willing to lose them.

Becoming a Multiplier

Counsel from two bold colleagues was just the dose of self-awareness that Bill needed. He could see his need for a course correction, and he made it. He started by listening more and telling less. He began to develop a deep appreciation for what his colleagues knew. As he recognized the diminishing effect he had on his management team, he began to detect other Diminishers in his organization. He began to counsel them. He recalled one person in particular who chronically needed to prove he was the smartest guy in the room. Bill sat him down and explained, "I don't care how brilliant you are yourself. If you keep this up, you are going to bring the organization to its knees. You are terrific, but you can't work here like this."

Bill became a better leader over time. It was a steady transition that happened naturally out of his desire to preserve his team and to realize the value of the incredible talent that he had attracted. By the time Bill became CEO at Intuit and led the company past the $1 billion revenue mark in 2000, he had uncovered the Multiplier inside of him.

A Multiplier of Multipliers

Even though Bill retired as the CEO, he remained on the Intuit board and also spent time coaching early-stage start-up companies. He played the role of mentor—a leader who had been there before, made the mistakes, and learned from those mistakes. He worked closely with venture capital partners to make sure their respective roles were clear: the VCs invested and Bill grew the talent. He assisted the CEO and the key leaders in developing the skills needed to allow the company to grow to its market potential.

What did Bill do to cultivate the CEOs? To a great extent, he built Multipliers. He taught what he had learned himself: "If it can be learned, it can be taught." He helped highly intelligent (and often young) CEOs learn how to leverage the intelligence inside their own organizations. The CEOs he coached have progressed to build some of technology's most prominent companies: Amazon, Netscape, PayPal, Google, and many more.

In 2010, Bill helped one CEO transform his executive staff meetings from bland, functional report-out sessions to rigorous debates on the jugular business issues. Before, the meetings had followed a predictable format: each person around the table would give their report, informing their colleagues of progress being made and issues within their function. Bill sat in on many of these staff meetings and saw the underutilization of the enormous brainpower in the room. He counseled, "You are not getting anything out of these staff meetings. You need to engage your people on your biggest issues." Bill asked the CEO to prepare five topics that were crucial to the company. The CEO then emailed the list to the team in advance and asked each person to think through each issue and come prepared with data and opinions.

The CEO opened the next meeting by asking his management team to take their functional hats off and put their company hats on. He then launched into the first issue: Should we be in the services space, or should we give this business to our partners? One executive cited the reasons they should stay in the space. Another argued the contrary. Each team member chimed in with his and her perspective. The CEO listened carefully, made the decision, and then outlined the implications and actions. One team member stepped up and said, "I've got it. I'll take it from here." The CEO then moved on to the next topic, and the next debate ensued.

Bill reflected on his work coaching and advising some of Silicon Valley's rock-star CEOs: "I can help them see it differently. I kick them out of their comfort zones, and I ask them the hard questions."

Bill began his career as a Diminisher who told people what to do and called every play. He then did the hard work to transform himself into a Multiplier where he asked the hard questions that made others think. But his leadership journey didn't end there. Bill Campbell was not just a Multiplier; he became a Multiplier of Multipliers, building other powerful leaders capable of extracting and multiplying intelligence and capability. Bill passed away in April 2016 after a long battle with cancer, but not before making an enormous impact. His biggest legacy in Silicon Valley was as a behind-the-scenes mentor to scores of its most important executives. Scott Cook, Intuit's cofounder, said the company wouldn't be what it is today without Campbell. "I don't think anyone had an impact as important and far-reaching on Silicon Valley's leaders and culture," Cook said. "He made us all better."

Bill's journey from Diminisher to Multiplier of Multipliers, which is similar to those of other leaders we studied, raises a number of questions. Can someone with Diminisher roots become a Multiplier? Can the transition be authentic? Does this journey happen passively, simply through accruing over time the wisdom that comes from maturity, or can it be accelerated through active effort?

In this chapter we address these questions and explore the journey of becoming a Multiplier. We'll offer examples of leaders who have made the transition, and we provide you with a framework and a set of tools to help you both lead more like a Multiplier and build a Multiplier culture around you.

Resonance, Realization, and Resolve

As various people have heard these ideas and read this book, I have observed a nearly universal three-step reaction:

1. RESONANCE. We hear from people everywhere that the distinction between Diminishers and Multipliers resonates deeply with them. Many say, "Yes, I have worked for that manager." They have seen diminishing in action (and/or multiplying), and it vividly describes the realities of the business world.

2. REALIZATION OF THE ACCIDENTAL DIMINISHER. Virtually all readers have confessed that they see some degree of diminishing behaviors in themselves. For some, there are only trace amounts. For others, there is a chronic pattern of behavior. They realize that their well-meaning management practices are, in all probability, having a diminishing effect on the people they work with.

3. RESOLVE TO BE A MULTIPLIER. After identifying their own diminishing tendencies, they have a genuine desire to become more of a Multiplier. Their conviction builds, but they are often overwhelmed by the Multiplier standard and the apparent magnitude of the task of achieving it.

Insight and resolve are a start, but they aren't sufficient to sustain oneself on the journey to Multiplier leadership. To effect operational change, a path must be forged between your personal insight and the impact you seek to have on others: a path paved with action—small steps in the right direction—and successive wins to deepen commitment.

And there's a second challenge. While we may personally aspire to being a Multiplier, few of us are the sole leader of our enterprise. When it comes to leading, most of us have other leaders with whom we work and coexist, who either aid or interfere with our new habits and our best attempts to create a hospitable work environment. How do you take other leaders with you or help the unaware leader realize the downside of their diminishing ways?

We'll address these twin challenges: 1) how can we advance from insight to impact? and 2) how can we inspire collective insight and action and create an entire Multiplier culture?

Becoming a Multiplier

From examples such as Bill Campbell and countless others, I've seen that Multiplier practices can be learned and developed. Some people will stumble in this direction, over time, on their own, but with the right approach the learning can be accelerated. The following five accelerators are proven fast-track practices—both for arriving sooner and for staying longer.

Accelerator No. 1: Start with the Assumptions

To score a strike in tenpin bowling, you need to hit the headpin. Hitting the headpin directly will knock down most of the pins behind it, and hitting it in just the right place, a little to the left or right, pretty much guarantees that all the pins will come tumbling down in a single strike. The assumptions of a Multiplier are the headpin. Because behavior follows assumptions, you can knock out a whole set of behaviors by adopting a Multiplier mindset.

Consider the following scenario and how you might approach it with either Diminisher or Multiplier assumptions:

Another executive has asked that you appoint someone from your division as a representative on a cross-divisional task force that will assess the company's competitive position and recommend changes to the current marketing programs. You decide to put Jyanthi on the task force and plan to use a one-on-one meeting to tee up the assignment.

WITH DIMINISHER ASSUMPTIONS: *People will never figure this out without me.* With this assumption, you would probably approach this meeting using Jyanthi as your representative, your eyes and ears into the project. She'll attend the meetings, gather information, and then report back, so you can weigh in on the issues.

What is the result of this approach? Jyanthi spends a lot of time attending meetings but contributes very little to the task force. She is careful not to overstep her role, so she passes up opportunities to speak out and steers clear of any controversial issues where she might be called on to influence a decision. Eventually, you hear through the grapevine that the task force leader commented on the lack of engagement from your division.

WITH MULTIPLIER ASSUMPTIONS: *People are smart and can figure it out.* You let Jyanthi know that you chose her for her understanding of the market and ability to assimilate the vast amounts of market data that the task force is assembling. You acknowledge that you are giving her a big job, as she will be representing the entire division and be fully responsible for implementing the task force's outcomes. You might recommend that she come to meetings armed with data so she can weigh in on the issues and think on her feet during the debates. You would let her know that this task force is her project, but that you are available as a sounding board if she wants to think through the issues jointly.

What is the result of this approach? Jyanthi engages fully in the task force, gains new understanding of the competitive landscape, and advocates for marketing programs that will have immediate benefit for your division. She impresses the task force leader, who thinks, *This group has great talent.*

The assumptions we hold shape our views and practices and, in the end, have a powerful effect on outcomes (often by being self-fulfilling prophecies). If you want to apply Multiplier skills and behaviors naturally and instinctively, try on the Multiplier Assumptions below and see how they guide your actions.

CORE ASSUMPTIONS

Discipline	Diminisher Assumption	Multiplier Assumption
Talent Magnet	People need to report to me in order to get them to do anything.	If I can find someone's genius, I can put them to work.
Liberator	Pressure increases performance.	People's best thinking must be given, not taken.
Challenger	I need to have all the answers.	People get smarter by being challenged.
Debate Maker	There are only a few people worth listening to.	With enough minds, we can figure it out.
Investor	People will never be able to figure it out without me.	People are smart and will figure things out.

Accelerator No. 2: Work the Extremes

In 2002, Jack Zenger and Joe Folkman published a set of fascinating research findings in their book *The Extraordinary Leader*.[1] They studied 360-degree assessment data for eight thousand leaders, looking for what differentiated the extraordinary leaders from the average leaders. They found that leaders who were perceived as having no distinguishing strengths were rated at the thirty-fourth percentile of effectiveness of all leaders in the study. However, when a leader was perceived as having just one distinguishing strength, his or her effectiveness shot to the sixty-fourth percentile. Having one towering strength almost doubled the effectiveness of the leader, provided the leader had no area of sharp weakness. Leaders with two, three, and four strengths jumped to the seventy-second, eighty-first, and eighty-ninth percentile respectively. The Zenger-Folkman study demonstrates that leaders do not need to be good at everything. They need to have mastery of a small number of skills and be free of show-stopping weaknesses.

What this implies for someone aspiring to lead like a Multiplier is that you do not need to excel at each of the Multiplier disciplines and master every practice. As we studied Multipliers, we noticed that each individual Multiplier wasn't necessarily, or even typically, strong in all five disciplines. The majority of Multipliers were strong in just three. There were many who were strong in four or even all five, but having strength in three of the disciplines appears to be a threshold for Multiplier status. We also noticed that these Multipliers were rarely in the Diminisher range in any of the five disciplines. A leader does not have to be exceptional in all five disciplines to be considered a Multiplier. A leader needs two or three strong disciplines and the others can be just good enough.

Instead of trying to develop strength in all five disciplines, an aspiring Multiplier should set an extreme development plan. Begin by assessing your leadership practices and then work the two extremes: 1) neutralize a weakness; 2) top off a strength.

NEUTRALIZE A WEAKNESS. A common misconception in executive coaching is that coaching or development can—or even should—turn your weaknesses into strengths. Clients have often told me, "I'm terrible at this, and I need to become really great at it." I suggest to them that, while not impossible, it is unlikely they will turn their biggest weaknesses into their biggest strengths. The truth is that you do not need to be fabulous at everything. You just can't be bad. You need to neutralize the weakness and move it into the middle, acceptable zone. Having realistic goals frees up capacity to do the more important development work: turning your modest strengths into towering strengths.

TOP OFF A STRENGTH. As Zenger and Folkman and many others have found, leaders with a small number of strengths are viewed more highly than leaders who have a broad base of capabilities. Of the five disciplines, identify your strongest area and then build a deep and broad repertoire of practices that allows you to excel at this discipline. Become a world-class Challenger or a resounding Talent Magnet. Invest your energy wisely and progress from good to great by topping off one of your strengths. The following chart illustrates these two development strategies:

WORKING THE EXTREMES DEVELOPMENT STRATEGY

MULTIPLIER	Talent Magnet	Liberator	Challenger	Debate Maker	Investor
Towering Strength	⬆**2**				
Competency		◯	⬆**1**	◯	◯
Vulnerability					
DIMINISHER	Empire Builder	Tyrant	Know-It-All	Decision Maker	Micro-manager

Based on our research, we've developed a multirater assessment tool, which you can access at www.multipliersbooks.com. Taking this

360-degree assessment will get you started in identifying your relative strengths along the Diminisher–Multiplier continuum. When reviewing your report, look for your extremes. Which discipline is your strongest? Are any disciplines dangerously within Diminisher territory?

Accelerator No. 3: Run an Experiment

Effective and enduring learning involves small, successive experimentation using new approaches—testing new behavior, analyzing feedback, adjusting, and repeating. The experiments in appendix E have been designed as starters for the larger Multiplier disciplines. Pick an experiment from the Multiplier discipline you aspire to, or choose an experiment to help ameliorate an Accidental Diminisher tendency. What's important is that you pick one (and preferably only one) and experiment with a new approach.

When these small experiments produce successful outcomes, the resulting energy fuels the next, slightly bigger experiment. Over time, these experiments form new patterns of behavior that establish a new baseline. Try extending your experiment over a thirty-day period. Why thirty days? Research published in the *European Journal of Social Psychology* shows that it takes approximately sixty days of concentrated effort to form a new habit.[2] A thirty-day challenge gets you to "halftime" and offers a chance to reflect and strategize for the second half of new habit formation. Like any good researcher, you should record your experiences in a journal, learning from what works and what doesn't.

Here's a glimpse into what happened when four leaders, and in some cases their management teams, turned an experiment into a thirty-day challenge.

LABELING TALENT. Jack Bossidy[3] was the team leader in a manufacturing plant. He could see that some members of his team dominated meetings while others withdrew. Curiously, the person who spoke most in the meetings was the same person who felt most underutilized and undervalued.

Jack decided to take a thirty-day challenge and began by genius watching. He took note of the native genius of each member of his team. In his next staff meeting, he spoke about each person, why they were needed on the team, and the unique capabilities they brought. He went beyond labeling each person's genius one-on-one and labeled it in front of the whole group. The team then reviewed the work that needed to get done over the next quarter and determined assignments. Although not explicitly asked of them, the team naturally ensured each person had an assignment that demanded one or more of their unique capabilities.

What do you suppose happened to the undervalued but overly dominating team member? He talked less, listened more, and began to draw out the capabilities of others. Under the leadership of an aspiring Multiplier, he went from dominating to multiplying. He told Jack, "It feels like we are really working as a team now."

LIBERATING LOKESH. Christine faced a common management challenge—how to get the most out of Lokesh, a smart but timid colleague. Lokesh always showed deference to other people's ideas. Instead of offering his own opinion, he would just go with what other people recommended, giving the impression that he didn't have any ideas. Christine found that it was easy to dominate meetings with Lokesh. Without meaning to, she would end up overexpressing her views and speaking 80 percent of the time. The more she tried to rescue him, the worse things seemed to be. The more she "mentored" Lokesh, the less he seemed to contribute.

Christine took a thirty-day challenge and focused on being a Liberator to Lokesh by making more space for him. She began by asking, "How is Lokesh smart?" The question snapped her out of her more judgmental Diminisher assumptions and put her into inquiry mode. As his abilities came into focus for her (his years of experience and his ability to break complex activities into actionable plans), she found it easier to ask him questions and to give him space to answer them.

Christine noticed an immediate change. Lokesh started to offer opinions. He spoke 50 percent or more in their interactions. He volunteered for the majority of the action items. He stepped into the role of a creator. And within days, one of the clients had commented to Christine about the difference. Christine summarized her learning by saying, "The silence creates the space. The space creates results. The results are valuable. And I have already seen a payoff!"

DEBATING THE DEAL. Gary Lovell is a Project Manager for HP Enterprise Services in Cape Town, South Africa. When a client purchased a new business unit that had to be integrated into their existing spend-management system, Gary and his team were tasked with finding the best product solution for the client. Specifically, they would need to recommend an integration strategy, considering time and resource-related implications. This was a high-stakes decision for the client, so Gary decided to turn to debate.

Gary needed to engage two sides of the business that normally disagreed and get them to create an aligned, compelling solution. Naturally, he was expecting apprehension from both the client and his technical team. Even though Gary had a gut feeling about which solution he should present to the client, he initiated a debate with the technical team. Throughout the debate, Gary asked each team member to assume untypical "job" roles to hash out the pros and cons of potential decisions. This process prompted nearly everyone to change their initial opinion at least once.

In the end, a solution was agreed upon by all. When they presented their final solution, the client's IT director posed many questions not only to Gary but to the HP technical team as well. Because they had previously dealt with those types of questions while "switching sides" during the debate, the entire team was prepared. Seeing the HP team's united front, the client's apprehension turned to confidence, and they moved forward with an innovative, outside-the-box solution that secured a much larger opportunity for the company.

INVESTING IN RENEWABLE ENERGY. Gregory Pal is a thoughtful and intense MIT graduate with an MBA from Harvard who works as a manager in an alternative energy start-up. Gregory is known for his ability to solve complex problems. As a reviewer of the early versions of this book, he admitted to feeling torn between his growing desire to lead like a Multiplier and the mounting pressures he faced at work. He found a way through his dilemma by taking on the thirty-day challenge, with a clear and focused target in mind.

Gregory had recently hired Michael, a talented individual with rich experience as an employee of the Brazilian embassy, but wasn't fully utilizing him. Michael was the only team member working remotely and was often "out of sight, out of mind." Michael estimated he was being utilized at 20 to 25 percent.

Gregory began the challenge by making a few simple investments. He gave Michael full ownership for capturing their Brazilian partnership strategy on paper for a critical board meeting. He then integrated Michael virtually into company-wide meetings so his ideas could be heard. He touched base with him often, but didn't take over his work. Within just a couple of weeks, Michael said he felt like he was being utilized at 75 to 80 percent. That represents a threefold utilization gain!

Yet the real gain, according to Gregory, came from a slight change in perspective. Once he started looking at the people around him through the lens of a Multiplier, he said, opportunities started presenting themselves. Instead of feeling frustrated at having to step in and redo work, he found ways to help other people take their thinking to the next level. He could take charge without taking over. He began to do things differently because he began to see his role differently.

Accelerator No. 4: Brace Yourself for Setbacks

Moving from inspiration to impact requires addressing the original assumptions *and* creating new Multiplier habits. The process is neither automatic nor immediate. But, with sufficient know-how and a few tools, you can transform your old assumptions into new habits.

Because the Multiplier disciplines are easy to grasp, a common trap is thinking that implementing the ideas is as easy as understanding them. Rarely is knowledge alone sufficient to transform into a Multiplier. Much more often, replacing diminishing habits with Multiplier behaviors comes only through persistence and resilience. It is therefore vital to anticipate—and create tools to withstand—possible setbacks along the way.

After all, changing diminishing behaviors is not like knee-replacement surgery, in which a worn-out joint is simply replaced with a new one. Desire to transform current assumptions will not, on its own, spontaneously override old habits. The seeds of the new Multiplier assumptions must be planted and cultivated while the old habits are gradually uprooted.

The good news is that the part of the brain that stores consciously cultivated new assumptions is the same part that unconsciously builds new habits.[4] Yet—and here is the kicker—until a new habit is formed (by creating new neural pathways through consistent behavior), the subconscious will think you *should* be operating in your old diminishing ways, even though those ways contradict your new Multiplier assumptions. The danger of this difficult interim period is that these "should" judgments will demotivate you—and might even lead you to quit the journey before you can develop and implement your new assumptions.

There is a trick to help you get through this period. First, give yourself permission to stumble as you cultivate new Multiplier behaviors while transforming old habits. Know that it will be hard; you're likely to take two steps forward and then a step back as you develop new mindsets and skills. Using the following strategy will

help you cut yourself some slack until those habits are fully transformed:

1. My new Multiplier assumption is [people are smart and
   will figure it out], so I need to develop a new habit [giving
   space].
2. As I'm becoming a Multiplier, old habits will be mixed
   with new assumptions.
3. Until those habits are fully uprooted, I will continue making mistakes diminishing others by [jumping in], while I'm
   trying to learn to multiply others by [giving space].

Second, share your strategy with colleagues who are likely to
encourage you along the way. If you are making a 180-degree shift,
talking it out with a few team members will reduce the freak-out factor
that your changes might create—quickly moving from diminishing
behaviors to multiplying ones might be viewed as suspect if demon-
strated without warning. Further, it will help you commit to your plan
while also garnering some much-needed support at the same time.

Accelerator No. 5: Ask a Colleague

If you really want to accelerate your development as a Multiplier
leader, let a colleague—an employee, peer, or boss—choose your
experiment for you. Pick someone who can see your Accidental
Diminisher tendencies and who also knows your good intentions.
Give them the worksheet in appendix E on pages 340–42 and tell
them you are choosing one new practice to help you become a better
leader. Then ask this question: *If I want to bring out the best in the
people I lead, which one of the nine experiments would help me the
most?* But, be warned, this step isn't for the lackadaisical learner or
accidental leader. It's rocket fuel for the aspiring Multiplier—it will
get you there faster.

My team and I have been inspired as we witnessed senior leaders and frontline managers around the world take experiments and become comfortable with their new gait and rhythms. For many, merely watching their employees' reactions was sufficient evidence to keep them moving forward. For others, the proof came when they realized their new approach was liberating for themselves as well as their employees. Dave Havlek, the investor relations executive who put his team in charge (see the Give It Back experiment on page 336), reflected, "Suddenly the burden of me having to make every decision, every call, was lifted. It felt good to let go, and it felt even better when the team delivered a solid result. I am starting to feel like I don't have to work until midnight each night." As Dave successfully shifted the burden of thinking to his team, they moved faster and made smarter decisions, and Dave redefined his role as a leader.

While the ripple effect of a single leader can be felt across an organization, no leader leads in isolation. Each leader is part of a system, and it takes leaders at all levels to build an environment where intelligence is deeply utilized.

Building a Multiplier Culture

Mike Felix is a strong, well-established leader with a knack for transforming struggling businesses and teams. In 2012, after successfully leading a turnaround in Alaska as the president of Alascom (an AT&T subsidiary), Mike was asked by AT&T to move to the Midwest to lead almost 8,500 people in the Midwest Internet and Entertainment Field Services division. This move was part of the global telecommunications giant's larger transformation to become the premier integrated communication company in the world. To accomplish this the company was working to build an agile workforce that could take smart calculated risks as well as create a culture where every voice was heard and every mind mattered.

In his new role, Mike would be responsible for leading a management staff of seven directors, sixty-eight area managers, and almost five hundred frontline managers. And to make this big job even bigger, the Midwest division had been perennially in last place among the five divisions (by virtually every business measure). It was an organization that appeared to have been chronically overmanaged and underled.

An Awakening

Mike spent most of his first year "wandering" around the Midwest, observing behaviors, listening to conversations, and asking questions, getting a sense for attitudes and behaviors that were holding the team back. He made a clarion discovery: many of the managers had been promoted because they were good technicians but had never been taught how to lead and coach. So he created a mentoring program where area managers could learn the new skills of leadership and get the best, consistent performance with their teams.

A year into his assignment, Mike attended a global leadership summit where he heard about Multipliers and, more important, about the notion that even really good leaders can become Accidental Diminishers. As a natural leader, the idea resonated with him; it gave him words to describe his own positive leadership practices and also crystalized the diminishing assumptions that had been holding his division back. It struck a chord, and it also hit a nerve. He said, "It really challenged me. It helped me see the areas where I was an Accidental Diminisher." Mike read *Multipliers* and found ways to minimize his Accidental Diminisher tendencies. Instead of overwhelming his staff with his vision and energy, he would simply seed ideas and then step back and ask more questions. He also used the Multiplier practices to offer bigger challenges and shift ownership to others, which took his own mentoring and coaching to a new level.

No leader—even one with superior skills and exceptional self-awareness—can transform an organization single-handedly. To turn around an 8,500-person organization, Mike knew he needed to hone his own leadership capability, but more important, he needed to build a broad Multiplier culture. It would require that the more than 500 managers become better leaders and cocreate a system of shared beliefs across the entire organization.

A Call to Action

Mike began by introducing the language of Multipliers. As a perpetual student of leadership and organization, he understood that changing a culture meant changing the conversation. And, to change the conversation, people would need new words, especially words about behaviors that would lead to winning results. Mike asked all his managers to read *Multipliers* and take the Accidental Diminisher quiz (which you can find at www.multipliersquiz.com). Soon all his managers were using the same vocabulary, especially the lexicon of the Accidental Diminishers. They talked about being Always On and Pacesetters and began pushing back on other's well-meaning attempts as Rescuers and the like. Mike said, "It gave us a common language and permission to call out diminishing actions."

But calling out ineffective behavior was just the beginning—they had to define the new leadership behaviors necessary to shape a culture of trust and high performance. Mike spent more time in the field, understanding what people needed from their managers in order for them to perform at their best and achieve their business goals. Mike didn't construct an elaborate competency model; he kept it simple, capturing the behaviors and learning progression he expected on a piece of paper only two inches square. After several tours across the Midwest and tens of thousands of miles of driving and flying, Mike had met with all sixty-eight of his area managers and more than four hundred frontline managers, discussing these winning behaviors and teaching managers how to lead and coach the rest of the team. As Mike modeled the new leadership approach, the directors and area managers followed. An Ohio area manager said, "I try to teach and not tell. I ask a question, find out what they know, and then help guide them to a solution. I try to let them be the smartest person in the room." While the directors and area managers were the teachers, they weren't the proctors. Instead of trying to catch and correct all behavioral infractions, they encouraged and coached their teams to self-assess and adjust.

But Mike didn't just expect the managers below them to learn new behaviors, he himself continued to make personal leadership adjustments. For example, at the conclusion of every town hall meeting, Mike would ask his direct reports for feedback on his tone and any unintentional messages he might have sent. Mike said, "People can often see where they are Multipliers, but not necessarily where they are Diminishers. For this you need feedback, and I'm lucky to have a whole posse of people who will give me this information." When a group of his managers was asked about Mike's Accidental Diminisher tendencies, they laughed. One said, "He's got every one of them! But it isn't diminishing because he calls himself out. He says, 'Maybe I approached that wrong.' It doesn't matter if it is in a small group or on a conference call with four thousand people, he'll say he got it wrong." A Chicago area manager said, "It means we aren't afraid to make mistakes or make decisions on our own. If we fail, we try to fail fast and move on."

After coming to a clear consensus on the behaviors allowed, Mike and his team stood ready to make up-front people decisions. Key leadership decisions were made with a clear principle that Mike had established: "Past results don't predict future results; actually past behavior predicts future behavior, which then drives future results." Leaders who exhibited the right mindsets and behavior were pulled up, while some who could not make the transition were moved out. Mike and his leadership team made a point of reaching into the organization and shining a spotlight on good leadership. For example, one frontline manager, who created a game show to reinforce the importance of safety, became a bit of a local hero. He and other new heroes became role models, giving the larger organization a chance to tell new stories and build new success beliefs. Innovative action sprang up across the organization.

Mike and his team could see the need to increase trust. People needed to know they were trusted and, in turn, could trust their management to have their best interests at heart. Mike could have preached the trust message and conducted seminars on trust, governing from a closed office and dispatching staff people to look for signs of noncompliance. Instead, Mike and his management team started to build trust by extending trust to employees and by asking a lot more questions. They weren't interrogating, gotcha questions; they were sincere questions, the ones that say, *I want to know what you think, and why.* They were questions that conveyed the message that *I trust you.* It wasn't a blind faith that *I trust you to get it right*; it was a more deeply held confidence that *I trust you to learn how to get it right.* As the managers consistently asked questions, the technicians and the staff got the message: they were expected to think for themselves, and they would be allowed to recover from mistakes.

A Common Culture

New beliefs are initially tenuous and need reinforcement and validation to become inculcated and deeply rooted. Mike and his team created visible programs to celebrate and share progress. For example, area managers whose organizations were accident free for an entire quarter were awarded a Circle of Safety coat—a reminder to the whole team that the safety of the team mattered as much as financial and operational targets. The mentoring program that Mike established became a regular monthly practice. To no surprise, Mike still speaks to every class and makes sure they all know that *Multipliers* is first up on the reading list. He talks about his own Accidental Diminisher tendencies and encourages others to do the same. Talking about a manager's vulnerabilities had previously been the subject of furtive, closed-door conversations; now it is out in the open and a breath of fresh air. Three years ago, the idea of manager as genius maker was novel. Today it's the new normal, just part of how things work there.

By the end of 2015, just three years after Mike Felix took the helm,

AT&T's Midwest IEFS division was on its way to winning its third consecutive JD Power Award for Customer Satisfaction with U-verse TV service, finishing with the best financial performance among the five divisions, and, in any given month, was in the number one or number two position in operational metrics. It was a journey from perennially last to definitively first. Mike's mentees nominated him for the 2015 Multiplier of the Year contest and cheered him on to become one of the finalists.

Mike didn't just change himself; he changed an entire culture. While it started with a singular, sudden insight, he achieved sustained impact by building a culture—a common language, a system of shared assumptions, and a set of norms about the way to win collectively and to continually get smarter and more capable.

If you want to build a brilliant organization, don't just settle for your own aha moment: build a Multiplier culture, one that generates Multiplier moments every day and between everyone in the organization.

Cultivating Growth

So, how do you build a Multiplier culture—an environment where the mindsets and the practices of Multipliers are shared and the new normal? To begin developing new cultural norms, we must understand what culture is and how a strong culture is formed. Let's start with the classic definitions of culture. From the anthropological perspective, culture is "the beliefs, customs, arts, etc., of a particular society, group, place or time." From the business perspective, culture is "a way of thinking, behaving, or working that exists in a place or organization."[5] Strong cultures typically exhibit the following traits:

➤ *Common language:* Words and phrases that hold a common meaning within a community based on opinions, principles, and values[6]

➤ *Learned behaviors:* A set of learned responses to stimuli[7]
➤ *Shared beliefs:* The acceptance of something as true[8]
➤ *Heroes and legends:* People who are admired or idealized for their qualities, behavior, and/or achievements and the stories told about their heroic actions[9]
➤ *Rituals and norms:* Consistent behavior regularly followed by an individual or a group[10]

Consider a powerful culture where these elements work together to shape new behavior and produce positive outcomes. Alcoholics Anonymous is a mutual aid fellowship of more than 2 million people in 170 countries whose primary purpose is to help alcoholics "stay sober and help other alcoholics achieve sobriety." Though AA has no governing body and is a globally dispersed, loosely connected fellowship, it maintains a strong culture throughout. No matter where you attend an AA meeting, your experience will be consistent. Why is that?

In AA, members exhibit common language through references to the Big Book, the Twelve Steps, and the Twelve Traditions. They hold shared beliefs, like admitting that they are powerless over alcohol and need help from a "higher power." In AA, people combat alcoholism through a number of learned behaviors: one way is by building accountability through attending meetings and talking regularly with a sponsor. In AA, each person becomes a hero because they all share their stories with each other—and by telling their stories, they help both themselves and others with their sobriety; they create legends. Some of the rituals of Alcoholics Anonymous include regular meeting attendance, saying specific prayers together, and the well-known introduction, "Hi, my name is [Oliver], and I am an alcoholic."

Regardless of what any of us think about AA, we can universally acknowledge that its culture is powerful. Culture is powerful because it redirects and shapes our behavior; its forces overpower individual intent and reject individual behaviors that are not acceptable or normative. In AA, any type of person can show up and belong, but the culture mandates that if that person hinders the group from fulfilling its primary purpose, he or she will no longer be welcome. Plato offers this insight: "The overwhelming majority of individuals will prove incapable of resisting the voice of the culture that surrounds them: in the typical case, their values, their beliefs, indeed, their very perceptions will tend to mirror those of the surrounding culture."[11]

Diving into the Deep

Most companies and their leaders recognize the need to rid their organizations of old, unproductive habits and to introduce new behaviors more fit for the future needs of the organization. Attempting to build new norms, these well-meaning companies expose their management ranks to new ideas, often through keynote speeches, generally giving little thought to integrating the new practices into the daily working of the business or operation. These efforts seek to inspire, assuming that the epiphany will generate the momentum required to counteract the gravitational pull of current practices and status quo thinking. But there is a short shelf life on inspiration without action.

While introducing ideas and generating conversation is a good start, it doesn't go far enough. It is much like when a patient begins taking a prescribed course of antibiotics and fails to complete the full course of treatment, thus running the risk that the bacteria will survive, mutate, and become resistant. Similarly, incomplete attempts to introduce a new culture cannot only fail to produce results but can also cause residual resentment that can become resistant to future initiatives.

A rapidly growing software company became intrigued with Multipliers as a key to their growth, innovation, and talent retention strategy. Managers were asked to read the book and inject its concepts into their management and new hire training programs. Quickly, talk of Multipliers, Diminishers, and Accidental Diminishers was heard in the halls of the workspace and between the walls of conference rooms. Known Diminishers were exposed, and would-be Multipliers were inspired. However, when the company hit a few bumps on their growth curve, many managers retreated to their default style—not because it was better but simply because it was easier. As the company returned to steady growth, they realized they had lost sight of their aspirations. Today they are regrouping and recommitting to build and sustain a true Multiplier culture. This time, they aren't just starting a conversation, they are building deep internal capability to teach the ideas and integrate them into their talent and performance management practices.

Building a culture is neither a one-time injection nor a sheep dip; it requires connection to the deep layers of the culture—it necessitates going from surface-level cultural elements (such as shared language and behavior) to affect the deeper cultural elements (such as rituals and norms), as the chart below illustrates.

LAYERS OF CULTURE

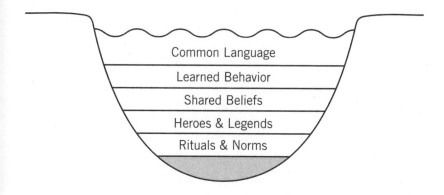

Common Language

Learned Behavior

Shared Beliefs

Heroes & Legends

Rituals & Norms

Engaging in the surface-level practices is like dipping your toe into a pool of water—feeling the temperature of the water but skimming the surface. As your organization engages in the deeper practices, surface-level insights become deeply embedded beliefs and new behaviors are routinized into standard operating practices. When new ideas become new norms, you have cultivated a sustainable culture.

Building Deep Culture

How do you create new norms? This section offers a set of practices that will assist you in building the essential elements of culture (see the chart below), starting from surface-level elements like creating a shared language to deeper practices such as integrating Multiplier behaviors into manager assessment and hiring practices.

Each practice is illustrated with an example of how one company is putting this strategy to work. In most cases, these companies are deploying a number of practices; however, only a small sample of the larger work they are engaged in is highlighted below.

10 PRACTICES TO BUILD A MULTIPLIER CULTURE

Cultural Element	Multiplier Practice
Common Language	1. Hold a book talk 2. Discuss Accidental Diminishers
Learned Behavior	3. Introduce Multiplier mindsets 4. Teach Multiplier skills 5. Fuse Multipliers with daily decisions
Shared Beliefs	6. Codify a leadership ethos
Heroes & Legends	7. Spotlight Multiplier moments 8. Measure managers
Rituals & Norms	9. Pilot a Multiplier practice 10. Integrate practices with business metrics

Common Language

When a group shares a common vocabulary, they can more easily name desirable and undesirable behaviors that would otherwise be slippery or invisible. Many leadership models name desirable behaviors but fail to spark discussion about undesirable behaviors. Having a common vocabulary gives people the chance to talk about diminishing, which is a discussion that all too often exists only in shrouded conversations and hushed tones. To strengthen a culture, create a safe space for people to talk about leadership—not just in theoretical, aspirational terms but also in real daily experiences and interactions. Use either of the two practices below to help people name and express what is working and not working for them and their colleagues.

PRACTICE 1: *Hold a book talk.* Ryan Sanders, the COO of Bamboo HR, a rapidly growing software-as-a-service company, introduced Multipliers to his company. He went in highly cognizant of two principles that he learned from managing triple-digit growth. First, underperformers could easily hide in high-growth companies. Second, bad management and lack of leadership development compound the problem. He began his leadership development efforts by having his senior leadership team read this book and discuss the need for Multiplier leadership across their growing business in a series of weekly staff meetings.

PRACTICE 2: *Discuss Accidental Diminishers.* In addition to discussing the ideas in the book, the senior leaders at Bamboo HR each took the Accidental Diminisher quiz and compared their self-assessments. The conversations were real and vulnerable, with team members confronting each other's diminishing behaviors and lauding their Multiplier moments. Tears weren't uncommon. While many companies start the dialogue, this management team kept it going, creating a comfortable space to call each other out on diminishing behaviors and work together to replace those behaviors with multiplying practices. Their collective point of view allowed them to lead a cultural transformation and increase their retention of top talent. Most important, the conversation continues within all ranks of the company.

Learned Behavior

When we watch our boss or another successful leader micromanage in high-stakes situations, we are learning "appropriate" behavior and are likely to default to this behavior when presented with a similar situation. The behavior becomes naturalized or unconscious. To acquire a set of new learned behaviors, people must move from unaware Diminisher to automatic Multiplier, as summarized in the following chart.[12]

SHIFTING FROM UNAWARE DIMINISHER TO AUTOMATIC MULTIPLIER

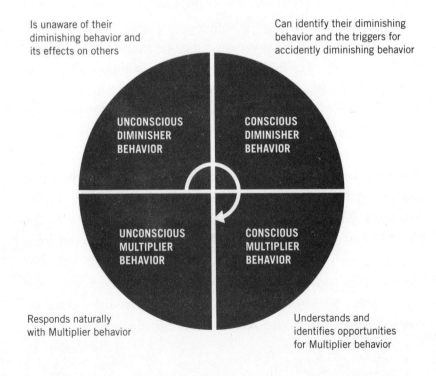

Is unaware of their diminishing behavior and its effects on others

Can identify their diminishing behavior and the triggers for accidently diminishing behavior

UNCONSCIOUS DIMINISHER BEHAVIOR

CONSCIOUS DIMINISHER BEHAVIOR

UNCONSCIOUS MULTIPLIER BEHAVIOR

CONSCIOUS MULTIPLIER BEHAVIOR

Responds naturally with Multiplier behavior

Understands and identifies opportunities for Multiplier behavior

Initially, people need to discover the downside of an old, negative behavior. Once they understand the downside, they need to learn to spot the triggers, the situations that bait and activate diminishing responses. Once they've been introduced to new Multiplier behaviors, they need to experiment with those behaviors and experience success. However, to make that behavior permanent, our response to the stimulus needs to become habituated or automatic. The following practices can help managers unlearn diminishing behaviors and spot opportunities to replace them with Multiplier practices.

PRACTICE 3: *Introduce Multiplier mindsets.* Mike Felix, the leader described earlier, wasn't an anomaly; his actions were part of a larger movement across AT&T. As employees of a large company know, it's easy to be underutilized inside big companies, becoming lost in red tape, political silos, and corporate structure. In AT&T's quest to become the world's premier integrated communications company, they needed a better way to tap into intelligence inside the company and to create a culture of trust and transparency where people could speak up. And they needed a fresh and efficient way to reach more than 100,000 leaders. AT&T began their efforts to flatten the hierarchy by starting at the top. Under the direction of their CEO, AT&T University held a series of seminars for the 150 company officers. The seminars introduced the Multipliers mindsets and practices and prompted conversation among the senior leaders—not about what they wanted leaders below them to do (as is all too common inside corporations) but about their own vulnerabilities as Accidental Diminishers. The new framework became a powerful lens to view how leaders with positive intent could have negative effects and how hidden mindsets shape both action and outcome.

As senior officers experimented with Multiplier practices, others in the organization took notice, witnessing how seemingly small shifts in behavior could have major impact. For example, Brooks

McCorcle, the president of AT&T Partner Solutions, had such a positive experience with "playing fewer chips" (see page 322) that managers throughout her team began trying their hand with the exercise. While AT&T's effort began at the top of the organization, it didn't stop there. AT&T University distributed a copy of the book to all 6,700 general managers and then held a Multipliers webinar viewed by over 125,000 leaders worldwide (roughly 46 percent of their overall employee population). Along with the webinar came a forty-eight-page discussion guide encouraging managers to convert ideas into daily business practices.

While the effort certainly hasn't eradicated all diminishing behavior or all Diminishers, it has established a collective ambition and introduced ways of working that are reducing hesitation and dismantling hierarchy. Employees are more likely to hear their managers asking questions, listening, and saying things such as "There is no one right answer here" or "What's on your mind?" or "Let's jump on a call and debate this." One senior leader made a point of giving his more junior managers greater access to company officers (who often get shielded from ideas-in-process). The junior managers, sensing the trust being placed in them, put more rigor into their thinking, not less. But they also weren't afraid to suggest something seemingly outrageous. The senior leader said, "This flatter, more collaborative style is a much faster operating model."

People also feel greater permission to call out well-intentioned yet diminishing behaviors. For example, when an overly eager colleague was dominating a conversation, someone else jumped in with a lighthearted "Whoa, slow down, cowboy." The message was sent quickly and humorously rather than festering or getting queued for inclusion in an annual performance review. Just as we saw with Mike Felix's organization, when managers learn to recognize the triggers for diminishing behavior and turn these into Multiplier moments, the Multiplier way of leading becomes normalized.

PRACTICE 4: *Teach Multiplier skills.* To develop the talent and innovation necessary to transform from a commodity-based business to a specialty chemical company, Eastman Chemical held a series of immersive two-day leadership workshops under the direction of Mark Hecht, a seasoned executive coach inside the company. The workshops introduced the Multipliers framework and taught only the Multiplier practices that supported their business objectives. In addition to teaching skills, they utilized a 360-degree assessment to provide data to enable the leaders to recognize their blind spots and monitor their progress. Some leaders took it a step further in skill development by adding "Multiplier Moments" to their natural team meeting agenda to assist leaders in sharing pivotal moments when they could turn diminishing actions into opportunities to magnify the best in their employees.

PRACTICE 5: *Fuse Multipliers with daily decisions.* The Multipliers framework fit nicely with Intuit's business values, but the company wanted to ensure that ideas would translate from training-room scenarios to real-time business decisions in the leaders' daily practice. Instead of just teaching skills, they used a business leadership simulation from the consulting firm BTS. In the simulation, teams managed a fictitious business modeled after Intuit, and faced a series of strategic and tactical decisions wherein they had to choose the actions that would both deliver the desired business results while simultaneously utilizing and multiplying the company talent. As the teams played through the simulation, leaders learned how to approach the most difficult business problems with a Multiplier mindset and behaviors. When they were faced with similar business decisions back on the job, they understood the trade-offs and were prepared to lead as a Multiplier.

Shared Beliefs

In a strong culture, people not only share a set of beliefs about what is true, they also share a set of assumptions about how the world works. The peaks and perimeters are clearly defined—members know what conduct earns someone hero status and what conduct gets someone kicked out of the tribe. In a Multiplier culture there is clarity on what constitutes good leadership, and people who behave in ways that are congruent with the leadership ethos rise to the top. Each time people who uphold the beliefs are rewarded, the culture is strengthened; likewise, every time diminishing behavior is over-looked, that culture is diluted. To build a strong culture, define the core beliefs about leadership and ensure those beliefs are validated more frequently than they are violated.

PRACTICE 6: *Codify a leadership ethos.* In 2011, Nike, the global athletic powerhouse, was bolstering their efforts to build a strong, sustaining management culture. The company analyzed the leadership required to support their global growth and established a manager Manifesto, a code from CEO Mark Parker that defined the purpose and standards of excellence for managers across Nike. With the concept of Multipliers as a cornerstone, this code defined Nike's expectations for managers: Managers who extract and extend the genius of others get vastly more from their people. They are a force to multiply team performance and fuel business growth through leading, coaching, driving, and inspiring their teams. This manifesto sounded a clarion call to all managers: Your job is to unleash the full potential of each person on your team.

Heroes And Legends

Individuals who embody sought-after leadership values can be powerful role models, propelling hopeful or even reluctant managers forward. Not only can these leaders have a contagious effect on the organization, they can become cultural legends, leaving a lasting imprint long after they've left the organization. The heroes in a Multiplier culture might be those truly inspiring leaders who exemplify

Multiplier mindsets and practices. However, your most powerful role models just may be the aspiring Multipliers—the leaders who earnestly seek to understand and confront their own diminishing ways.

Dawn Cunningham is a leader who has become legendary at 3M. After attending the 3M Amplify program, Dawn (who runs the Customer Insights function) embarked on a mission to redeem herself from her Accidental Diminisher tendencies, even phoning former colleagues to apologize for past actions that she now understood to be diminishing. She made such an impression on her colleagues that she was invited to speak to the company's top one hundred executives. Courageously, she shared her self-assessment and challenged the top executives to consider how their best intentions might be stifling the innovation they so earnestly sought.

PRACTICE 7: *Spotlight Multiplier moments.* When Casey Lehner, senior director of Design Operations at Nike, won the Multiplier of the Year contest[13] in 2012, Nike went all-out. The company made an internal announcement and held an awards ceremony at company headquarters, during which Lehner's staff spoke ebulliently about working for her. One said, "She believes we are capable, so we believe we are capable." Following the tribute, her colleagues presented her with a custom pair of sneakers designed and produced in her honor. You don't need to wait until someone from your company earns an award; you can spotlight leaders inside your company for exemplifying Multiplier leadership. Make heroes out of these genius makers who bring out the best in others.

PRACTICE 8: *Measure managers.* Companies can reinforce Multiplier practices by periodically but regularly assessing how well managers incorporate Multiplier behaviors into their daily leadership practices. After all, as the adage goes, what gets measured gets done. Some companies use the Multipliers 360-degree assesssment as one of a suite of management assessments. Other companies incorporate the behaviors into their existing manager assessments. For example, Nike invites employees to rate their managers once a year against a set of eight habits of winning managers based on the Multipliers practices. NBN, an Australian broadband network provider, mapped the Multipliers practices to their core leadership competencies and use a 180-degree assessment tool to measure their managers. This data is not only incorporated into their midyear performance reviews but also aggregated into a company-wide heat map revealing the collective strengths and vulnerabilities of their leaders.

Rituals And Norms

The Multiplier way of leading becomes institutionalized as you integrate its disciplines into operational practices of the organization, such as performance management, talent planning, and financial incentives. What was once experimental, and perhaps even went against the grain, becomes an integral part of the fabric of the organization. The following two practices can normalize once novel ideas.

PRACTICE 9: *Pilot a Multiplier practice.* Chris Fry, formerly the senior vice president of product development at Salesforce, held a two-day Multipliers workshop for his management team. At the conclusion of the workshop, Chris suggested his team focus their efforts by putting just a single idea into practice. He offered this challenge to the group: "I want us to get 1 percent better across the whole team." Aiming to promote free movement and growth of talent inside the company, the team focused on the Talent Magnet discipline. They established a guiding principle: It should be easier to transfer inside the company than to pursue an opportunity outside the company. They sketched out a new transfer policy called "opportunity open market" that allowed software developers to transfer to new teams after each quarterly release in their agile product development cycle. After each release they held an internal job fair that advertised internal opportunities. Existing managers were not allowed to veto transfers, which offered individuals the opportunity to move freely inside the company. The pilot was so successful and popular with employees (and managers) that the program was implemented across the broader company.

PRACTICE 10: *Integrate practices with business metrics.* When Rick de Rijk of the Dutch consultancy firm Leadership Natives was working on a leadership development program with the global bank ABN AMRO, they went beyond a set of competencies and training programs. They began by correlating the Multiplier traits with the new leadership language that had been defined by ABN AMRO. Finding a 96 percent overlap, Multipliers became their new training method to achieve their desired leadership language. In training programs, participants created a business leadership plan that connected the Multiplier behavior with their business impact goals and Key Performance Indicators. These business leadership plans were then tied to the corporate strategy to establish clear lines of sight between the most critical business metrics and the leadership behavior that would enable these outcomes. When the impact of their pilot program was measured, they found a 163 percent return on investment.[14]

The practices described above are by no means an exhaustive list or a one-size-fits-all program. They are offered as examples of purposeful action taken to imbue a set of mindsets and practices into an organization, which can permeate the surface layer of culture and create a strong foundation for an intelligent organization—one that isn't just an aggregation of smart people but a team with collective brilliance.

Building Momentum

It is a commonly held belief that change, especially cultural change, must start at the top—and *with* the top executives. While it is prudent for cultural norms to cascade from the top (as is the case at AT&T), it isn't the only strategy. My colleagues and I have noticed that most successful implementations typically start in the middle. Here's why. When middle managers experiment with the Multipliers mindsets and practices inside their organizations, they produce pockets of success— anomalies that catch the attention of senior executives and corporate staffers who are highly adept at detecting variances (both negative and positive). When senior executives notice positive outcomes, they are quick to elevate and endorse the new practices, in turn spreading the practices to other parts of the organization. In other words, most senior executives are adept at spotting a parade and getting in front of it! (Incidentally, this is one of several executive skills you won't find documented on any official leadership competency model.)

If you don't yet have the political capital to lead a company-wide initiative, run a pilot with a few rising middle managers. Shine a spotlight on their success and let the practices spread to their peers. Expose their good work to the executive team and make yourself available to turn the parade into a movement.

Whatever starting point you choose is inconsequential compared to how you will sustain the momentum you've generated. Unfortunately, most new initiatives—be they corporate change initiatives or personal improvement plans—begin with a bang but fizzle out in what I call "the failure to launch" cycle depicted in the following chart.[15] Instead, start small and build a series of successive wins. As illustrated in the next chart, each win provides the energy needed to carry the work into the next phase. These series of wins generate the energy and collective will needed to complete the cycle of success. As that cycle spins, nascent beliefs become more deeply entrenched and old survival strategies get supplanted by new methods to not just survive but thrive inside the organization.

Lastly, you can also draw on the power of community as a way to spark and sustain momentum, especially when you encounter set-backs. As like-minded leaders gather in tribes, they create a safe space

FAILURE TO LAUNCH VERSUS A SUCCESS CYCLE

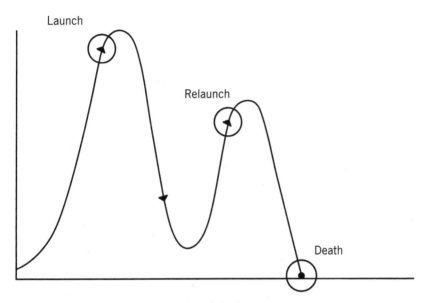

FAILURE TO LAUNCH

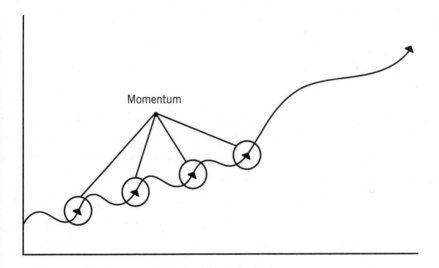

SUCCESS CYCLE

to experiment with new practices and incubate the successes that can grow into cultural legends. A tribe can also provide the positive peer pressure to sustain momentum. The most successful participants of the thirty-day challenge worked collectively or had a partner who served as both a sounding board and accountability point.

You might start small by finding a couple of colleagues or friends who read this book and want to take the challenge. You might then create an online learning community. Or you may choose to join a community of leaders around the world who aspire to lead like a Multiplier. By joining forces with a community, you need not have all the answers—or even all the questions. You can look to the genius of the group to guide you.

The Multiplier Effect Revisited

When my colleagues and I teach the Multiplier ideas to teams and organizations, we often ask our classes, "Does any of this matter?" How does leading like a Multiplier matter to you, to your organization, or even to the world at large? Let us consider each in turn.

First, it matters to you because people will give you more. My research showed consistently that even high-performing people gave Multipliers 2× more than they gave their Diminisher counterparts. People don't give a little more; they give a lot more. They give all of their discretionary effort and mental energy. They dig deep and access reserves of brainpower that they may not even know exist. They apply the full measure of their intelligence. They reason more clearly, comprehend more completely, and learn more quickly. In the process they get smarter and more capable.

Your people will give you more, and in return they get a richly satisfying experience. "Exhausting but exhilarating" captures what people continually told us it was like to work for a Multiplier. One woman said, "It was exhausting, but I was always ready to do it again.

It is not a burnout experience—it is a buildup experience." As you become more of a Multiplier, people will flock to you because you will be "the boss to work for." You will become a Talent Magnet, attracting and developing talent while providing extraordinary returns to the company as well as to your direct reports.

Second, it matters to the organization you work for. Many organizations face the double whammy of new challenges and insufficient resources. Perhaps you can relate to one start-up that experienced years of extraordinary growth. Their strategy had been to "throw people at the problem." But, as their growth declined, they had to try to outperform their market without adding headcount. Suddenly resource leverage was as strategically important as resource allocation. A leader in a Fortune 500 company recently shared with us that in one particular division, one in three of his people was utilized below the 20 percent level! Organizations led by Multipliers can more than double the capability of their people and hence their organizations.

This is a particularly timely message. In down markets and times of scarcity, managers seek ways to get increased capability and productivity from current resources. Corporations and organizations need managers who can migrate from the logic of addition, where more resources are required to handle the increased demands, to the logic of multiplication, where leaders can more fully extract capability from their current resources. Resource leverage has the power of relevancy: it is timely, and it is also timeless.

It is timeless because even in times of abundance and growth, companies need leaders capable of multiplying the intelligence and capability of their colleagues and increasing the brainpower of the organization to support growth demands. In down markets or growth markets, leading like a Multiplier matters to the organization you work for.

Third, leading like a Multiplier matters to the world at large. Albert Einstein is credited with saying, "The significant problems we face cannot be solved at the same level of thinking we were at when we created them." What if we could access twice the levels of available intelligence and channel it to our perennial problems? What solutions could be generated if we could access the underutilized brainpower in the world? Surely we need leaders who can extract and utilize all available intelligence to solve our most complex and vital challenges. We need more than just geniuses at the top of our organizations; we need genius makers.

Genius or Genius Maker?

When Philippe Petit illegally connected a tightrope wire between the 1,368-foot Twin Towers in New York City, he still had the chance to change his mind. The moment of truth came later, when he stood with one foot perched on the building and another on the wire in front of him. The wire was bouncing up and down from the airflow between the buildings; his weight was still on his back leg. Recall how Petit described that critical moment as he stood on the edge overlooking the chasm: "I had to make a decision of shifting my weight from one foot anchored to the building to the foot anchored on the wire. Something I could not resist called me [out] on that cable." He shifted his weight and took the first step.

At the conclusion of this book, you may feel like Petit, with one foot anchored to the building of the status quo and the other anchored to the wire of change. You can remove your foot from the wire, lean back, and continue to lead the way you have in the past. Or you can shift your weight onto the wire and lead more like a Multiplier. Inertia will keep you on the building, where it is comfortable and safe. But for many of us there is also a force pulling us out onto the wire and to a more impactful and fulfilling way of leading others.

Leading like a Multiplier is a choice we encounter daily or perhaps in every moment. What choices are you making? How will these choices affect what the people around you become? Is it possible that the choice you make about how you lead can impact not just your team, or even your immediate sphere of influence, but generations to come? A single Accidental Diminisher turned Multiplier can have a profound and far-reaching impact in a world where the challenges are great and full intelligence underutilized.

It seems possible that there are Diminisher assumptions holding whole businesses back. What could happen if one aspiring Multiplier introduced people around them to these ideas? What would happen if an organization currently operating on 50 percent of its intelligence moved to 100 percent? When Accidental Diminishers become Multipliers, they are like Sir Galahad, whose "strength was as the strength of ten." This is because Multipliers are the key to everyone else's intelligence. A Multiplier is the key to unlocking capability. A single Multiplier matters.

It is plausible that Diminisher assumptions are underlying failing schools. What would transpire at one school if one principal learned to lead like a Multiplier and found a way to give teachers, parents, and students greater ownership for the success of the school? What if these students and teachers learned and adopted these new assumptions together? How would families be transformed if parents led like Multipliers in their homes?

Many governments are suffocating, even collapsing. Is it possible for our civic leaders to seed challenges and then turn to the community for answers? Could answers to our most vexing challenges be found through rigorous debate and the extraction of the full intelligence of the community? Could Diminishing leaders be replaced by true Multipliers, inspiring collective intelligence and capability on a mass scale?

I believe that the diminishing cultures we see in organizations, schools, and even families are not inevitable. Indeed, in the last analysis, diminishing cultures may simply be unsustainable. To the extent that these cultures are based on incorrect assumptions, they violate the truth about how people work and thrive. Like many historical empires, they will eventually collapse. It may be that the only institutions left standing in turbulent times are those that know how to harvest the abundance of intelligence available and operate on Multiplier assumptions.

Finally, the way you choose to lead not only matters for the type of organizations we build and for the people you lead, it can matter for you as well. It will shape how you think about yourself, and it will define the legacy you leave. How do you want to be remembered as a leader? Someone with a big personality? Or someone around whom other people grew? To be a Multiplier, you don't need to shrink. To grow people around you, you need to play in a way that invites others to play big. I think you'll find that as you bring out the best in others, you also bring out the best in yourself.

We began this inquiry with an intriguing observation about two political leaders paraphrased by Bono, musician and global activist. He said, "It has been said that after meeting with the great British Prime Minister William Ewart Gladstone, you left feeling he was the smartest person in the world, but after meeting with his rival Benjamin Disraeli, you left thinking you were the smartest person." The observation captures the essence and the power of a Multiplier.

Perhaps you stand with one foot on the building and the other on the wire, deciding whether to shift your weight and take that first step. The choice matters. Which will you be: a genius? Or a genius maker?

Chapter Nine Summary

Becoming a Multiplier

Starting the Journey

1. Resonance
2. Realization of the Accidental Diminisher
3. Resolve to be a Multiplier

The Accelerators

1. Start with the assumptions
2. Work the extremes (neutralize a weakness; top off a strength)
3. Run an experiment
4. Ask a colleague
5. Brace yourself for setbacks

Elements of a Culture

- *Common language:* Words and phrases that hold a common meaning within a community based on opinions, principles, and values
- *Learned behaviors:* A set of learned responses to stimuli
- *Shared beliefs:* The acceptance of something as true
- *Heroes and legends:* People who are admired or idealized for their qualities, behavior, and/or achievements and the stories told about heroic actions
- *Rituals and norms:* Consistent behavior regularly followed by an individual or a group

Building a Multiplier Culture

Cultural Element	Multiplier Practice
Common Language	1. Hold a book talk
	2. Discuss Accidental Diminishers
Learned Behaviors	3. Introduce Multiplier mindsets
	4. Teach Multiplier skills
	5. Fuse Multipliers with daily decisions
Shared Beliefs	6. Codify a leadership ethos
Heroes and Legends	7. Spotlight Multiplier moments
	8. Measure managers
Rituals and Norms	9. Pilot a Multiplier practice
	10. Integrate practices with business metrics

Acknowledgments

It should be obvious by now that this book is the work of many people, not just one or two. I am indebted to so many and would like to thank everyone who has offered insights and put their thumbprint on this work.

The first group is perhaps the least obvious and the most essential: the nominators—the original people we interviewed, who told us of their experiences working with the Multipliers and Diminishers throughout their careers, and the dozens of people who shared their experiences and strategies for dealing with diminishing bosses. The witness protection program requires that I don't list their names, but they know who they are. This book exists because they have shared their experiences and insights. Of course, there are the Multipliers who allowed us to study them and who have shared their stories, and appendix C, "The Multipliers," lists these. These leaders, and the other rock stars whose stories I couldn't fit into the book, were a constant inspiration. It is my hope that their way of leadership inspires countless more leaders like them.

Next, the book was made stronger by a team of reviewers who read early versions of the book and helped polish the ideas. Your comments both kept me on track and kept me going. For the first edition, a big shout-out goes to: Evette Allen, Shannon Colquhoun, Sally Crawford, Margie Duffy, Peter Fortenbaugh, Holly Goodliffe,

Sebastian Gunningham, Ranu Gupta, John Hall, Kirsten Hansen, Jade Koyle, Matt Macauley, Stu Maclennan, Justin McKeown, Sue Nelson, Todd Paletta, Ben Putterman, Gordon Rudow, Stefan Schaffer, Lisa Shiveley, Stan Slap, Hilary Somorjai, John Somorjai, Fronda Stringer Wiseman, Ilana Tandowsky, Guryan Tighe, Mike Thornberry, Jake White, Alan Wilkins, Beth Wilkins, John Wiseman, Britton Worthen, and Bruce and Pam Worthen. For the second edition, my thanks go to: Ellen Gorbunoff, Deborah Keep, Dustin Lewis, Rob Maynes, Eunice Nichols, Ryan Nichols, Ben Putterman, and Andrew Wilhelms.

There were several people who went so far and above the role of reviewer that I need to broadcast a special thank-you to them. These folks offered new ideas, interesting stories, voluntary rewrites, plus good old-fashioned moral support. If this were a crime scene investigation, the following people would have more than thumbprints on the work—their DNA would be all over it: Jesse Anderson, Heidi Brandow, Amy Hayes Stellhorn, Mike Lambert, Matt Lobaugh, Greg Pal, Gadi Shamia, and Kristine Westerlind. For the second edition, the following individuals are master practitioners of Multipliers and offered insights, examples, reviews, and more: Heidi Brandow, Rick de Rijk, Rob DeLange, Jennifer Dryer, Elise Foster, Alyssa Gallagher, Jon Haverley, Hazel Jackson, Megan Lambert, and Jeffrey Ong. And I owe a particular debt to my mother and on-demand editor, Lois Allen. For both the first and the second edition, she pretended this was just another high school term paper and reviewed every word and fixed countless errors so others could review the ideas without being distracted. Mom, you continue to make me better.

The following people offered critical data analysis for our numerous surveys: Jared Wilson and Jim Mortensen of BYU; Crystal Hughes, Derek Murphy, and Josh Sheets at the Booth Company; and Chad Foster, a brilliant engineer who so readily and generously shares his native genius with us. Credit for the graphics work goes to the brilliant team at Big Monocle and to Anthony Gambol.

I was fortunate to land a highly experienced and collaborative publishing team at HarperCollins. While many authors feel beat up, I felt built up by the team. This was made possible by my insightful editor, Hollis Heimbouch. Hollis, thank you for "getting it" instantly, for guiding me, and for so deeply embracing what it means to be a Multiplier in your own work. And thanks to Matthew Inman and Stephanie Hitchcock and the team at HarperCollins for your diligent labors on behalf of this book. To Shannon Marven, my agent at Dupree-Miller, thanks for signing up with us, for your tenacity, and for making this all possible.

There are a few people whose role has been much broader than just this book that I must acknowledge. I have been fortunate to have many great mentors who have let me borrow their minds and see the world through their most brilliant lenses. Here are a few who have shaped my views and who have influenced this book profoundly. The late Dr. C. K. Prahalad, a great management thinker, taught me the importance of reaching deep into an organization for intelligence and how to build collective intent. C. K. encouraged these ideas, helped me unearth the core assumptions, and guided the book in many ways. I have always been proud just to be C. K.'s student, and now I am proud to be among those who continue his work and honor his legacy. Dr. J. Bonnor Ritchie, professor and peace broker, early on shared with me (and each of his students) his insatiable intellectual curiosity and inspired us to truly embrace ambiguity. Ray Lane, an extraordinary business leader, taught me how to lead, and was a Multiplier to me and so many others. Kerry Patterson, writer and great teacher, raised my sights and encouraged me to write this book not just for corporate managers but for leaders all across the world. Kerry, thank you for coaching and pushing me harder, even when it involved a good beating.

My sincere appreciation goes to my early collaborator and thought partner Greg McKeown. This book is better thanks to his fanatical need for clarity, high aspirations, and his relentless pursuit of truth in all he does. Thank you for being instrumental in this journey. This second edition would not be possible without the brilliant team at The Wiseman Group: Karina Wilhelms has served as project manager, editor, and my thought partner through every step in this process. Her ability to think deeply and move quickly while keeping her cool inspires me every day. The team was completed by Alyssa Gallagher, who conducted research and contributed an important update of the Multiplier experiments, Shawn Vanderhoven, who contributed critical thinking for Chapter 9 and who lent his brilliance to the graphics work, Judy Jung, who managed the entire interview process and who makes it possible for me to continue teaching and learning, and Heidi Brandow who has not only contributed ideas and reviews, but who has spend the last five years teaching practitioners around the work how to teach managers how to be Multiplier leaders, a role she has played brilliantly and passionately. Thank you all for challenging me and making work a pleasure.

My deepest appreciation goes to my husband, Larry, for believing in this project from day one, for guarding my space to work like a watchdog, and for making me feel like a genius every day of my life.

To each of the above, thank you for so generously contributing your time and energy in bringing forward these ideas. I hope that I have done justice to what you've given me.

The Research Process

Here you will find a detailed account of the research conducted to study the differences between Diminishers and Multipliers. We outline the research process in four phases: 1) the foundation work for the research; 2) the research itself; 3) the development of the Multiplier model; and 4) dealing with diminishers research.

Phase 1: The Foundation

RESEARCH TEAM. While Greg and I were the primary members of the research team, C. K. Prahalad served as an important, informal research adviser. While many people contributed to the research in the book, our core was as follows:

Liz Wiseman, Master of Organizational Behavior, Marriott School of Management, Brigham Young University

Greg McKeown, Master of Business Administration, Stanford Graduate School of Business

C. K. Prahalad, Paul and Ruth McCracken Distinguished University Professor of Corporate Strategy at the Ross School of Business of the University of Michigan

RESEARCH QUESTION. Through an iterative process, we refined our research question to this one (which has two parts): "What are the vital few differences between intelligence Diminishers and intelligence Multipliers, and what impact do they have on organizations?"

A contrast is inherent in this question. We reasoned that it wasn't enough to study Multipliers. As Jim Collins has explained, if you studied exclusively gold medalists at the Olympics, you might erroneously conclude that they won because they all had coaches. It is only by contrasting winners with the people who lost that you realize that everyone has a coach, so having a coach cannot be the active ingredient in winning.[1] We were looking for the active ingredients or differentiating factors.

DEFINITION OF KEY TERMS. To be able to answer our research question, we first defined our three key terms: Diminisher, Multiplier, and intelligence.

> **DIMINISHER:** a person who led an organization or management team that operated in silos, found it hard to get things done, and, despite having smart people, seemed to not be able to do what it needed to do to reach its goals.

> **MULTIPLIER:** a person who led an organization or management team that was able to understand and solve hard problems rapidly, achieve its goals, and adapt and increase its capacity over time.

> **INTELLIGENCE:** In our literature review we found a paper that identified more than seventy definitions of intelligence.[2] One paper that was important to us throughout the research process was signed by fifty-two researchers in 1994. They agreed that intelligence was "the ability to reason, plan, solve problems, think abstractly, comprehend complex ideas, learn quickly and

learn from experience. It is not . . . narrow. . . . [I]t is a broader and deeper capability for comprehending our surroundings—'catching on,' 'making sense' of things, or 'figuring out' what to do."[3] Beyond this, we included the ability to adapt to new environments, learn new skills, and accomplish difficult tasks.

INDUSTRY SELECTION. Having first observed the Diminisher/Multiplier phenomenon at Oracle, a software company, we opted to research the phenomenon in other companies within the broader technology industry. These companies included:

Technology Industry	Company
Biotech	Affymetrix
Online Retailing	Amazon
Consumer Electronics	Apple
Networking and Communications	Cisco
Internet Search	Google
Microprocessors	Intel
Computer Software	Microsoft
Enterprise Software Applications	SAP

Phase 2: The Research

NOMINATORS. Instead of trying to identify Diminishers and Multipliers ourselves, we found people who would nominate these leaders for us. We used two criteria in the selection of our nominators. The first was that they should be successful professionals. It was important that these individuals had positive career experiences to draw from. We reasoned that interviewing people who had an "ax to grind" could skew the data. The second criterion was that these nominators have approximately ten years' management experience themselves. We wanted practical insight from people who had grappled with challenges of leading others. It is worth noting that nominators at many of the above companies pointed us to both Multipliers and Diminishers they had worked with at entirely different companies and often industries.

RESEARCHER-ADMINISTERED SURVEY. We asked the nominators to rate the Multipliers and Diminishers they had identified on a five-point scale against forty-eight leadership practices. We designed the list to be comprehensive, drawing upon standard competency models, popular leadership frameworks, and practices we hypothesized would differentiate Diminishers from Multipliers.

The survey included *skills* (e.g., "Focuses on the customer"; "Demonstrates intellectual curiosity"; "Develops the talent of the team"; and "Business acumen") and *mindsets* (e.g., "Sees their role as a primary thought leader" and "Sees intelligence as continually developing"). We collected the results of this survey and analyzed the data in several ways. We looked for the largest deltas between Multipliers and Diminishers, the top skills and mindsets of Multipliers, and the skills most correlated with the top mindsets of Multipliers and Diminishers.

THE RESEARCH PROCESS

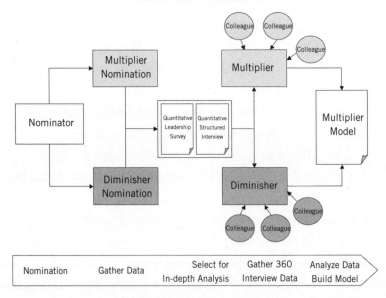

STRUCTURED INTERVIEWS. In the original interviews with the nominators, we followed a structured format. We used the same questions in the same order to minimize context effects, or at least hold them constant, so we could ensure reliable aggregation and comparison of the answers we received across different interviews and time frames.

All the interviews were conducted between October 2007 and October 2009, with the first round taking place in 2007. The interviews averaged between sixty and ninety minutes and were conducted in-person or by telephone. We kept written transcripts of all the conversations so we would have a permanent record of quotations and examples. While we followed a structured format, we allowed ourselves some latitude in determining how much time to devote to each question. Our typical format for an interview kept to the following narrative structure:

1. *Identification of two leaders:* one who stifled intelligence and the other who amplified it
2. *Identification of an experience or story working with each leader*
3. *Context for working with Diminisher:* experience, setting
4. *Impact on nominator:* percentage of nominator's capability used
5. *Impact on group:* role played in group process, perception in broader organization
6. *Leader's actions:* what was done or not done to impact others
7. *Result of actions:* outcomes, deliverables accomplished
8. Repeat questions 3 through 7 for the nominated Multiplier

IN-DEPTH INTERVIEWS. We conducted a second round of interviews to gather more information about the strongest Multipliers. This included: a) interviews with the Multipliers themselves; b) second interviews with the nominators to gather greater detail and understanding; and c) an in-depth 360 process interviewing both former and current members of the Multiplier's management team.

INDUSTRY EXPANSION. As we extended our research to eventually include 144 different leaders, we found more examples within our original target companies, added more companies within the technology and biotech industries, and went beyond these industries entirely to include others in the for-profit sector as well as nonprofits and government agencies. Our research journey took us across four continents and introduced us to a rich and diverse set of leaders (see appendix C, "The Multipliers"). The following is a list of organizations where we studied Multipliers. In order to provide confidentiality, we are not publishing the list of companies where we studied Diminishers.

Industry	Example Companies
Biotech	Hexal, Affymetrix
Green Tech	Bloom Energy, Better Place
Education	Stanford University, VitalSmarts
Entertainment	DreamWorks Studios
Government	White House, Israeli Army
Manufacturing	GM Daewoo, Flextronics
Nonprofit	Boys and Girls Club of the Peninsula, Green Belt Movement, Bennion Center, Unitus
Private Equity and Venture Capitalists	Advent International, Kleiner Perkins Caufield & Byers
Professional Services	Bain & Company, McKinsey & Company
Retailing	Gap, Lands End, Gymboree
Sports	Highland High School Rugby, North Carolina State University women's basketball program
Technology Industry	Amazon, Apple, Cisco, Infosys Technologies, Hewlett-Packard, Intel, Intuit, Microsoft, SAP, Salesforce
Workers' Union	Self-Employed Women's Association

Phase 3: The Model

We gathered approximately four hundred pages of interview transcripts, read them multiple times, and collated them for cross-interview analysis. We then took this theme analysis and calibrated it against the quantitative data we had gathered from the leadership survey. Finally, we adhered to a disciplined and rigorous debate methodology for crafting each of the disciplines that eventually became chapters for the book.

Both Greg and I claim to have been severely beaten up by each other during this debate process. We hope the research is stronger for it.

Phase 4: Dealing with Diminishers

While the original research for this book was conducted in 2007 through 2009, the research for chapter 8, "Dealing with Diminishers," was conducted in 2016. The goal of the research was to better understand the depth and breadth of impact caused by Diminishers and to ascertain strategies for minimizing the damaging, reductive effect of these Diminishers. The research was conducted by Liz Wiseman, Karina Wilhelms, Alyssa Gallagher, and Jared Wilson, all of The Wiseman Group. The research comprised the following:

IN-DEPTH INTERVIEWS. I conducted twenty-four interviews with successful professionals to understand how to survive, and potentially thrive, under diminishing bosses and colleagues. Interviewees were selected based on two criteria: 1) their overall career success and skill in navigating complex organizational situations; and 2) their understanding of the concept of Multipliers and Diminishers. In each interview, interviewees identified situations in which they worked for a Diminisher and then answered a series of questions to explore their coping strategies and to assess the effectiveness of these strategies.

BROAD SURVEY. The Wiseman Group conducted a survey of approximately two hundred participants with the objective of uncovering the best strategies for dealing with Diminishers, to understand why some people seem to be more easily diminished than others, and to understand if individuals who have been chronically diminished are more or less likely to become Diminishers to others. The survey provided many useful insights on both effective and ineffective strategies for dealing with Diminishers, as well as some of the factors that cause some people to experience a greater diminishing effect than others. The survey did not yield conclusive data on whether or not those who have been chronically diminished are more likely to lead like Diminishers themselves. More data is needed to adequately address this issue.

TESTING OF STRATEGIES. After formulating the thirteen strategies outlined in chapter 8, we invited several people (who had participated in the above-mentioned survey) to test out the strategies with their Diminisher bosses for a fourteen-day period. The goal of the fourteen-day challenge was to determine if the strategy could make a marked difference in the situation in just 2 weeks. We then collected information about the result of their experiment and held a conference call to review results. Five people completed the experiments and all five reported a marked (if not remarkable) change in the relationship with their diminishing colleague or with their overall happiness and outlook. My favorite was the person who chose to "turn down the volume" and, instead of obsessing about work, channeled his energy into experimenting with new recipes and cooking delicious meals for his wife and children each night. Not only was he happier at work and in general, but his wife was pretty thrilled, too.

LITERATURE REVIEW. We scanned the existing "victim" literature for insights on positive coping strategies. In general, we found little crossover into the workplace setting and therefore focused on the interview and survey data to formulate the best coping strategies.

Frequently Asked Questions

ARE PEOPLE EITHER DIMINISHERS OR MULTIPLIERS OR ARE THERE PEOPLE IN THE MIDDLE?

We see the Diminisher–Multiplier model as a continuum with a few people at the extremes and most of us somewhere in between. As people have been introduced to this material, they almost always see some of the Diminisher and some of the Multiplier within themselves. One leader we've worked with is illustrative. He was a smart and aware individual who didn't fit the archetype of a Diminisher, and yet when he read the material he could see how he sometimes behaved in a diminishing manner. When we study this leadership phenomenon as a contrast, we see the model as a continuum or spectrum, with the majority of us somewhere in the middle.

COULD I BE A DIMINISHER TO SOME PEOPLE AND A MULTIPLIER TO OTHERS?

Yes, the secret to understanding this dynamic is to better understand the assumptions that you hold about the two different people. In fact, you might even be behaving in similar ways around both, but your assumptions might cause your behavior to be construed in different ways.

COULD I BE A MOST-OF-THE-TIME MULTIPLIER AND AN OCCASIONAL DIMINISHER?

Certain situations can bring out the worst in us. Most leaders, even the best ones, tend to have some Diminisher tendencies that are awakened in certain situations, particularly when: a) there's a crisis (see the question below); b) when the stakes are high; c) when time is short; and d) when they are generally stressed. What's important is having awareness of the situations that provoke our diminishing tendencies and then finding workarounds.

Rob Delange, Multiplier master practitioner, described it this way: "When you lead like a Multiplier by rule, you can be a Diminisher by exception"—meaning, if you have built a strong foundation of trust with your team, they are likely to forgive your diminishing moment. This is especially true if you call attention to your diminishing moments, explain your reasoning, and then return to your more normal Multiplier style. The real key is to string together as many Multiplier moments as you can.

ARE THERE TIMES (PARTICULARLY DURING A CRISIS) WHEN DIMINISHER LEADERSHIP IS CALLED FOR?

Yes, there are situations where there is a legitimate crisis and a leader needs to jump in and manage by fiat. But these situations don't need to be diminishing. Wise leaders can keep these situations from having a diminishing effect by doing the following:

1. **TREAT THEM LIKE TRUE EXCEPTIONS.** When a manager leads like a Multiplier by rule, they can get away with operating like a Diminisher by exception. Here's an illustration. While I was teaching a leadership seminar at a hospital for the Yale Medical School, several physician-leaders who over-

see residency programs voiced an intriguing frustration. While they wanted to give the resident physicians space and freedom to do their best work, the life-and-death nature of their work forced them to micromanage and bark orders. They insisted that there was no room for learning or being a Multiplier leader when someone is flatlining on the operating table. I agreed and asked, "What percentage of your time is spent in these situations?" They suggested it was probably 3 to 5 percent of their time. I acknowledged their dilemma, but suggested that the other 95 percent of their time might warrant a different leadership approach. Several months later, I had a similar conversation at the US Navy Postgraduate School with a group of officers who commanded military ships. They estimated that, at most, 2 to 3 percent of their time dealt with life-or-death moments. Yes, these critical situations aren't Multiplier moments. But the other 95 to 97 percent of the time just might be.

2. **LET PEOPLE KNOW WHAT YOU ARE DOING.** Instead of randomly micromanaging or dictating, let people know you are in one of those 3 to 5 percent moments and need to take over. Better yet, ask for their permission. When you are done, return control to your team. Or you can let your team know the parts of the business that you need to manage very closely yourself (and explain why). Tell them that you want them to step up and be big in the other parts of the business.

In allowing for these exceptional situations, I would still emphasize that most situations, even extreme ones, can be viewed through either a Diminisher or Multiplier lens. Situations people often think call for a Diminisher approach can be exactly the time to call upon the full intellectual horsepower of the people around you. When the stakes are high, when the challenges are complex and nonlinear—

those may be just the times when the Multiplier approach is most relevant.

THIS IS GREAT FOR TOP TALENT, BUT WHAT ABOUT MY BOTTOM PERFORMERS?

While everyone has something to contribute, not everyone is contributing at the same level. Multipliers see talent less like an industrial park (a sprawling collection of near identical three-story buildings) and more like a city skyline, where buildings of varying heights and colors create a jagged, irregular profile. To Multipliers, people are such skylines. They appreciate the rich diversity of intelligence and talent around them. They acknowledge that not everyone is at the same level of capability, but they believe that everyone's capability can increase. Instead of trying to bring everyone to the same level, they uplevel each person, building a floor or two of capacity at a time.

Here are some suggestions for leading people who appear to be low performers:

1. Start with the assumption that the person is smart and capable of being a top performer. Sometimes people need someone to expect and demand more from them.

2. Instead of asking, "Is this person smart?" ask, "In what way is this person smart?" You may not be able to turn them into your version of a top performer, but you will find out what they are brilliant at, and then can look for ways to put it to work on your top challenges.

3. Remember that low performers are often former (or potential) superstars who have been historically diminished by their leaders (often accidentally or through neglect). Even if you do all the "right" things to be a Multiplier, he or she may not respond immediately because either they aren't accustomed to being given challenging work or they have learned not to trust their managers. Start small and earn their trust.

Just because you are leading like a Multiplier doesn't mean you won't encounter performance problems. If you have chronic low performers, take care of the situation and help them move to an environment or team where they can contribute more.

HOW DO THESE DYNAMICS CHANGE ACROSS CULTURES?

The research was done in thirty-five companies on four continents. We find the Multiplier way of leading (and the positive impact it has) to be pervasive across cultures. However, we find that in cultures with high levels of hierarchy, the diminishing impact tends to be greater (with the average Diminisher receiving between 30 and 40 percent of people's intelligence instead of the global average of 48 percent). We also found that in these more hierarchical cultures, leaders need to make extra efforts and greater precautions to establish the levels of intellectual, emotional, and organizational safety people need to fully contribute their best thinking.

Mostly, remember that Multipliers don't all lead in the same way. While their individual leadership practices vary, what they share is a common mindset and assumption: a belief that the people they lead are smart and will figure it out. Also, they are aware of the impact that their own intelligence and presence has on their team and actively work to create room for others to contribute. These actions may follow different forms to be culturally appropriate.

THERE ARE SOME LEADERS YOU MENTION WHOM YOU HAVE IDENTIFIED AS MULTI-PLIERS BUT WHO ARE SOMETIMES KNOWN TO DIMINISH THE PEOPLE THEY WORK WITH. HOW DO YOU EXPLAIN THE CONTRADICTION?

Yes, this was interesting to us, too. Even in our original data pool, we occasionally found that some leaders were named as both a Diminisher and a Multiplier by different people. On closer inspection, we found this a paradox rather than a contradiction. As just one illustration, we found that some leaders had figured out how to involve their direct reports but hadn't learned to scale their leadership up and out to the broader organization. The farther removed people were from the leader, the more diminished they felt. It was a classic case of Accidental Diminishing. It appears that being a Multiplier to *everyone* takes deliberate intention and effort. A leader needs to think consciously of the people at the periphery of the organization in order to be a Multiplier to them.

WHAT ABOUT LEADERS LIKE STEVE JOBS (OR OTHER ICONIC, SUCCESSFUL LEADERS WHO APPEAR TO HAVE STRONG DIMINISHING TENDENCIES)?

Many founders and visionary leaders have a mixed bag of Diminisher and Multiplier traits. For many of these high-profile leaders, the news media focus on their Diminisher tendencies (because this story tends to be more interesting to readers). As you consider the Diminisher qualities of company founders and other iconic leaders, consider the following: 1) strong leaders (especially founders) often have Diminisher characteristics, but they often have a couple of even stronger Multiplier characteristics that compensate for their diminishing tendencies; 2) top leaders (e.g., CEOs) with Diminisher characteristics often compensate by bringing in other leaders (e.g., a president or COO) who have strong multiplier characteristics; 3) leaders with strong diminishing tendencies might be well suited to lead organizations in stable environments but struggle in complex, changing environments; and 4) company founders often start companies on the strength of their own ideas. Companies can grow to a certain size based on the strength of the founder's intelligence, but for a company to grow, become successful, and endure, at some point these leaders need to develop into Multipliers or surround themselves with other leaders who have the Multiplier effect.

WHEN YOU SAY MULTIPLIERS GET 2× MORE FROM THEIR PEOPLE, THAT SEEMS LIKE A REALLY BIG CLAIM. IS IT REALLY THAT MUCH?

Yes, the number seemed high to us at first, but for several reasons we believe the ratio is correct.

First, we asked the nominators to contrast Multipliers to Diminishers, rather than contrast Multipliers to an average manager. The 2× effect assumes a best-to-worst comparison. Second, we repeated this question to people across industry, function, and management level and have confirmation that this ratio holds true as an average. Third, the surprisingly high difference may be the result of discretionary effort. As managers we can observe whether someone is working at, above, or below their usual productivity level. What is harder to know is how much a person is holding back. The way people answer this question suggests that people believe they hold back a considerable amount around certain managers.

We have concluded that while it is an amazing difference, Multipliers really do get, on average, 2× more than their Diminisher counterparts.

DO YOU FIND SIGNIFICANT DIFFERENCES IN HOW MEN AND WOMEN LEAD?

While there may be some actual differences in how men and women lead, there seems to be far more variation within a given gender than between the genders. We don't have any data that suggests that one gender is more likely to diminish, in fact both Diminisher and Multiplier levels are remarkably consistent. However, we do find that there may be some variance in how men and women *accidentally* diminish, perhaps driven by historically narrow views of male and female leadership styles. For example, many women who began their careers in earlier generations have contorted themselves to fit into a male-defined world, choosing between ill-fitting models of leadership. Some adopted the "man-up" model and acted tougher than nails, showed no fear, and attempted to out-men the men. Others fell into the "mama bear" archetype in which they nurtured, protected, and rescued people and projects in danger. Both caricatures can have massively diminishing effects. Leaders bring out the best in others when they are authentic—being themselves rather than acting out a role, which happens when the full range of leadership styles and strengths are available to women and men.

ARE MULTIPLIERS MORE SUCCESSFUL THAN DIMINISHERS?

Yes, they are more successful *at getting more out of people.* This was amazingly consistent throughout the research. Even high-powered executives, icons in their own right, who hammered their people simply could not get as much out of people as their Multiplier counterparts. We didn't study the career trajectories of Diminishers and Multipliers themselves, but we did study the success of the people they worked around. We found that people and their careers thrived and became more successful around Multipliers than around Diminishers.

CAN EVERYONE BECOME A MULTIPLIER OR ARE THERE SOME PEOPLE WHO ARE TOO MUCH OF A DIMINISHER TO CHANGE?

Anyone who can see their Diminisher behavior can change. Anyone can be a Multiplier if they're willing to shift their center of weight and look beyond themselves. There may be a few people who are so staunchly invested in their Diminisher approach to leadership that they won't be able to change, but we think of them as outliers.

In our work teaching and coaching, we have seen people make significant changes. For example, one leader we worked with had some strong Diminisher tendencies. He worked hard to adopt a more Multiplier approach to his leadership. People noticed the difference. Then, after he took a larger role at another company, he was able to start with a clean slate and a new approach. He is now seen as a Multiplier and has even introduced these ideas to the people in his organization.

We aren't under the delusion that every Diminisher *will* change, but we believe that the vast majority can make the shift. It begins with awareness and intent.

SHOULD COMPANIES FIRE THEIR DIMINISHERS?

Smart companies don't have to fire every Diminisher, but they should remove them from key leadership roles. If someone insists on being a Diminisher, they may need to be isolated or contained where they can't do great damage. If they are removed from key leadership roles, other people's capability gets released and the Diminishers are less likely to inspire managers underneath them to adopt Diminisher leadership practices.

This is easier said than done. Diminishers are, by definition, smart and intimidating. The course of least resistance is to keep them in their leadership roles. But once you start to calculate the high cost of Diminishers in your organization, you will be better prepared to take action. For example, if you had a machine that was a bottleneck, causing the rest of your production line to operate at 50 percent capacity, you would see immediately how expensive that machine was to your operation. If you replaced that one machine, you could double the capacity and throughput of your entire production line! That is what is at stake with every Diminisher you have in a key leadership role. Even if they are operating at full capacity, they operate as a bottleneck to everyone else around them. So, while the answer may not be to fire every Diminisher, we suggest that it's just too expensive to leave them in key leadership roles.

SHOULD I EVEN TRY TO HAND THIS BOOK TO A RAGING DIMINISHER?

Yes, drop it and run! Or perhaps you can send it from one of your other Diminisher colleagues!

More seriously, if you share the book from a Diminisher's perspective, by judging and dictating, you are likely to make them close down and continue the Diminishing cycle. However, if you approach it as a Multiplier, and make it safe for someone to learn new ideas, you might find surprising levels of receptiveness and impact. Here are two Multiplier strategies:

1. **FOCUS ON YOUR OWN EXPERIENCE.** You might begin by acknowledging how each of us can be an Accidental Diminisher at times, and say something like, "This book has shown

me how I sometimes diminish people without meaning to." Or you can focus on the impact it has had for you and introduce it with, "I've been working on being more of a Multiplier and I'm seeing how it is increasing performance on my team. I thought you might be interested, too."

2. **FOCUS ON THE UPSIDE TO THE ORGANIZATION.** Most managers would be interested in doubling the capacity of their organization. You could introduce the ideas with, "I think we have more intelligence in our organization than we've been able to tap into. I think there are some things that we could do as a leadership team to raise the IQ level of our organization."

Additionally, you could introduce the ideas indirectly by holding a brown-bag lunch discussion or by sharing a single idea or Multiplier practice. We believe that there is a way to share this material with almost anyone, but you are more likely to succeed if you approach it like a Multiplier. You can't diminish people into being Multipliers!

DO I NEED TO HAVE ALL FIVE OF THE MULTIPLIER DISCIPLINES TO BE A MULTIPLIER LEADER?

No, a leader doesn't need to be brilliant at all five of the disciplines to be a Multiplier and to get the Multiplier effect across their team. In fact, very few of the leaders that I studied had strength in all five—most had three or four strong disciplines. You can use the Multipliers 360 assessment to determine your relative highs and lows. A good development strategy is to identify your strongest discipline and get really great at it. Then make sure you don't fall into Diminisher territory in any one discipline. After this, do what you can to build strength in one or two more of the Multiplier disciplines.

IF I COULD DO ONE THING TO GET ON THE PATH OF MULTIPLIER, WHAT SHOULD IT BE?
The one thing we would suggest you do is to ask really insightful and interesting questions that make people think. This is a practical step and it applies across all of the disciplines. For example, whether you are trying to become a Liberator, a Challenger, or a Debate Maker, asking insightful and interesting questions will get you started down the correct path. So, if you are looking to build one skill, start with questions.

If you want to work on one assumption, we would suggest trying *People are smart and will figure it out.* One way to do this is ask, "How is this person smart?" That one question can interrupt any tendencies to judge people in a binary fashion and can work like a fast pass into the Technicolor world where Multipliers live.

APPENDIX C

The Multipliers

The following is a list of the "Hall of Fame" Multipliers featured in this book. Several appear in multiple chapters, but they are listed only once below, in the chapter where they are featured most prominently.

Multiplier	Featured Role	Current Role
Chapter 1: The Multiplier Effect		
Commander Abbot	Commander, U.S. Navy	
George Schneer	Division Manager, Intel	Executive-in-residence, Sevin Rosen Funds; partner, Horizon Ventures
Tim Cook	COO, Apple Inc.	CEO, Apple Inc.
Deborah Lange	SVP, taxation, Oracle Corporation	Retired
George Clooney	Actor	Actor; activist
Chapter 2: The Talent Magnet		
Mitt Romney	Consulting Manager, Bain & Company	Political Leader
Andreas Strüengmann	Cofounder, Hexal, Germany	Investor
Thomas Strüengmann	Cofounder, Hexal, Germany	Investor

Multiplier	Featured Role	Current Role
Larry Gelwix	Head Coach, Highland High School Rugby	CEO, Columbus Travel
Alyssa Gallagher	Assistant superintendent, Los Altos School District	Director of Global Leadership Development Practice, The Wiseman Group
Marguerite Gong Hancock	Girls' camp director	Executive director, Exponential Center, Computer History Museum
K. R. Sridhar	CEO, Bloom Energy	CEO, Bloom Energy
Chapter 3: The Liberator		
Robert Enslin	President, SAP North America	President of global customer operations, SAP AG
Ernest Bachrach	Managing partner, Advent International, Latin America	Director and special partner, Advent International Corporation
Steven Spielberg	Film director	Film director
Patrick Kelly	8th-grade social studies and history teacher	8th-grade social studies and history teacher
Casey Lehner	Senior director of global design operations, Nike Inc.	Senior director of global workplace experience, Nike Inc.
Ray Lane	President, Oracle	Investor
John Brandon	Vice president, channel sales, Apple Inc.	Vice president, international sales, Apple Inc.
Mark Dankberg	CEO, ViaSat	CEO, ViaSat
Chapter 4: The Challenger		
Matt McCauley	CEO, Gymboree	Retired
Irene Fisher	Director, Bennion Center	Community activist
C. K. Prahalad	Professor, University of Michigan	Passed away April 16, 2010

Multiplier	Featured Role	Current Role
Alan G. Lafley	CEO, Procter & Gamble	Executive chairman, Procter & Gamble; coauthor, *The Game Changer*
Sean Mendy	Director, Center for the New Generation, Boys and Girls Club of the Peninsula	Senior director, Development at Boys and Girls Club of the Peninsula
Wangari Maathai	Founder, Green Belt Movement, Africa, 2004 Laureate, Nobel Prize for Peace	Passed away September 25, 2011
Chapter 5: The Debate Maker		
Arjan Mengerink	District police chief, Eastern Netherlands	District police chief, Eastern Netherlands
Lutz Ziob	GM, Microsoft Learning, Microsoft Corporation	Dean, 4Afrika Academy, Microsoft Corporation
Tim Brown	CEO and president, IDEO	CEO and president, IDEO
Sue Siegel	President, Affymetrix	CEO, GE Ventures, Licensing, & Healthymagination, General Electric
Chapter 6: The Investor		
Jae Choi	Partner, McKinsey & Company, Korea	Executive managing director, chief strategy officer, construction equipment, Doosan Infracore, Korea
Elaben Bhatt	Founder, SEWA, India	Member, The Elders World Council
John Chambers	CEO, Cisco Systems	Executive chairman, Cisco Systems
John Wookey	Executive vice president, Oracle; executive vice president, SAP	Executive vice president, industry applications, Salesforce

Multiplier	Featured Role	Current Role
Michael Clarke	Division president, Flextronics	President and CEO, Nortek Inc.
Kerry Patterson	Cofounder, Interact Performance Systems	Author; cofounder, VitalSmarts
Jubin Dana	Coach, California Youth Soccer Association	Coach, California Youth Soccer Association; lawyer
Narayana Murthy	CEO, Infosys, India	Chairman emeritus, Infosys; political and business thought leader, India
Chapter 8: Dealing with Diminishers		
Sean Heritage	Commander, US Air Force	Cryptologic warfare officer, US Navy
Chapter 9: Becoming a Multiplier		
Bill Campbell	CEO, Intuit	Passed away April 18, 2016
Mike Felix	VP, Internet and entertainment field services—Midwest, AT&T	VP, Internet & entertainment field services—Midwest, AT&T

Multipliers Discussion Guide

This guide contains a set of questions for discussing Multiplier ideas as a team. As you plan your discussions, you might look for ways to create a Multiplier experience while discussing Multiplier ideas.

Chapter	Discussion Questions
The Multiplier Effect	Should a successful Diminisher try to become a Multiplier? Why?
	Can you be a Multiplier if you work for a Diminisher?
	Are there certain people who bring out the Diminisher in you? Why?
The Talent Magnet	How long does it take to develop a reputation as "the boss to work for"?
	When should you hire new people, as opposed to developing the talent of the people you already have?
The Liberator	A liberating climate gives a lot of space and expects a lot at the same time. How do you know when you have gone too far with either element?
	Does being a Liberator mean you have to be both "loathed and loved," the way Mr. Kelly is at his school? (See page 75.)

Chapter	Discussion Questions
The Challenger	How can you share your own knowledge and opinions without diminishing the people you lead? What one thing could Richard Palmer do to shift from leading like a Diminisher to leading like a Multiplier? (See page 99.)
The Debate Maker	Imagine you have only thirty minutes to make a high-stakes decision. Should you still approach the decision as a Debate Maker? If no, why? If yes, how? Being a Debate Maker means driving sound decisions through a rigorous process. How do you know when there has been enough debate and it is time to make a decision?
The Investor	What is the difference between being detail oriented and micromanaging? How can you give people full ownership without becoming disengaged yourself?
Becoming a Multiplier	If you had to define one idea that is common across all five disciplines, what would it be? What discipline could you make the most progress on in the least amount of time? Is it feasible to focus on a single area of development for a year? Where is your weight on the metaphorical wire? (See page 118.)
	Of the various organizations you are part of (business, community, family), where could you implement the Multiplier approach with the greatest impact? Why?

If you'd like to lead a more structured event, you can download a full Multipliers Facilitator Guide at www.multipliersbooks.com. Use it to bring Multiplier leadership into the conversation at your workplace!

Multiplier Experiments

NAME THE GENIUS

Identify the native genius of each person on your team.

Find the native genius of individuals on your team and find novel ways to utilize their genius more fully. Do this individually or as a team so that everyone understands the native genius of each person on the team.

MULTIPLIER DISCIPLINE

Talent Magnet
Remedy for **Idea Guy**, **Always On**, and **Strategist** Accidental Diminisher

MULTIPLIER MINDSET

Everyone is brilliant at something.

MULTIPLIER PRACTICES

For Individuals:

1. **Identify it:** Find the things that this person does natively. Ask:
   - What do they do better than anything else they do?
   - What do they do better than the people around them?
   - What do they do *easily* (without effort or even awareness)?
   - What do they do *freely* (without being asked or being paid)?

2. **Label it:** Give their native genius a short name (e.g., "synthesizing complex ideas" or "building bridges" or "identifying root causes"). Test your hypothesis with the person's colleagues and with the person. Refine it until it captures their genius.

3. **Put it to use:** Identify roles or tasks that will utilize and extend this person's genius. Go beyond formal jobs and identify ad hoc roles. Have a conversation with the individual and allow them to identify the best ways to utilize their genius.

Across an entire team:

1. Define the concept of native genius.
2. Ask each person to identify the native genius of each colleague.

3. Bring the group together.
4. Focus on one individual at a time.

- Have each team member describe that person's native genius
- Ask the person to offer their own perspective
- Discuss ways to best utilize this person's genius

Lab Results

Stephanie Post, Director of Sales and Customer Training for Sysmex America, learned about "native genius" during a Multipliers workshop and was determined to find out what genius was lurking inside her new team. She recognized this as an opportunity to "get them on projects and tap into what makes them excited about coming to work." As a team they discovered the genius of each team member, and one in particular—"Kimmy, the resource genius"—stood out. She's that person that's got your back when you can't recall the name of the restaurant or a beloved spot of one of your high-profile clients…that person that remembers your boss's birthday when you can't. She's got them googled and texted to you within minutes. But more than that, she can't help herself from exploring and researching things, anything really. When it comes to her role, she's curious, exploring processes, procedures and more, without hesitation. After Stephanie named Kimmy's native genius, she then gave her the space to "in-source" a major component of their work, which resulted in financial savings and ultimately laid the groundwork for the exciting opportunity to market a new line of business.

Your Turn: Prepare for success with Multiplier practices. Use this grid to plan and reflect on your experiments.

Look for Opportunity	Increase Your Impact
Where and how might you use this experiment?	Where and how might you use this experiment?
Maximize Your Learning	**Develop Your Skill**
What happened and what is your evidence?	Where can you use this again?

SUPERSIZE IT

Give someone a job that
is a size too big.

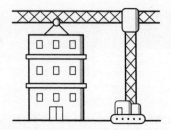

Acknowledge that everyone on your team is at different capability levels.
But everyone is capable of growth. Carve out roles and responsibilities the
way you shop for shoes for preschoolers...one size too big. And then let the
person grow into their new responsibilities.

MULTIPLIER DISCIPLINE

Talent Magnet, Challenger, Investor
Remedy for **Pacesetter** and **Protector** Accidental Diminisher

---

MULTIPLIER MINDSET

Everyone can grow.

MULTIPLIER PRACTICES

1. Map out the capability levels of your team, acknowledging that they
   will probably look more like a jagged skyline than a high-jump bar.

2. Pick one or two people who are ready for a stretch.

3. Map out a set of responsibilities beyond their current capabilities
   that will cause them to really stretch. Let them know you are giving
   them "a job" that might feel a bit too big. Affirm your belief in their
   ability to learn and grow into the role.

4. Maintain a vacuum that must be filled...by them, not you.

5. Do the same across all the individuals on your team.

Lab Results

Jessica Parisi, CEO at BTS, a business and leadership strategy company, was twelve months into launching a new approach to leadership development for their clients and realized they would need a leader at the mid level and another at the front line in order to scale the new approach. During a regularly scheduled team meeting, Megan, a relatively new BTS employee, expressed both a passion and an interest in developing the frontline leadership program. Jessica recognized that Megan was capable and had recently managed two front line leadership programs, so she took the opportunity to Supersize her role. Jess didn't care that Megan was only twenty-four years old; she saw an opportunity to partner Megan's passion with her growing expertise. Initially surprised, Megan became the go-to person globally for frontline leadership offerings. Having Megan in this role not only improved global teamwork, it also helped the more senior consultant accelerate their own adoption of the model and served as an example of what BTS expects from all partners.

Your Turn: Prepare for success with Multiplier practices. Use this grid to plan and reflect on your experiments.

Look for Opportunity	Increase Your Impact
Where and how might you use this experiment?	Where and how might you use this experiment?
Maximize Your Learning	**Develop Your Skill**
What happened and what is your evidence?	Where can you use this again?

PLAY FEWER CHIPS

Play fewer chips in a meeting.

Before a meeting, give yourself a budget of "poker chips," with each chip representing a comment or contribution to the meeting. Use your chips wisely, and leave the rest of the space for others to contribute.

MULTIPLIER DISCIPLINE

Liberator
Remedy for **Always On** and **Strategist** Accidental Diminisher

---

MULTIPLIER MINDSET

By being small, others get a chance to be big.
By being big less often, your own ideas will be more impactful.

MULTIPLIER PRACTICES

Here are some ways you might Go Big and play your chips, and when you might want to Go Small:

Go Big	Go Small
Open the meeting by framing the issue (what is the issue/decision, why is it important, how will it be discussed/ decided)	When you have the urge to say, "yes, I think that too"
Ask a big question	When you want to reframe what you heard into your own idea
Offer an idea of your own (that isn't already surfacing)	When you want to say, "I did some research, and the data validates that."
Redirect the conversation or get it back on track	
Summarize	

Lab Results

Mahmoud Mansoura, a global support delivery manager for HP Enterprise in Morocco, was inspired to rethink his contributions as a leader. After attending a Multipliers Workshop, Mahmoud could see that he was taking up too much space with his team—he realized he was always talking. He met with his team weekly and followed a practice of opening the meeting by sharing announcements and news, and giving directions to team members. This was a practice he had done for years, but now he started to pay attention to the impact on the team and wondered if others might contribute more if he talked less. Mahmoud decided to limit his contributions using the poker chips. He stopped opening the meetings with his remarks, and instead began every meeting with a roundtable where all team members were invited to share. Mahmoud was able to listen to the team share successes and challenges and watch them problem-solve. He now only intervenes when the team can use some redirection or he feels that a well-timed comment from him could have a positive impact on the team. Mahmoud has successfully shifted the amount of space he consumes in meeting through intentional practice and "poker chips."

Your Turn: Prepare for success with Multiplier practices. Use this grid to plan and reflect on your experiments.

Look for Opportunity	Increase Your Impact
Where and how might you use this experiment?	Where and how might you use this experiment?

Maximize Your Learning	Develop Your Skill
What happened and what is your evidence?	Where can you use this again?

TALK UP YOUR MISTAKES

Invite experimentation and learning by sharing your own mistakes.

Let people know the mistakes you have made and what you have learned from them. Make public how you have incorporated this learning into your decisions and current leadership practices.

MULTIPLIER DISCIPLINE

Liberator
Remedy for **Pace Setter**, **Optimist** and **Perfectionist** Accidental Diminisher

---

MULTIPLIER MINDSET

Mistakes are part of the natural learning and achievement process.

MULTIPLIER PRACTICES

1. Get personal. Reflect on your own leadership journey by charting the highs and lows of your career. Identify several of the big mistakes you've made. The bigger the better! For each mistake, identify:

   - What you did

   - What happened

   - Where you went wrong (actions or assumptions)

   - What you learned from it

   Look for opportunities to share these stories. You might share one before someone is about to tackle a challenging assignment or at the moment they make a distressing mistake.

2. Go public. Instead of talking about your and your team's mistakes behind closed doors or just one-on-one, bring them out in the open where the person making the mistake can clear the air and where everyone can learn. Try making it part of your management ritual.

   For example, you might add "screwup of the week" onto your regular team agenda. If any member of the team, including yourself, had a blunder, this is the time to go public, have a laugh and move on.

Lab Results

Quynh Vu, an Inpatient Pharmacy Manager, was inspired to "Talk Up Her Mistakes" after reading *Multipliers*. Quynh, a relatively new manager, is responsible for overseeing forty pharmacy technicians in an environment where thousands of doses are accurately prepared and efficiently delivered each day to patients admitted to the hospital. Pharmacies utilize a double-check system, which significantly reduces the error rate, but it certainly doesn't completely eliminate them. There can be errors in how medications are labeled, stored, dosed, or even dispensed. Quynh not only shared a minor mistake she had made but also took it a step further by working with other members of her department leadership in creating a "daily safety huddle" that lasts no longer than ten minutes for the 10 to 12 people on duty. During the huddle, team members are given the opportunity to share mistakes and invite team troubleshooting. Quynh said, "This safety huddle is where we invite people to openly discuss 'near misses,' which are mistakes that were caught before leaving the pharmacy, so that we can all learn from them. It also allows us to discuss opportunities for improvement."

Your Turn: Prepare for success with Multiplier practices. Use this grid to plan and reflect on your experiments.

Look for Opportunity	Increase Your Impact
Where and how might you use this experiment?	Where and how might you use this experiment?
Maximize Your Learning	**Develop Your Skill**
What happened and what is your evidence?	Where can you use this again?

MAKE SPACE FOR MISTAKES

Define a space where people can experiment, take risks, and recover.

Create a safe environment where people can take risks. Clarify the area where: a) your team members have room to experiment; and b) where the stakes are too high to allow failure.

MULTIPLIER DISCIPLINE

Liberator
Remedy for **Rescuer**, **Optimist**, **Protector** and **Perfectionist**
Accidental Diminisher

MULTIPLIER MINDSET

People learn best from the natural consequences of their actions.

MULTIPLIER PRACTICES

Create a clear "water line" above which people can experiment and take risks and still recover, but below which any mistakes or "cannon balls" might cause catastrophic failure and "sink the ship." Work with your team to understand this waterline.

1. On a white board or flipchart, make two headings.

2. Using Post-it notes, ask each individual to list a number of scenarios where it is OKAY TO FAIL and some where it is NOT OKAY TO FAIL.

3. Allow individuals to move the Post-it between categories and debate which category each belongs in. Physically move the notes until the group reaches a shared understanding.

4. Push the thinking, encouraging as many scenarios as possible to go into the "Okay to fail" category. Draw "the water line" between the categories.

5. Group like scenarios together.

6. Define the themes in each of the categories. For example:

a. It's OKAY to fail when: a) the learning is greater than the cost; b) we have time or resources to recover; or c) when customers or students are not harmed, etc.

b. It's NOT OKAY to fail when: a) it violates our ethics or values; b) it does damage to our brand/reputation in the market; c) it is career ending for someone (including the leader), etc.

7. Record the key principles above and below the water line. Share this with the team.

Lab Results

When the executive leadership team for apparel company, Banana Republic, signed up for a Multipliers workshop, they were seeking ways to enable their employees to take smart risks and innovate. They decided to create space for mistakes by identifying the parts of the business where it was OKAY to experiment and fail versus the parts of the business where success was critical. Members of the executive team captured their views on sticky notes and then placed them on a large white board, with one side labeled "OKAY TO FAIL" and the other labeled "NOT OKAY TO FAIL." The team discussed and negotiated each idea, moving sticky notes from one side of the board to the other until consensus was reached. The group of executives then stepped back and looked for a theme in each category. Within a minute or two it became abundantly clear where it was NOT OKAY TO FAIL. It could be expressed in a single word–December. The president's observation sounded like this: "Eleven months out of the year it is OKAY to experiment with product, price, promotion, etc., but we can't jeopardize December," the all-important holiday shopping season. Imagine how clarifying and liberating this was when they shared this distinction with their broader management team.

Your Turn: Prepare for success with Multiplier practices. Use this grid to plan and reflect on your experiments.

Look for Opportunity Where and how might you use this experiment?	**Increase Your Impact** Where and how might you use this experiment?
Maximize Your Learning What happened and what is your evidence?	**Develop Your Skill** Where can you use this again?

EXTREME QUESTIONS

Kick-start your curiosity by leading a conversation asking only questions.

This means everything you say ends in a question mark! Or, better put: Can you make sure that everything you say ends with a question mark?

MULTIPLIER DISCIPLINE

Challenger
Remedy for **Idea Guy**, **Always On**, **Rescuer**, **Rapid Responder**, **Strategist** and **Perfectionist** Accidental Diminisher

---

MULTIPLIER MINDSET

They want to learn from the people around them and understand.

MULTIPLIER PRACTICES

Access what the other people know. Make your points known through the questions you ask. Go all the way and only ask questions!

Think of it in terms of hours, not minutes. Challenge yourself to ask different types of questions.

- Leading questions: Lead someone toward a specific outcome

- Guiding questions: Help another see what you can see

- Discovery questions: Create an idea or solution together

- Challenge questions: Surface and question prevailing assumptions

Challenge: Questions Prevailing Assumptions

Discovery: No One Has an Answer Yet

Guiding: Helps Another See What You Can See

Leading: Directs Toward an Outcome

Open: Elicits Ideas of Explanation

Closed: Yes or No

Lab Results

Tom Mottlau, Senior National Account Manager of Healthcare Sales for LG Electronics, was asked to take ownership for bringing Mike, a new member of the sales team, on board. In the past, this assignment would have taken at least a full day of Tom's time and mostly consisted of LG employees sharing their wealth of expertise and information with new employees. After engaging in Multiplier executive coaching, Tom saw an opportunity to use Extreme Questions. Instead of making assumptions about what Mike knew, Tom prepared for their time together by writing a list of questions. Through the use of questions Tom was able to learn more about Mike's previous experiences and gauge what aspects of the onboarding process would be of most value to both Mike and LG. Starting with questions allowed Mike to cover more ground in a shortened amount of time, and what would have been a full day of meetings only required four hours of Tom's time. Even better, Mike shared that the LG induction was the most unique and potent "first day" experience he has ever had.

Your Turn: Prepare for success with Multiplier practices. Use this grid to plan and reflect on your experiments.

Look for Opportunity	Increase Your Impact
Where and how might you use this experiment?	Where and how might you use this experiment?
Maximize Your Learning	**Develop Your Skill**
What happened and what is your evidence?	Where can you use this again?

CREATE A STRETCH CHALLENGE

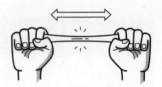

What hard thing might your team or organization be capable of?

Engage your team members by giving them a "mission impossible," something hard that will challenge them or even the entire organization. Help them see what might be possible, extend an intriguing, vivid challenge, and, then generate belief that it just might be possible.

MULTIPLIER DISCIPLINE

Challenger
Remedy for **Pacesetter**, **Protector**, and **Strategist** Accidental Diminisher

---

MULTIPLIER MINDSET

People are capable of doing hard things.

MULTIPLIER PRACTICES

- Identify the hard thing your team member or organization might be capable of doing.

- Create an intriguing, vivid, and believable challenge to engage their best thinking.

- Identify a first step that is achievable to generate belief.

- Now turn your challenge into a question that will capture their imagination.

- Ask your question; and then don't answer it. Let your team find solutions.

Lab Results

Jason Grodman, a government employee for the Pima County Regional Wastewater Reclamation Department, was given a mandate to increase productivity in his department. As the leader of ten employees focused on inspections, Jason wrestled with the best approach to take. He gathered data on the previous years and realized that the highest numbers of inspections the team had ever completed in one year was 750. Armed with this information and a desire to empower his team, Jason posed a challenge: "What would we need to do to complete 1,000 inspections in 2016?" He wasn't clear on how the team would do it, but Jason engaged their best thinking and turned the creation of the plan over to the inspectors. Not only did the inspectors create a plan, but they continually revisited the plan with new questions and insights. During the first seven months of 2016, the team had already surpassed their best year ever. Not only are they on track to meet the goal, but they will likely exceed 1,000 inspections this year. While it is motivating for the team to crush their previous record and meet the challenge head on, it is even more exciting for Jason to see the increased engagement levels across his department and experience firsthand the power of creating a stretch challenge.

Your Turn: Prepare for success with Multiplier practices. Use this grid to plan and reflect on your experiments.

Look for Opportunity	Increase Your Impact
Where and how might you use this experiment?	Where and how might you use this experiment?
Maximize Your Learning	Develop Your Skill
What happened and what is your evidence?	Where can you use this again?

MAKE A DEBATE

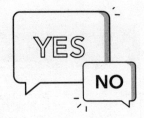

Use debate to build collective intelligence and speed to execution.

Identify an important decision. Frame the issue. Spark a debate. Reach a decision.

MULTIPLIER DISCIPLINE

Debate Maker
Remedy for **Rapid Responder** and **Optimist** Accidental Diminisher

---

MULTIPLIER MINDSET

Bring together the people who need to be involved in the decision. When people understand the logic, they know what to do.

MULTIPLIER PRACTICES

1. Frame the issue

   - Define the question: A good debate question has clear options from which to choose.

   - Explain why it is a critical question and requires debate.

   - Form the team: Ask people to come prepared with information/ data/evidence as support.

   - Clearly communicate how the decision will be made.

2. Spark the debate

   - Ask the debate question.

   - Ask people to support their positions with evidence.

   - Ask everyone to weigh in.

   - Ask people to switch positions and argue the other side.

3. Drive a sound decision

   - Re-clarify the decision-making process.

   - Make the decision.

   - Communicate the decision and the rationale.

Lab Results

Clay Gilbert, President of Thornton Brothers, Inc, a company that prides themselves on being experts in innovative janitorial, package, and safety solutions, experimented with "Make a Debate" after losing a senior member of their leadership team to an industry competitor. If Clay had followed past practice, he would have pulled in the two other executives that comprise the leadership team for a closed-door discussion. Instead, after reading Multipliers, Clay saw an opportunity to allow others in the company to share their best thinking prior to any decisions being made. Clay planned a debate. He set a meeting date, invited a cross section of employees, and asked them to come prepared with their argument. When debate day came, Clay framed the meeting with a core question centered on the company's purpose and core values. He remained neutral throughout the meeting, only interjecting to help shift thinking or stir up further debate. As a group they generated creative and solid responses, which Clay is currently working through. Although the final outcome is unknown, Clay found the experience of framing and sparking debate "freeing." Regardless of the outcome, the process required everyone to offer their best thinking, resulting in greater confidence in the decision-making process as the team moves forward.

Your Turn: Prepare for success with Multiplier practices. Use this grid to plan and reflect on your experiments.

Look for Opportunity	Increase Your Impact
Where and how might you use this experiment?	Where and how might you use this experiment?
Maximize Your Learning	Develop Your Skill
What happened and what is your evidence?	Where can you use this again?

GIVE 51% OF THE VOTE

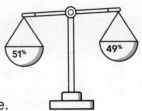

Put someone else in charge by giving that person the majority vote.

Instead of delegating work, let people know that they (not you) are in charge and accountable. Tell them they get 51% of the vote, but 100% of the accountability.

MULTIPLIER DISCIPLINE

Liberator and **Investor**
Remedy for **Always On**, **Rescuer** and **Perfectionist** Accidental Diminisher

---

MULTIPLIER MINDSET

People operate at their best when they are in charge and held accountable for their work.

MULTIPLIER PRACTICES

1. Identify the project you are going to transfer to a team member.

2. Describe the project and answer questions to ensure understanding.

3. Give them the majority vote and give it a number to make it concrete.

For example, tell them they have 51% of the vote and you have only 49%. Or, go wild and make it 75/25%. Anything over 50% will carry the message: You are in charge. You get final decision.

Be sure they understand what 51% (or more) means:

- You are in charge (hence, I am not).

- You get to make the final decisions (I will weigh in, but if we disagree, you make the call).

- I expect you to be the one to move things forward (I will participate, but will follow your lead).

You can really punctuate the point by saying (with a twinkle in your eye!):

"You're 51%. I'm 49%. So, I'm taking this off my to-do list."

Implication: "I'll assume it is on yours!"

Lab Results

Stacey and Jim were leading an early-morning theology class for high school students. These teachers had a vision for a big, end-of-year showcase where the students could show off what they had learned to their parents, much like a back-to-school night. This was not only a new idea, but also something Stacey and Jim wanted the students to lead themselves, especially the older students who would be graduating soon. So, they gathered the seniors together one evening at Stacey's house for dessert. Stacey and Jim shared their vision, gave the students some parameters and then told them they were in charge and could plan any type of event that met the criteria. The students began discussing ideas but kept deferring to the teachers. Stacey made it clear that the students were the ones who were actually in charge, and told them they had the deciding vote. To make it clear, Jim and Stacey got up and left the room. Stacey made herself busy in the kitchen and Jim sat down at the piano and played. When they returned to the room ten or fifteen minutes later, they discovered that the students had come up with a fun idea, made assignments, and had a list of things they needed from the teachers. The students continued to lead the planning and pulled off an absolutely spectacular event that was above anything Stacey and Jim could have imagined (or organized themselves).

Your Turn: Prepare for success with Multiplier practices. Use this grid to plan and reflect on your experiments.

Look for Opportunity	Increase Your Impact
Where and how might you use this experiment?	Where and how might you use this experiment?
Maximize Your Learning	Develop Your Skill
What happened and what is your evidence?	Where can you use this again?

GIVE IT BACK

Give ownership back
to the person it belongs to.

When someone brings you a problem that you think they are capable of solving, give it back to them and ask for the "F-I-X." (See page 186.) Play the role of coach rather than problem solver.

If someone legitimately needs help, jump in (take "the pen") and contribute, but then clearly give ownership back.

MULTIPLIER DISCIPLINE

The Investor
Remedy for **Idea Guy** and **Rescuer** Accidental Diminisher

---

MULTIPLIER MINDSET

People are smart and will figure it out.

MULTIPLIER PRACTICES

1. **Ask for the F-I-X:** When someone brings you a problem, ask them to complete the thought process and provide a solution (an F-I-X). Use coaching questions like these to offer help, but maintain their ownership for the work:

   • What solution(s) do you see to this problem?

   • How would you propose we solve this?

   • What would you like to do to fix this?

2. **Give the "pen" back:** When your team members are struggling, offer help, but have an exit plan. Here are some statements and questions that will help you clarify that you are giving back ownership.

   • I'm happy to help you think this through, but you are still the lead on this.

   • Those are thoughts to consider. You can take it from here.

   • I'm here to back you up. What do you need from me as you lead this?

Lab Results

Dave Havlek is a capable executive who describes himself as "super-stressed and super-opinionated." He is the head of Investor Relations for Salesforce .com, a high growth cloud computing business known for its fast innovation and perpetual change. Despite working frequently till 12:30 a.m. and beyond, Dave still was a bottleneck to his group. People were left wondering what they should be doing while he figured things out and gave directions. When faced with a pressing need to determine a staffing plan to get his resource-strapped team through an eight-week crunch, but out of time to come up with the solution himself, Dave (who had spent the day in a Multipliers leadership training program) broke from his usual management modus operandi. Instead of figuring out the answer himself, he decided to give the task back to his team in the form of a question. The team was instantly energized, thrilled to accept responsibility for this task themselves. They then worked together to build a cogent plan faster than Dave could have done on his own.

Your Turn: Prepare for success with Multiplier practices. Use this grid to plan and reflect on your experiments.

Look for Opportunity	Increase Your Impact
Where and how might you use this experiment?	Where and how might you use this experiment?
Maximize Your Learning	**Develop Your Skill**
What happened and what is your evidence?	Where can you use this again?

SHOPPING FOR A NEW BOSS

If you want a job that will bring out your best, don't just look for the right company or job/role; shop for your boss. Here's a shopping guide that will help you find a Multiplier.

---

1. **Look for signs of Multiplier and Diminisher behavior.** The three traits most correlated with Multiplier leaders are: intellectual curiosity, asking great questions, and customer focus. Similarly, the traits most negatively correlated with Diminisher leaders are: entertains debate and contrary views, empowers others, seeks to understand, and has a sense of humor, so be on the lookout for those, too. Here are a few telltale signs and questions to help spot the Multipliers and Diminishers.

Multiplier Signs:

☐ Has a low talk/listen ratio

☐ Asks follow-on questions out of curiosity

☐ Asks "why" to better understand

☐ Shares multiple perspectives on issues

☐ Shows sincere self deprecation & laughs

Diminisher Signs:

☐ Has a high talk/listen ratio

☐ Accepts surface-level answers

☐ Asks about "what" and "how"

☐ Is emphatic with ideas

☐ Takes themselves very seriously

2. **Ask revealing questions.** Ask questions that expose mindset and core assumption.

- [ ] **Do they have a growth or fixed Mindset?**
  Ask: How have you become better as a leader? Listen for: Do they demonstrate an awareness of their vulnerabilities and do they actively seek out information about their blind spots? Has feedback from colleagues fueled self-improvement? Do they see the downsides of their good intentions?

- [ ] **Are they self or team focused?**
  Ask: Tell me about your team? Listen for: Not what they say, but how long they can talk. If they are self-focused, the conversation will come back to them quickly.

- [ ] **How do they view their role?**
  Ask: What is the fundamental role that leaders play here? How would others describe your role on the team? Listen for: Do they see themselves as a thought leader or a catalyst?

- [ ] **How do they view intelligence?**
  Ask: What type of people are seen as highly intelligent here? Listen for: Is there a singular view of intelligence or do they think people bring unique types of capabilities.

- [ ] **How much responsibility and ownership do they give others?**
  Ask: What is an example a project that is currently owned by someone at my level? Listen for: Do they describe a set of tasks or a large project or initiative?

3. **Check the reviews.** Sleuth around to find out what it's like to work for this boss. Talk to the people who are currently working for him or her or use tools like Glassdoor.com.

4. **Try before you buy.** If you have any doubts, ask to work initially as a contractor or consultant. If this isn't feasible, ask to sit in a team meeting or participate on a conference call to better understand how the team works.

Note: If the prospective manager is uncomfortable with you asking or doing any of the above, you've just received all the information you need.

MULTIPLIER EXPERIMENTS

STEP 1: Once you've identified your Accidental Diminisher tendencies, select an experiment that will remedy that vulnerability and help you be more of a Multiplier. Need to revisit your Accidental Diminisher tendencies? Take the quiz at www.multipliersbook.com.

ACCIDENTAL DIMINISHER TENDENCY

EXPERIMENT	Idea Guy	Always On	Rescuer	Pacesetter	Rapid Responder	Optimist	Protector	Strategist	Perfectionist
Name the Genius Identify what the people on your team do easily and freely so you can better utilize their native genius.	✓	✓						✓	
Supersize It Give someone a job or a task that is a size too big and help them "level up" and grow into the role.				✓			✓		
Play Fewer Chips In a meeting give yourself a budget of chips, with each chip representing a comment or contribution to the meeting.	✓							✓	
Talk Up Your Mistakes Invite experimentation and learning by sharing your own mistakes.				✓		✓			✓

ACCIDENTAL DIMINISHER TENDENCY

EXPERIMENT	Idea Guy	Always On	Rescuer	Pacesetter	Rapid Responder	Optimist	Protector	Strategist	Perfectionist
Make Space for Mistakes Define a space (projects, types of work or aspects of the business) where people can experiment, take risks, and recover from mistakes.			✓			✓	✓		✓
Ask the Questions Lead a meeting or conversation by only asking questions.	✓	✓	✓		✓			✓	✓
Create a Stretch Challenge Instead of giving people a goal, lay down a concrete challenge—define an intriguing puzzle to be solved or a question to be answered.				✓			✓	✓	
Make a Debate Instead of offering a fast answer on a critical decision, outline the options and ask people to weigh in with data and their point of view.					✓	✓			
Give 51 Percent of the Vote Put someone else in charge by giving that person the majority vote on an issue or project.		✓	✓						✓
Give It Back If someone needs help, jump in and contribute, and then clearly give ownership back to the other person.	✓		✓						

STEP 2: If you want to accelerate your development as a Multiplier leader, pick a colleague—an employee, peer, or boss—to choose your experiment for you.

STEP 3: Ask your colleague:

> ➤ Which of the Accidental Diminisher tendencies is my vulnerability? (In other words, in which way do you see me shutting down good ideas and action in others, despite having the best of intentions as a leader?)
>
> ➤ Which experiment would help me get the most out of other people? Why?
>
> ➤ What insights can you offer that would help me be a better leader to you and the team?

The Multipliers Assessment

Are You an Accidental Diminisher?

In our research, we were surprised to discover how few Diminishers understood the limiting effect they were having on others. Most had moved into management having been praised for their personal—and often intellectual—merit and assumed that their role as boss was to have the best ideas. Others had once had the mind of a Multiplier but had been working among Diminishers for so long, they had gone native.

Accidental or not, the impact on your team is the same—you might be getting only half of the true brainpower of your team.

The Accidental Diminisher Quiz is a quick assessment that will allow you to:

- Reflect on ten common management scenarios and how closely they describe your own approach to management.
- See to what extent you may be inadvertently diminishing your people. You'll get an instant AD score—the smaller, the better!
- Get an immediate report analyzing your responses with suggestions for how you can adjust your leadership practices to lead more like a Multiplier and get more from your team.

To access the Accidental Diminisher Quiz, go to
www.multipliersbooks.com.

Click on the Accidental Diminisher Quiz link
to complete the online assessment.

To conduct a complete 360-degree assessment or to measure how much intelligence you or your team is accessing from the people around you, contact:

The Wiseman Group at www.TheWisemanGroup.com
or send an email to info@TheWisemanGroup.com.

Notes

Foreword

1. Peter F. Drucker, *Management Challenges of the 21st Century* (New York: Harper Business, 1999), 135.

Preface

1. David R. Schilling, "Knowledge Doubling Every 12 Months, Soon to Be Every 12 Hours," *Industry Tap*, April 19, 2013; "Quick Facts and Figures about Biological Data," *ELIXIR*, 2011; Brian Goldman, "Doctors Make Mistakes. Can We Talk About That?," TED Talks, November 2011; Brett King, "Too Much Content: A World of Exponential Information Growth," *Huffington Post*, January 18, 2011.
2. The name has been changed.
3. http://www.gallup.com/poll/165269/worldwide-employees-engaged-work.aspx.
4. https://www.shrm.org/ResourcesAndTools/hr-topics/employee-relations/Pages/SHRM-Job-Security-Is-No-Longer-Top-Driver-of-Satisfaction.aspx#sthash.x5fhRn2v.dpuf.
5. This data comes from the Multipliers 360 assessment and utilization index that was conducted for 1,626 managers between 2010 and November 2016. In this assessment, a manager's colleagues, employees, and boss assess how fully the manager is utilizing their intelligence and capability.

Chapter 1: The Multiplier Effect

1. Bono, "The 2009 Time 100: The World's Most Influential People," *Time*, May 11, 2009.
2. The name has been changed.
3. The name has been changed.
4. Research method and data available in appendix A.
5. Carol Dweck, *Mindset: The New Psychology of Success* (New York: Random House, 2006).
6. Nicholas D. Kristof, "How to Raise Our I.Q.," *New York Times*, April 16, 2009.
7. Ibid.; Richard E. Nisbett, *Intelligence and How to Get It: Why Schools and Cultures Count* (New York: W. W. Norton & Company, Inc., 2009).
8. Gary Hamel and C. K. Prahalad, *Competing for the Future* (Boston: Harvard Business School Press, 1994), 159.

9. The name has been changed.
10. Dweck, *Mindset*, 6.
11. Ibid., 7.
12. Adrian Gostick and Scott Christopher, *The Levity Effect: Why It Pays to Lighten Up* (Hoboken, NJ: Wiley, 2008), 12. Pat Riley, speech to SAP (Miami, July 12, 2011).
13. Joel Stein, "George Clooney: The Last Movie Star," *Time*, February 20, 2008.

Chapter 2: The Talent Magnet

1. The name has been changed.
2. Carol Dweck, *Mindset: The New Psychology of Success* (New York: Random House, 2006).
3. Jack and Suzy Welch, "How to Be a Talent Magnet," *BusinessWeek*, September 11, 2006.

Chapter 3: The Liberator

1. The name has been changed.
2. Students scoring either "proficient" or "advanced" levels have increased from 82 to 98 percent. Students scoring "below basic" or "far below basic" levels have decreased from 9 to 2 percent.
3. The Multiplier of the Year award is an annual contest sponsored by The Wiseman Group and given to leaders who exemplify the ideals and impact of Multipliers based on nominations from their employees. Information can be found here: http://multipliersbook.com/nominate-leader-2016-multiplier-year-award/.
4. Peter B. Stark and Jane S. Flaherty, *The Only Negotiating Guide You'll Ever Need* (New York: Random House, 2003).

Chapter 4: The Challenger

1. Larry Huston and Nabil Sakkab, "Connect and Develop: Inside Procter & Gamble's New Model for Innovation," *Harvard Business Review*, March 2006.
2. Interview with Riz Khan, *One on One*, Al Jazeera broadcast January 19, 2008.
3. Noel Tichy, *The Leadership Engine* (New York: Harper Business, 1997), 244.

Chapter 5: The Debate Maker

1. Standing in the Rose Garden on Tuesday, April 18, 2006, amid pressure to remove Defense Secretary Donald Rumsfeld from his cabinet position, Mr. Bush described his approach to making decisions. He explained, "Don Rumsfeld is doing a fine job . . . I hear the voices, and I read the front page, and I know the speculation. But I'm the decider, and I decide what is best. And what's best is for Don Rumsfeld to remain as the secretary of defense."
2. Joe Klein, "The Blink Presidency," *Time*, February 20, 2005.
3. Michael R. Gordon, "Troop 'Surge' Took Place Amid Doubt and Debate," *New York Times*, August 30, 2008.
4. Quoted in Adam Bryant, "He Prizes Questions More Than Answers," *New York Times*, October 24, 2009.
5. Ibid.
6. Shared inquiry is a method of learning developed and taught by the Junior Great Books Foundation.

Chapter 6: The Investor

1. Nic Paget-Clarke, interview in Ahmedabad, August 31, 2003, *In Motion* magazine.
2. "The Big Picture" was developed by Catalyst Consulting.
3. *The Economist* ranking for Murthy/Infosys: http://www.marketwired.com/press-release /worlds-most-admired-ceos-2005-microsofts-bill-gates-named-most-admired-global -leader-nasdaq-wppgy-571937.htm.
4. Based on our research survey on the leadership practices of Multipliers and Diminishers. See appendix B.

Chapter 7: The Accidental Diminisher

1. Carol Dweck, *Mindset: The New Psychology of Success* (New York: Random House, 2006).

Chapter 8: Dealing with Diminishers

1. For a detailed description of the research conducted for "Dealing with Diminishers," see the latter half of appendix A.
2. Freedman, Joshua. "Hijacking of the Amygdala" https://web.archive.org/web/2009 1122194535/http://www.inspirations-unlimited.net/images/Hijack.pdf (PDF). Archived from the original on November 22, 2009. Retrieved 2010-04-06.
3. Elinor Ostrom and James Walker, *Trust & Reciprocity: Interdisciplinary Lessons from Experimental Research* (New York: Russell Sage Foundation, 2003), 3–7.
4. The name has been changed.
5. www.speedoftrust.com/How-The-Speed-of-Trust-works/book.
6. For example, glassdoor.com, greatplacetowork.com, and vault.com.
7. This data comes from the Multipliers 360 assessment that was conducted for 1,626 managers between 2010 and November 2016. In this assessment, a manager's colleagues, employees, and boss assess how fully the manager is utilizing their intelligence and capability.

Chapter 9: Becoming a Multiplier

1. John H. Zenger and Joseph Folkman, *The Extraordinary Leader* (New York: McGraw-Hill, 2002), 143–47.
2. Phillippa Lally, Cornelia H. M. van Jaarsveld, Henry W. W. Potts, and Jane Wardle, "How Are Habits Formed: Modelling Habit Formation in the Real World," http://onlinelibrary .wiley.com/doi/10.1002/ejsp.674/abstract (July 16, 2009).
3. The name has been changed.
4. David D. Burns, *Feeling Good: The New Mood Therapy* (New York: William Morrow and Company, 1980).
5. "culture," *Merriam-Webster.com*, 2016, https://www.merriam-webster.com (October 24, 2016).
6. Saritha Pujari, "Culture: The Meaning, Characteristics, And Functions." *Yourarticlelibrary .com: The Next Generation Library*. http://www.yourarticlelibrary.com/culture/culture -the-meaning-characteristics-and-functions/9577/.
7. Ibid.
8. Kim Ann Zimmermann, "What Is Culture? | Definition of Culture," http://www .livescience.com/21478-what-is-culture-definition-of-culture.html (February 19, 2015).
9. Ifte Choudhury, "culture; some definitions," https://www.tamu.edu/faculty/choudhury /culture.html, Texas A&M.

10. "culture," *BusinessDictionary.com*, 2016, http://www.businessdictionary.com/definition/culture.html.
11. "Elements of Organizational Culture," http://www.kautilyasociety.com/tvph/communication_skill/organizational_culture.htm.
12. Daniel Pekarsky, PhD, "The Role of Culture in Moral Development," *Parenthood in America*. Published by the University of Wisconsin-Madison General Library System. http://parenthood.library.wisc.edu/Pekarsky/Pekarsky.html, 1998.
13. The Multiplier of the Year award is an annual contest sponsored by The Wiseman Group and given to leaders who exemplify the ideals and impact of Multipliers based on nominations from their employees. Information can be found here: http://multipliersbooks.com/nominate-leader-2016-multiplier-year-award/.
14. ROI of 163 percent was measured by the ROI Institute Europe and approved by Jack & Patti Phillips.
15. This failure-to-launch cycle is from the Multipliers workshop and is a derivative of the Gartner Hype Cycle, which begins with a technology trigger, has a peak of inflated expectations, then proceeds with a trough of disillusionment and then continues in a steady upward climb (enlightenment and productivity). Unlike this broad market cycle, personal and organizational change cycles often get killed rather than progress up this slope of enlightenment.

Appendix A: The Research Process
1. James C. Collins, *Good to Great: Why Some Companies Make the Leap—and Others Don't* (New York: Harper Business, 2001), 7.
2. Shane Legg and Marcus Hutter, *Technical Report: A Collection of Definitions of Intelligence* (Lugano, Switzerland: IDSIA, June 15, 2007).
3. Linda S. Gottfredson, "Mainstream Science on Intelligence: An Editorial with 52 Signatories, History, and Bibliography," *Intelligence* 24, no. 1, (1997): 13–23.

Index